Key Performance Indicators

FOR

DUMMIES

A Wiley Brand

Key Performance Indicators FOR DUMMIES®

A Wiley Brand

by Bernard Marr

Key Performance Indicators For Dummies®

Published by: **John Wiley & Sons, Ltd.,** The Atrium, Southern Gate, Chichester, www.wiley.com

This edition first published 2015

© 2015 John Wiley & Sons, Ltd, Chichester, West Sussex.

Registered office

John Wiley & Sons Ltd, The Atrium, Southern Gate, Chichester, West Sussex, PO19 8SQ, United Kingdom

For details of our global editorial offices, for customer services and for information about how to apply for permission to reuse the copyright material in this book please see our website at www.wiley.com.

For general information on our other products and services, please contact our Customer Care Department within the U.S. at 877-762-2974, outside the U.S. at (001) 317-572-3993, or fax 317-572-4002. For technical support, please visit www.wiley.com/techsupport.

For technical support, please visit `www.wiley.com/techsupport`.

A catalogue record for this book is available from the British Library.

ISBN 978-1-118-91323-9 (paperback) ISBN 978-1-118-91325-3 (ebk)

ISBN 978-1-118-91324-6 (ebk)

Printed in Great Britain by TJ International, Padstow, Cornwall.

10 9 8 7 6 5 4 3 2 1

Contents at a Glance

Introduction *1*

Part I: Getting Started with Key Performance Indicators *5*
Chapter 1: Introducing Key Performance Indicators (KPIs) 7
Chapter 2: Types, Targets and KPI Mistakes...19
Chapter 3: Creating a Culture of Fact-Based Decision-Making.................................29
Chapter 4: Organising Your KPIs 43

Part II: Implementing and Using KPIs Effectively *63*
Chapter 5: Developing a KPI 65
Chapter 6: Use it or Lose it: Turning KPIs into Insights...91
Chapter 7: Spreading the Word: Reporting and
Communicating KPIs Effectively 105

Part III: Developing Financial KPIs *121*
Chapter 8: The Holy Grail of Business: Revenue and Profit KPIs 123
Chapter 9: The Ones You Can't Take Your Eyes Off:
Liquidity and Cash Flow KPIs 135
Chapter 10: Reporting to the Masters: Shareholder and Value-Added KPIs 145
Chapter 11: Measuring Your Financial Efficiency 153

Part IV: Developing Customer, Sales and Marketing KPIs *163*
Chapter 12: The Customer is Always Right: Measuring
Your Customer Success...165
Chapter 13: Measuring the Market and Your Place in It 183

Part V: Developing Operational and Internal Process KPIs *197*
Chapter 14: Measuring Project Performance 199
Chapter 15: Measuring Internal Efficiency and Quality 207
Chapter 16: Measuring IT Performance 227

Part VI: Measuring Your Most Important Assets: Developing HR and People KPIs.............. 237

Chapter 17: Measuring People Performance...239
Chapter 18: Measuring Human Resources Performance 253

Part VII: The Part of Tens 263

Chapter 19: Ten Tips for Developing Effective KPIs..................................265
Chapter 20: The Ten Biggest KPI Mistakes to Avoid 269
Chapter 21: The Top Ten KPIs to Use 275

Index 281

Table of Contents

Introduction 1

About This Book 2
Foolish Assumptions 3
Icons Used in This Book 3
Beyond the Book 3
Where to Go from Here 4

Part I: Getting Started with Key
Performance Indicators 5

Chapter 1: Introducing Key Performance Indicators (KPIs). 7

Why Every Company Needs KPIs 8
    The Fishing Analogy 8
    The Datafication of our World 9
    KPIs as vital decision support tools 10
Making KPIs Work in Your Business 11
    Create a KPI culture 12
    Decide on the right KPI framework 12
    Develop the right KPIs 13
    Analyse and report 14
Assessing Your Financial KPIs 14
    Revenue and profit 14
    Liquidity and cash flow 15
    Shareholder value 15
    Financial efficiency 15
Assessing Your Customer KPIs 16
    Customer satisfaction and loyalty 16
    Market share 16
Assessing Your Operational KPIs 16
    Project performance 17
    Efficiency and quality 17
    IT 17
Assessing Your Employee KPIs 18
    Employee engagement 18
    Talent retention 18

Chapter 2: Types, Targets and KPI Mistakes **19**

Understanding that KPIs can be Strategic or Operational 19
  The pear tree analogy 20
  Why we can measure everything and how to do it 21
Creating the Right Set of KPIs 22
  What is a good number of KPIs? 23
  Tracking the tangible and intangible.. 23
  The leaders and the laggers 23
Setting the Right Targets for Your KPIs... 24
  KPIs vs. targets.. 25
  Making targets specific 25
  Making targets realistic and achievable 26
Knowing Where People Go Wrong with KPIs.................................... 26
  Measuring everything that walks and moves.............................. 27
  Collecting the same measures as everyone else 27
  Not choosing the relevant KPIs.. 28

Chapter 3: Creating a Culture of Fact-Based Decision-Making **29**

Implementing the Key Components of Fact-Based Management 30
  Establishing senior management buy-in...................................... 30
  Introducing KPIs for the right reasons...................................... 32
  Establishing the processes and culture...................................... 33
Creating Improvement and Performance Preview Meetings 37
  Introducing strategy revision meetings 37
  Establishing strategic performance preview meetings.................. 38
  Putting in place operational performance
    improvement meetings.. 39
  Aligning personal performance discussions 39

Chapter 4: Organising Your KPIs **43**

Understanding the Need for KPI Frameworks 43
  Weighing the options 43
  Selecting the right framework.. 44
Introducing the Balanced Scorecard 46
  Getting a grasp of the four BSC perspectives.............................. 47
  Tackling the financial perspective.. 48
  Making sure you're delivering to your customers........................ 50
  Looking at your internal processes 51
  Improving and driving future value.. 54
  Putting it on paper and mapping it out 55
Looking at Alternative KPI Frameworks 60
  Using Quality or Lean Frameworks 60
  Using Project Management Frameworks 62
  The Risky Side of Business 62

Part II: Implementing and Using KPIs Effectively 63

Chapter 5: Developing a KPI 65

The Question is The Answer: Developing Key
Performance Questions (KPQs) 66
    Harnessing the power of questions 66
    Creating good key performance questions (KPQs) 67
Deciding on the Right KPIs 70
    Step 1: Linking KPIs to strategic objectives................................. 70
    Step 2: Identifying the unanswered questions 70
    Step 3: Isolating the decisions to take... 71
    Step 4: Checking for existing data and methods......................... 71
    Step 5: Collecting meaningful data in time 71
    Step 6: Assessing the usefulness to answering the question 72
    Step 7: Assessing the usefulness to decision-making................... 72
    Step 8: Creating awareness of cheating 73
    Step 9: Are the costs and effort justified?..................................... 73
    Step 10: Collecting the data... 73
    Making it work: the ten-step template in action 74
Deciding on How to Collect the Data 75
    Identifying types of data 76
    Applying quantitative methods... 76
    Understanding qualitative methods 77
    Combining data to improve insights 80
    The big data challenge 81
Finalising Your KPIs: Applying the KPI Design Template....................... 81
    The basics.. 82
    Completing your KPI Template 83
    How good is the indicator?... 86

Chapter 6: Use it or Lose it: Turning KPIs into Insights 91

Testing Cause and Effect Relationships.. 92
    Why strategies are just assumptions 93
    Testing your assumptions 94
    Testing Business Assumptions at Google, Inc. 95
Learning from Business Experiments 96
Removing Bias through Business Experiments 97
Business Intelligence and Analytics.. 100
    Datafication... 100
    Analytics 102

**Chapter 7: Spreading the Word: Reporting and
Communicating KPIs Effectively** **105**

Getting the Attention of the Decision Maker 106
    The importance of communicating 106
    Keeping in mind the target audience 107
    Using best practice performance reports 108
    Publishing analogy 108
    Headline, photo and narrative 109
Visualising KPIs: Using Graphs and Charts 110
    Bar graph 111
    Line graph 112
    Pie chart 113
    Scatter chart 113
    Bullet graph 114
    Speedometer dials or gauges 115
    Using innovative ways to visualise data 115
Developing Management Dashboards 116
    Seven dashboard design tips 117
    Making use of software tools 118

Part III: Developing Financial KPIs *121*

Chapter 8: The Holy Grail of Business: Revenue and Profit KPIs . . . 123

The Bottom Line – Gauging Profit 123
    Profit means prizes 125
    Understanding the different perspectives on profit 125
    Why profit only matters in context 127
    Measuring profit in practice 128
Measuring Profit Margins 129
    Why margins are so vital 129
    Knowing the different profit margins 130
    Measuring profit margins in practice 131
The Top-Line: Measuring Revenue Growth 132
    When revenue isn't everything 133
    Why you should track revenue over time 133
    Measuring revenue in practice 133

**Chapter 9: The Ones You Can't Take Your Eyes Off:
Liquidity and Cash Flow KPIs** **135**

Tracking Your Cash 135
    Why cash is king 136
    What cash flow tells you about your business 137
    Measuring cash flow in practice 137

Looking Out for Liquidity 140
    The often unseen danger 141
    Measuring liquidity in practice 141

**Chapter 10: Reporting to the Masters: Shareholder and
Value-Added KPIs** **145**
    The Ultimate Value Metric: EVA 145
        Why profitable companies might not create value 146
        Understanding opportunity cost 146
        Measuring opportunity cost in practice 147
    Keeping an Eye on Your Share Price 148
        It's all relative: comparing businesses 149
        Measuring P/E ratio in practice 149
    Tracking Total Shareholder Return (TSR) 150
        Competition is stiff on the stock market 150
        Measuring TSR in practice 151

Chapter 11: Measuring Your Financial Efficiency **153**
    Assessing the Return on Investment 153
        Every investment must yield a return 154
        Measuring ROI in practice 155
    Measuring the Return on Capital Employed 156
        Understanding ROCE 157
        Measuring ROCE in practice 157
    Gauging Return on Equity (ROE) 158
        Why should you measure ROE 159
        Measuring ROE in practice 159
    Understanding Return on Assets (ROA) 160
        Why does ROA matter to companies? 161
        Measuring ROA in practice 161

*Part IV: Developing Customer, Sales and
Marketing KPIs* *163*

**Chapter 12: The Customer is Always Right:
Measuring Your Customer Success** **165**
    Asking if Your Customers Would Recommend You (NPS) 165
        How NPS drives loyalty and profitability 166
        Understanding the NPS formula 167
        Measuring NPS in practice 168
    Measuring How Satisfied Your Customers Are (Satisfaction Index) 169
        Identifying what makes your customers happy 170
        Creating your unique index 171
        Measuring CSI in practice 171

Tracking How Likely Your Customers are To Leave
(Retention/Churn) 173
Churn and retention matters! 173
Measuring it in practice 174
Gauging Whether All Customers are Equal (Profitability) 176
Understanding where the profits are made 176
Tracking customer profitability 176
Measuring it in practice 177
Calculating Your Customers' Value (Life-Time Value) 178
The ultimate customer KPI! 178
Measuring it in practice 179
Measuring Whether Your Customers are Truly Engaged 180
Understanding the different levels of engagement 181
Measuring engagement in practice 182

Chapter 13: Measuring the Market and Your Place in It 183
Painting a Picture of Your Market (Market Growth Rate) 183
Understanding the health of your market 184
Options for measuring market growth rate 185
Measuring market growth rate in practice 186
Understanding Your Place in the Market (Market Share) 187
Why market share matters 187
Getting a good picture of your market can be tough 189
Measuring relative market share in practice 190
Gauging Your Market Success (Customer Acquisition KPIs) 190
Knowing the cost of finding new customers 191
Options for gauging customer conversion 191
Measuring cost per lead in practice 192
Charting the Power of Your Brand 194
What brand equity means for your business 194
Finding your unique formula 195
Measuring brand equity in practice 195

**Part V: Developing Operational and
Internal Process KPIs 197**

Chapter 14: Measuring Project Performance. 199
Why Project Performance Matters 199
Introducing the Three Components of Project Performance 200
Tracking whether your projects are on time
(Project Schedule Variance) 201
Measuring whether your projects are on budget
(Project Cost Variance) 201
Checking whether your projects are delivering
the right value (Earned Value) 202
Measuring the KPIs in practice 202

Chapter 15: Measuring Internal Efficiency and Quality **207**

Assessing Quality, Lean and Six Sigma KPIs 207
    Why Lean matters 208
    What does Six Sigma really mean? 209
    Finding your ways to track quality 210
    Measuring the KPIs in practice 211
Calculating Your Internal Productivity 213
    Looking at waste levels 213
    Monitoring rework levels 216
    Scrutinizing order fulfilment 218
    Dissecting delivery 219
    Investigating inventory 221
Asking Yourself Whether You're Future Proof 222
    Your innovation pipeline 223

Chapter 16: Measuring IT Performance **227**

Why IT Matters More Than Ever 227
    Measuring IT service delivery 228
    Measuring IT project performance 233

*Part VI: Measuring Your Most Important Assets:
Developing HR and People KPIs* **237**

Chapter 17: Measuring People Performance **239**

How Satisfied and Engaged are Your People? 240
    Satisfaction and engagement matters 240
    Measuring satisfaction and engagement in practice 241
Would your Employees Recommend Your Business? 244
    Measuring the trends 244
    Measuring staff advocacy in practice 245
Looking All Around – 360 Degree Feedback 247
    Understanding the need for a full picture 247
    Measuring 360-degree feedback in practice 248
How Much Value Are Employees Generating? 250
    Measuring the value your employees generate in practice 251

Chapter 18: Measuring Human Resources Performance **253**

Charting How Well You're Recruiting 253
    Finding and keeping talent 254
    Moving beyond the trivial 255
    Measuring recruitment effectiveness in practice 255
Analysing How Well You're Training 259
    The pitfalls and challenges of measuring training 259
    Measuring it in practice 260

Part VII: The Part of Tens 263

Chapter 19: Ten Tips for Developing Effective KPIs 265
  Map Your Strategy 265
  Identify the Questions You Need to Answer 265
  Define Your Data Needs 266
  Evaluate All Existing Data 266
  Find the Right Measurement Methodology 266
  Assign Ownership 267
  Identify the Right Measurement Frequency 267
  Ensure Costs and Efforts are Justified 267
  Find the Right Supporting Data 268
  Finding the Right Picture to Communicate your KPI 268

Chapter 20: The Ten Biggest KPI Mistakes to Avoid 269
  Measure Everything That is Easy to Measure 269
  Measure Everything Everyone Else is Measuring 270
  Not Linking KPIs to Strategy 270
  Not Separating Strategic KPIs from Other Data 270
  Hardwiring KPIs to Incentives 271
  Not Involving Executives in the KPI Selection 271
  Not Analysing Your KPIs to Extract Insights 272
  Not Challenging Your KPIs 272
  Not Updating Your KPIs 272
  Not Acting on Your KPIs 273

Chapter 21: The Top Ten KPIs to Use 275
  Revenue Growth Rate 275
  Net Profit Margin 275
  Cash Conversion Cycle (CCC) 276
  Net Promoter Score 276
  Customer Engagement 277
  Customer Profitability 277
  Relative Market Share 278
  Capacity Utilisation Rate (CUR) 278
  Staff Advocacy Score 278
  Sustainability Index 278

Index 281

Introduction

*I*f you were to eavesdrop on just about any management or executive meeting, strategy session or performance review in any business you would hear the term 'KPI' mentioned many times in many different contexts. Most people in those discussions would know that the acronym stands for Key Performance Indicators but if you pressed each person to explain what a KPI actually is, it's likely that you would hear many different definitions.

Business is challenging, especially during difficult economic times. It is also extremely competitive and our customers are becoming increasingly discerning. As a result business leaders and senior executives are all looking to improve performance, minimise errors and seek out new and novel ways to gain the edge over their competition. KPIs – when properly understood and used effectively provide a powerful tool in achieving just that.

Key Performance Indicators for Dummies was written as the definitive guide to KPIs for anyone wishing to separate the rhetoric and flavour-of-the-month-management fad approach from the genuinely useful information. Whilst coving the relevant theory this book is focused squarely on practical solutions to persistent business problems that KPIs can and do solve.

KPIs are a ubiquitous in modern business. They are everywhere – common almost. And yet businesses that are using KPIs correctly and effectively are not common. Knowing about KPIs and understanding their relevance is of course important and we'll explore these essential topics in this book. But, when push comes to shove KPIs are only really useful if you identify the right ones to measure for *your* business and only measure those ones. They will only deliver mission critical data if you then use the KPIs and analyse what they tell you on a regular basis to inform and illuminate your decision making.

This book is therefore specifically designed to ensure that you design, implement and use KPIs correctly for the maximum impact with the minimum fuss. When used properly KPIs can become the compass that can guide you through even the choppiest of corporate waters leading your business to even greater success and prosperity.

About This Book

Key Performance Indicators for Dummies is your essential guide, or road map to effective KPIs and their successful implementation. It is jammed full of practical information, ideas, suggestions, tips, checklists, sample diagrams and figures designed to help anyone who wants to get the best out of KPIs. And that is true regardless of the type of business or industry you are in. KPIs are relevant to all businesses, in all industries as well as government departments and not for profit organisations.

The information contained in this book is deliberately accessible and covers everything you need to know about KPIs from the basics to more sophisticated insights that could further improve and fine tune existing KPI initiatives. As a result this book is essential reading whether you are new to business, in your first management role or a seasoned professional seeking some additional nuggets of wisdom to help squeeze just a little more value out of KPIs. If you are already familiar with KPIs this book will shine some light on the common problems or mistakes people make so you can rectify any errors that may be impairing your results. Re-inventing the wheel is time consuming and costly – learn from other people's mistakes instead and make your KPIs matter right now. Ensure that they are the useful, insight and powerful business tools they were designed to be right from the start.

Consider this book your KPI reference guide and come back to it often. Try out the ideas and band and shape the advice to suit your situation in your business. Make it your own and allow KPIs to revolutionise your performance, inform your decision making and drive your strategy.

In order to make reading this book as easy as possible certain things are treated consistently:

- ✔ All Web addresses appear in monofont
- ✔ New terms appear in italics and are closely followed by an easy-to-understand definition.
- ✔ Bold text indicates keywords in bulleted lists or highlights the action parts of numbered steps.

If you decide to visit a Website listed in the book then you just need to copy the Web addresses exactly as it appears in the book. This is true even if the address falls between two pages – we will not have inserted any extra characters (such as hyphens) into the text.

Foolish Assumptions

In order to write a book you need to think about the audience. Who is most likely to read this book and once you know that you need to speak to that audience. For this book I've assumed that you are a manger, senior executive or leader within a business, government department or not-for-profit organisation seeking to better understand and utilise KPIs and improve performance. And I've also assumed that you are in a position to make changes or at least table changes within your organisation so that you can actually action what you read.

Icons Used in This Book

No one likes huge blocks of daunting text! These little icons are used to break up the text so that it's easier and more enjoyable to read. They also flag important information and help you find that information again when you come back to the book.

These indicate expert advice or suggestions to fast track success. They are intended to help save time, effort, money or brain cells as you implement KPIs into your business.

This icon flags critical material that you should store away in your memory for later use. But don't worry – they are usually very short.

As the name would suggest this icon flags potential pitfalls that you need to avoid as you become more and more familiar with KPIs.

The quickest, easiest and often most enjoyable way to really 'get' something is to read a true story, case study or real world example of the theory in practice. This icon flags those stories so you can learn quickly – often from others who have already walked your path.

Beyond the Book

In addition to the material in the print or e-book you're reading right now, this product also comes with some access-anywhere goodies on the Web. Check out the free Cheat Sheet at `www.dummies.com/cheatsheet/kpis` for some helpful key checklists.

Furthermore, check out the website of the Advanced Performance Institute, which I founded and head up. There you will find many relevant case studies, white papers and reading material on KPIs and performance management: www.ap-institute.com.

Where to Go from Here

That's entirely up to you. You can read this book in order from Chapter 1 to Chapter 21, but you don't have to. So where you start reading will depend on how familiar and comfortable you are with KPIs already.

If you are new to KPIs, or are interested in or charged with designing a KPI agenda for your business, or changing the way KPIs are measured in your business then start at the beginning. Otherwise use the table of contents to find what you are most interested in and jump straight to that section. Whatever reading approach you take you will find a treasure trove of information that will allow you to unlock the power of KPIs for your business.

Part I

Getting Started with Key Performance Indicators

In this part . . .

- ✔ Understand how everything in your business can be measured.

- ✔ Get to grips with what KPIs are and how you can benefit from using them.

- ✔ Become aware of the importance of evidence-based decision making.

- ✔ Learn to use KPIs to enact and enhance your business strategy.

Chapter 1

Introducing Key Performance Indicators (KPIs)

In This Chapter

▶ Understanding KPI basics

▶ Identifying the most common errors

▶ Identifying the key business areas to measure

So what the heck are Key Performance Indicators (KPIs) anyway?

KPIs help organisations understand how well they are performing in relation to their strategic goals and objectives. In the broadest sense, a KPI provides the most important performance information that enables organisations or their stakeholders to understand whether the organisation is on track toward its stated objectives or not. In addition KPIs serve to reduce the complex nature of organisational performance to a small, manageable number of key indicators that provide evidence that can in turn assist decision making and ultimately improve performance.

If you think about it, this is the same logical approach we use in our daily lives. Say you are not feeling very well and decide to visit your doctor. She may ask you what is wrong but she's immediately searching for evidence to qualify your subjective opinion. She may, for example, take your blood pressure and measure your cholesterol levels, heart rate and body mass index as key indicators of your health. With KPIs we are trying to do the same in our organisations. And without them we are flying blind, relying on the often subjective assessment and opinion of key personnel.

In practice, the term KPI is overused and misunderstood. Too often, KPIs are assumed to be financial in nature or simply the numerical measures we can most easily count. However, such a definition is much too narrow. The data for KPIs can come from myriad sources, providing the best possible answer to your most important business questions. Anything, even the most esoteric or intangible elements of business can be measured simply by tracking the difference between one thing and another. If you can observe a move from one state, situation or element of performance to another that is strategically or operationally important to the success of your business then you can measure it. And if this is helping you to answer a critical business question then that measurement is a KPI.

Unfortunately there is often a disconnect between whether something *can* be measured and whether it *should* be measured. Instead of clearly identifying the information needed, and then carefully designing the most appropriate indicators to assess performance, businesses too often implement KPIs using what I call the 'ICE' approach:

- ✔ Identify everything that is easy to measure and count
- ✔ Collect and report the data on everything that is easy to measure and count
- ✔ End up scratching your head thinking, 'What on earth does this all mean and what are we going to do with all this performance data?'

This opening chapter is designed to cover the basics of KPIs, explain what they are and why companies need them, and offers as a brief glimpse into what I'll cover in more detail in the rest of the book.

Why Every Company Needs KPIs

KPIs act like navigation tools for your business and allow you to know where you are against where you think you are or where you want to be in the same way a compass would guide a fishing voyage.

The Fishing Analogy

As long as there have been fish, human beings have been fishing. Initially our efforts were probably pretty basic consisting of a net, a line and a stick! Over time we progressed to small boats and were able to search for fish further afield. By the 16th century fishermen had much larger boats capable of going to sea in search of bigger and bigger catches. Initially the ships would set out using little more than a compass, a sextant and some 'inside knowledge' passed down generations of fishing families. If they were sailing at night they would use celestial navigation techniques and plot a course by the stars in order to arrive in the right vicinity. When the fishermen arrived at the fishing grounds they would cast their nets and hope for the best.

Modern fishing, however, is very different. Huge trawlers, capable of travelling enormous distances and processing the fish on board, are also technology-rich, using high-tech navigation systems and GPS. Although shipbuilding technology helped, what really transformed fishing into the lucrative industry we see today was access to relevant information that allowed fisherman to know where they were on the ocean, where the fish were, where they would be tomorrow and when to cast their nets for maximum yield. Fishing has used KPIs to improve revenue and performance for centuries, and businesses must do the same if they are to prosper in an increasingly competitive world.

Just as GPS helps fishermen to navigate the ocean and find the fish in enough numbers to make money and be successful, KPIs, if used effectively, can help business leaders navigate the often treacherous waters of business to make better evidence-based decisions and implement their chosen strategy successfully.

Centuries or even decades ago an abundance of fish made success possible regardless of navigation tools. But that is no longer the case. And the same is true for business. Business must also go further – not just physically to new markets and territories opened up by globalisation but they must go further across the board including improved customer experience, quality control and efficiency. KPIs make that possible because they shine a light into the business, letting you see what's really happening.

Businesses need a way to assess where they are and whether they are on or off course against their strategy. They need to be able to correct quickly and adapt to the changing conditions of the market. The days where good enough was good enough and competition was minimal so everyone prospered regardless of quality or customer satisfaction are long gone. In the years following WWII for example countries needed to re-build so there was often no competition and quality was poor but it was better than nothing. Hopefully those days will never come again. If you want to succeed in a fiercely competitive market you need a way to measure progress (or otherwise) in real time not just after the fact. If your business doesn't have or use the right KPIs then, like the fisherman of old, you are effectively casting your nets and hoping for the best.

The Datafication of our World

The pressure to identify and perfect business navigation tools is only going to intensify as we get more and more access to more and more data. As in the previous section, the fishing analogy is useful in understanding the implications of the datafication of our world. If a fisherman is competing for fish in a lake, the information he needs is finite and restricted to information about the lake. But once he goes to sea the amount of possible data he could or should have access to increases exponentially.

Most modern businesses compete globally. Within those businesses and within those markets the amount of information we now have access to is truly mind-boggling. The massive uptake of social media, smart technology and quantum leaps in computer storage and computer power collectively means that we are now generating more information and more data than ever before. It is said that we are now producing five exabytes or billion gigabytes of data every two days! Behind closed doors many business leaders are already stressed about the amount of data they probably have in their business but don't have adequate or meaningful access to and that situation is only going to get worse if we don't start managing that data effectively.

When you identify and use the right KPIs for your business you can cut through the oceans of data that exists, could exist or should exist and get timely access to the nuggets of wisdom that you need to make better decisions and improve performance.

Without the right KPIs to navigate the swelling oceans of data that already exist and is increasing all the time you can so easily find yourself all at sea.

KPIs as vital decision support tools

When used effectively, KPIs provide the evidence and information required to make better, faster decisions without stress. Business experience matters, and clearly you sometimes need to make decisions when all the facts are not available but KPIs provide a vital decision support tool across the business that can reduce those occasions and minimise error and anxiety.

Using KPIs to answer your most critical business questions

Your business needs KPIs because they help to answer your most critical business questions. Depending on your strategy you will have a series of important business questions that you need to answer in order to work out if your business is doing what it needs to do to achieve that strategy or is moving away from it or going off course.

Once you know what those questions are you can work out what information you need in order to answer them. Once you know the information you need you can design the right KPI that will deliver that answer and use the KPI to guide the strategy.

Essentially KPIs allow you to measure performance accurately, which in turn allows you to:

- Learn from past outcomes and improve results in the future
- Report externally and demonstrate compliance
- Focus effort and monitor output

Using KPIs to learn and improve performance

When you have access to the information you need you are better able to make better, more informed decisions. These allow you to learn what's working and not working quickly, so you can improve performance.

KPIs also provide the real-world evidence that can be used to challenge strategic assumptions and ensure the business is always heading in the right direction.

Using KPIs to report externally and demonstrate compliance

KPIs can also be used to inform external stakeholders and comply with external reporting regulations and information requests.

When measuring for these purposes, any reports and associated indicators can be produced on a compulsory basis such as for annual financial statements, accounts, or performance reports for regulators or they can be produced on a voluntary basis such as environmental impact reports.

Using KPIs to focus effort and monitor output

KPIs can also be used to focus employee's behavior and effort and monitor their output. Although this may sound a little Machiavellian, KPIs can be extremely positive in opening dialogue up and down the company. Say you have a manager who is hell-bent on a particular approach even though his staff are not supportive – KPIs allow both sides to see the facts and make decisions about where to focus effort based on evidence, not assumption or opinion. Equally, if a member of your team is not pulling his or her weight then KPIs provide feedback on any unwanted variance between achievements and goals. It's not opinion or assumption: the KPI tells the story, which tends to defuse potentially difficult situations and allows both parties to move straight into solution mode.

The word *indicator* is deliberate – KPIs are not targets to pin reward and punishment on. They are indicators, guides that can help a business or individual know where they are in relation to where they should be.

Making KPIs Work in Your Business

Although the term KPI is common, the effective application and use of KPIs in business is not.

What normally happens is that there will be a KPI champion who will struggle to engage the rest of the group about the relevance of KPIs. Even if by some miracle that individual does garner support, if he or she leaves the whole KPI framework quietly disappears and everyone goes back to business as usual.

Alternatively too many KPIs are introduced without any real regard for how the information will be used. Over time the people collecting the data become disillusioned because nothing comes of their KPI collection and reporting. And when people are already busy it won't take long for the KPIs to fall by the wayside. See Chapter 2 for more on common errors in implementing KPIs.

This chapter is designed to give you quick overview of KPIs, how to decide on the right ones and organise them for maximum impact. as well as a sneak a peek at a few. For more detail on organising KPIs, check out Chapter 4.

Create a KPI culture

KPIs are incredibly effective navigation tools that can inform decision making and give you almost real-time access to what's actually happening in your business. However, they won't ever deliver on that promise until you take steps to shift the culture inside your business to embrace KPIs and see them for a positive, inclusive and collaborative way to understand and improve performance – without finger pointing and blame.

You don't need to instigate radical cultural change programs, though – the necessary culture shifts will come about naturally. The worst thing you can do when it comes to KPIs is to announce their arrival. Instead, initiate a subtle approach where you start with a few key KPIs, explain their relevance and what the information is going to allow you to do. Collect that data, and most importantly use the data to make new choices. When people begin to see that the data you are collecting is being used in the decision-making process and to inform choices instead of being jammed in a folder and forgotten about then the culture will change.

When that change begins, lock it in through regular and semi-regular KPI-focused meetings. Chapter 3 gives you more on creating an evidence-based culture in your business.

Decide on the right KPI framework

As you will see as you read the rest of this book, there are a huge number of KPIs to choose from. Even the ones mentioned in this book represent a handful of the possible KPIs that you could theoretically choose from.

Getting KPIs right is as much about how you choose and present them as it is about the ones you choose. You need to present he KPIs in context, otherwise they are just numbers and data. Most decision makers are already busy; they don't want to have to wade through mountains of information to scratch out the insights. They want to be able to get the information they need in a way that makes sense to them already.

As a result the best way to present your KPIs is to use an existing or familiar performance framework. For example if your business already uses the *Balanced Scorecard* (BSC) or *Six Sigma* then people inside the business are already familiar with that methodology. Adding KPIs around the already familiar framework makes it much more likely that mangers and decision makers will use the KPIs and derive meaningful benefit from them very quickly.

There is absolutely no point re-inventing the wheel so wherever possible, piggy back on an existing framework – be that a project management framework, quality framework or the BSC.

Develop the right KPIs

So which KPIs should you use? Well that depends on what you need to know. Too often people get excited about KPIs and go overboard. So they go from zero to hero and wonder why KPIs don't stick.

If you currently don't use any KPIs, or measure a few but don't really use them to inform strategy and decision making then plucking the sexiest 50 out of a KPI book – even this one – is going to fail.

You need to start with the questions you most need answers to in order to improve performance. If you are worried about staff turnover then you need to know the answer to 'How many people are leaving the company?' But that alone won't really tell you if you have a problem or not. You may want to revise that question to, 'How many of the people leaving the company do you regret leaving?' If you are only losing people you want to lose then you need to tighten up your recruitment process to ensure you don't recruit those people in the first place. If you are losing vital members of your team then you need to find out why and do all you can to rectify the problem.

The guiding principle for successful KPI selection is – only measure what matters. And in this context that means only measure what you need to measure in order to deliver your strategic objectives, improve performance and stay on track. Chapter 5 gives you the meat on developing effective KPIs.

Analyse and report

Even once you've decided on the right KPIs for you and they all service a purpose and help you answer performance critical questions you need to analyse the KPIs and make sure the people that need the information get the information in a way that makes sense to them.

Too often companies will decide to use KPIs and collect them all together in a big fat folder or distribute all the KPIs to all the managers and decision makers. The resulting document is often overwhelming so no one uses the information.

Remember KPIs are navigation tools. They need to be put in context and they need to be turned into insights that can direct strategy and decision making. KPIs also allow decision makers to identify and test assumptions that can improve performance. Ultimately a KPI is only useful if it's used in the course of normal business operations. And they are only useful if the analysis reaches the right people. Chapter 6 tells you how to turn KPIs into business insights, and Chapter 7 shows you how to communicate them effectively.

Assessing Your Financial KPIs

Financial KPIs are the most common type of KPI in most businesses. Whether a business is considered a success or not is largely measured by financial performance which is measured via a number of financial KPIs.

Revenue and profit

Business exists primarily to make money – that's the objective. There may be other objectives but commercial organisations are driven to create revenue and more importantly profit.

It's essential therefore that you understand the different types of profit – gross, net and operating and how to measure the various margins so you can figure out how much money is really being made by the business.

Revenue is considered a key metric for success and is especially important to investors or potential investors.Chapter 7 has the inside track on developing KPIs for revenue and profit.

Liquidity and cash flow

The biggest reason for business failure is not lack of sales, poor products or bad management. Most of the time businesses fail because they simply run out of money. They don't keep an eye on cash flow and liquidity and underestimate the inflows and outflows of cash from the business.

In any business cash is king. The more cash you have or the more cash you have access to quickly (*liquidity*), the more flexibility you have in how you run and grow the business. A cash-rich business doesn't have to borrow money or attract investors to grow. Debt finance and equity finance can be expensive options and dilute the control of the business, so knowing how much cash you have today and how much you will have tomorrow is critical for long term survival and growth. Chapter 8 introduces you to the key KPIs for liquidity and cash flow.

Shareholder value

In business, the shareholders wear the trousers. Whether they are the owners of a privately-owned business or the shareholders in a publicly-owned company, the owners are watching and they want to know how their investment is doing.

Shareholder KPIs allow owners, managers and investors to know how attractive a company is and how much value they can expect.

For publicly-listed companies, shareholder metrics are critical. If a share price is too low but the earnings are good then it leaves the company open to a takeover. Competition is harsh in the stock market and shareholders will go where they believe they will get the best return – you need to know whether that's you or not. Chapter 9 tells you what you need to know about shareholder and value-added KPIs.

Financial efficiency

Profit is a direct result of how efficiently you run your business. How well do you use the resources you have? What sort of returns are you getting on the capital you employ? Are your assets working hard enough? These are just some of the questions you need to know the answer to. Chapter 10 shows you how to get a handle on financial efficiency.

Assessing Your Customer KPIs

Your business isn't a business without customers. If you want to grow and prosper moving forward you need to know what your customers think about you and you need to know how about your market share.

Customer satisfaction and loyalty

Competition is fierce in most markets. Customers for the most part are much more discerning than they used to be. If you don't give them what they want when they want it then they are much more likely to jump ship and buy from your competitor.

Business has recognised the importance of at least trying to keep their customers happy for a long time but research has demonstrated that happy customers don't necessarily translate into loyal customers. Plus, just because a customer is loyal doesn't always mean that customer is profitable. You need to be able to classify your customers so you know who is making you money and who is costing you money.

You need to find the raving fans and encourage them to spread the word still further but you can't do that unless you implement some meaningful customer focused KPIs. Chapter 11 shows you how to measure customer satisfaction, and how to enhance your chances of keeping those customers loyal.

Market share

Do you currently know much about your market? Is it shrinking or expanding? How do your products and services fit into that market? Do you know your market share? All of these questions are important if you are to stay relevant to your customers and adapt to changing demands. Chapter 12 takes you through what you need to do to measure your market and your place in it.

Assessing Your Operational KPIs

How your business produces its products and services also have a very clear and direct link to revenue, profit and growth. Do you know how operationally efficient your projects and processes are? Are you aware of how much waste is built into your processes? Do you know how many defective products you produce and why? The answers to these questions are critical as you seek to minimise wasted time, resources and customer dissatisfaction.

Project performance

Most strategic objectives are broken down into projects to ensure that the strategy is executed. Without these projects strategic objectives can easily remain aloof.

It makes sense therefore that you wrap some key KPIs around those projects to ensure that the deliver what they were instigated to deliver. Without clear milestones and measurement protocols projects can easily fizzle out and come to nothing.

If a project is critical to the overall implementation of the corporate strategy then you need to measure performance using key project KPIs. Chapter 13 has the essentials on measuring project performance.

Efficiency and quality

There are two ways to create more profit – sell more products or make your products more efficiently. It makes sense to focus on both sides of the equation and that means understanding what is happening in your business on a daily basis and how your products or services reach your customers.

Do you know what level of quality your customers expect? It may be that you have built in levels of quality that are commercially irrelevant or you may be missing the mark too often. Whichever it is you need to know. Chapter 15 gives you what you need to handle efficiency and quality control.

IT

Information Technology (IT) is deeply embedded into most businesses – whether that is through accounts software, customer management software or the ordering system. There is no escaping the reach and importance of IT.

Like most things in life IT is a double-edged sword. On one hand it provides huge benefits in efficiency, data analysis and communication. At the same time the omnipotence of IT leaves us vulnerable to threats. Most businesses are hugely dependant on IT, and any failings in systems can cause havoc.

IT is an important business area that requires monitoring and the use of KPIs. Chapter 16 helps you out with assessing IT performance.

Assessing Your Employee KPIs

Your people are your greatest asset. For most businesses employees also represent the biggest cost. It makes sense therefore to know what's happening with your staff. Are they leaving in unusual numbers? Are they are productive as you would like them to be? Do you even know?

Employee engagement

There is a strong, recognised link between happy employees and happy customers, and another one between happy customers and profit. After all, if employees are happy they are much more likely to interact with customers in a positive, helpful manner. When customers experience pride and loyalty from the employees of a business they are much more likely to believe and trust that business.

Making sure your people are engaged and satisfied therefore makes a lot of commercial sense. Chapter 17 takes you through the metrics you need to understand your business's most important resource – its people.

Talent retention

We are experiencing an ongoing war for talent. Every business needs talent to execute its strategy, and competition to secure that talent is fierce.

Whether you win or lose the war often comes down to recruitment and training. How successful are you at attracting that talent in the first place? And once you have the talent how successful are you are keeping it? Talented individuals want to know that they are going to be developed further and they often expect high quality training once they are in the position so they can improve and develop.

Wrapping some KPIs around recruitment and training can help you answer these and other important HR questions. Chapter 18 covers those KPIs.

Chapter 2

Types, Targets and KPI Mistakes

In This Chapter

▶ Understanding the different types of KPIs

▶ Setting the right targets

▶ Identifying the most common errors

Successfully implementing KPIs involves more than meets the eye. Often the indicators themselves can be quite straightforward, so it's easy to under-estimate their relevance. This chapter is all about context, and making sure that you fully appreciate the various types of KPIs, and what they can and can't measure, as well as looking at how many KPIs you should have, how to set suitable KPI targets and the top three KPI mistakes to watch out for.

Understanding that KPIs can be Strategic or Operational

KPIs can be used to measure *strategic objectives*, that is, monitoring where you are now in relation to where you want to be in the future or to measure *operational objectives*, that is tools for monitoring operational performance on a daily basis. But the two outcomes are not the same – they require different types of KPIs.

Operational KPIs seek to get closer and closer to 'real time' measurement, so you can assess what's actually happening in the business on an hourly, daily, weekly and monthly basis. These insights help you to do things better. They offer up important information about where systems, processes or people are falling behind or veering off course so that you can take corrective action quickly, solving the issue before it escalates into a full-blown problem. This real-time performance monitoring is not required for strategic measurement.

You don't need to monitor strategic measures day-by-day, and certainly not hour-by-hour. Strategic KPIs are more about monitoring progress or trends toward a stated destination, and as your strategy shouldn't change that much, nor should the set of KPIs you use to measure progress toward that stated destination. It's important to monitor the same KPIs over time so you can get an accurate picture of progress.

Strategic and operational KPIs are equally important – they just provide different information for different purposes. However, a disconnect often exists between the metrics a company uses at a strategic, board level and those indicators people use on the shop floor to measure performance. For KPIs to yield all their promise strategic and operational KPIs must be linked together so that everyone in the business can see the connection between what they do and what the business achieves.

To get the most from your KPIs, you need to follow four main steps:

1. **Use KPIs to verify that your chosen strategy is valid.**

2. **Create high level strategic KPIs to help you establish whether you are on- or off-course against that strategy.**

3. **Create a performance framework (more on that in Chapter 4) to measure all the critical elements that will deliver on that strategy**

4. **Add operational KPIs which will allow you to measure those areas in real time.**

The pear tree analogy

Think of linking strategic and operational KPIs as being like a pear tree. The pears on the tree are the product or service you offer to your customers. Your product or service is the visible output of your business in the same way as the pear is the visible output of the pear tree. But the pear didn't arrive on the tree by magic: It is the product of a visible and invisible network of connections and interconnections, just like your product or service. The major branches of the tree represent the various departments within a business – each with their own operational objectives that make the pears possible.

Buried deep in the soil, invisible to anyone looking at the pear tree, are the hidden roots. The stabilising roots allow the tree to access the tangible and intangible resources it needs to grow the pears. The roots draw nutrients and water from the soil and direct it to the right part of the tree at the right time. In your business your tangible and intangible resources – for example money, people, systems and processes – work in the same way as the roots of the tree, drawing the needed nutrients and pushing them to the right place.

In the middle is the trunk of the tree which represents the core competencies of the business that support all the various departments and the common threads that run through the business such as finance, administration, and people. The trunk gives the tree strength and connects the resources to the departments that make the pears possible. See Figure 2-1

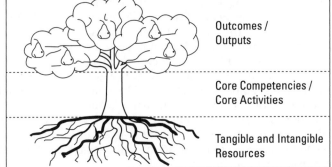

Figure 2-1:
Your business as a pear tree

Outcomes / Outputs

Core Competencies / Core Activities

Tangible and Intangible Resources

Your business is a single entity creating your product or service in the same way that a pear tree is a single entity creating pears. The trunk alone will never create pears. The branches without the roots will never create pears. Pears are only possible when the roots connect to the trunk which connects to the branches to create pears. In the same way your business will not produce your product or service efficiently and profitably unless your roots, trunk and branches know what you are seeking to create, why and how each part of the business connects and contributes to that objective.

Linking the strategic objectives to the operational objectives and using appropriate KPIs to measure how your business is doing against those targets is the only way to make this possible.

To be successful you must understand more than just your product, service or market. You need to know how to get the most out of your tangible and intangible resources so you can produce the best 'pear' possible and stand out from your competitors.

Why we can measure everything and how to do it

People can often shy away from KPIs because they get hung up on the idea of using them for measurement. Measurement implies the application of some unambiguous mathematical or numerical characteristic. Too often people think of KPIs in these narrow numerical terms. It is, after all, easy to quantify things like money spent, number of customers served, number of complaints, or units sold. But of course, not everything that matters can be defined in such a way, so skeptics discount the value of KPIs. They assume that it is not possible to measure things like employee engagement, customer satisfaction, strength of customer loyalty, reputation or culture because they are much too complex and fuzzy.

This assumption is wrong. Everything can be measured, as long as you define what you are actually trying to measure first. You might think, for example, that you can't measure the culture in your business. The omnipotent and mercurial nature of culture does make it impossible to measure – certainly at a first glance. But if you ask yourself what you mean by culture you can begin to uncover elements that you *can* measure. For example you may decide that happy, engaged employees are critical to your culture. How happy and engaged your employees are can be measured. You may decide that innovation is an important part of your culture. That can be measured. By drilling down and defining exactly what you want to know or observe about your culture, you can then ask the right questions and design KPIs that will measure those various aspects of company culture.

We really need to move away from the notion that KPIs are about providing an objective, uniform or quantified picture of reality. Certain KPIs such as profit, sales or return on investment can deliver rigorous, quantified data but not everything that matters is quantifiable. However, that doesn't make things which are less easily quantifiable any less relevant or important to monitor. As Albert Einstein once said, 'Not everything that can be counted, counts and not everything that counts can be counted!'

KPIs are called indicators for a reason – they indicate performance. Quantifying how many people are on welfare indicates how many people are living in poverty but it doesn't measure poverty. An intelligence test can indicate whether someone has a certain type of intelligence but it doesn't measure their intelligence. We've all met people who are incredibly bright and yet lack common sense. In the same way KPIs are indicators of performance but they don't measure performance or provide the whole picture.

Creating the Right Set of KPIs

Creating the right set of KPIs for your business is the secret to success. If you think of KPIs as a torch light, each KPI allows you to shine your light into a particular part of your business and illuminate performance. One KPI alone isn't much help because too much of your business remains in darkness. If however you create the right set of KPIs then you get a much broader, clearer and more informative view of the whole business.

What is a good number of KPIs?

I'm often asked how many KPIs is a good number to have. Unfortunately there is no right answer to this question. Ultimately how many KPIs are right for you will depend on your strategic and operational objectives and unanswered questions you have that you need to answer.

That may require 20 KPIs or it may require 30 or more. The number will depend on your business, but every KPI must have a specific purpose and provide a specific insight, or you should not include it.

As a general rule, I think that corporately a company should aim for between 15 and 25 high-level KPIs, and then have similar numbers for each business unit.

Tracking the tangible and intangible

To get a clearer picture of what is going on in your business it's important to include KPIs that measure the *tangible* and *intangible* aspects of your business. The KPIs for tangible things, such as number of customers or volume of sales, are usually the ones that people rush to first because they are easy to measure.

KPIs for intangible aspects of business that explore, for example, whether you have the right brand image and reputation or whether you have the right people in the right positions and how engaged those people are, may be a little more difficult to measure, but they are equally if not more insightful.

Going back to the pear tree analogy, it is often the intangible elements of business, the ones are not immediately visible (such as culture and customer satisfaction) that hold the greatest potential for elevated performance and results. You therefore must include both tangible and intangible KPIs in your performance measurement framework.

The leaders and the laggers

If you only measure outcomes such as the money you've made this quarter or the products you've delivered this month, then it's a bit like driving a car while only looking in the rear-view mirror. Your financial performance or your sales performance today is an outcome of having done certain things in the past. These indicators are not very good predictors of the future – they only measure performance in the past. These types of indicators are known as *lagging indicators*.

Lagging indicators are important to include in your chosen set of KPIs because they indicate how the business has done against targets. However the information you receive from lagging indicators is provided too late to intervene or change the outcome if necessary. They just tell you what has happened and nothing about what might, should or could happen in the future.

Obviously knowing about the past is not enough: You need access to information that will also help you predict future performance. Indicators that help to prevent problems before they escalate, or help to nudge performance back on track before the problems cause breakdowns in service, or irritate customers, are called *leading indicators*. Again, going back to the pear tree analogy, leading indicators tend to focus more on the trunk and roots of the tree than the tangible outputs.

Companies need a good mix of both leading and lagging indicators to provide the most complete and useful picture possible.

Setting the Right Targets for Your KPIs

For KPIs to be genuinely useful you need to assign a target to each one. A KPI without a target is useless because it's the target that puts the indicator into context and allows you to know where you are in relation to where you want to be.

For a commercial organisation these targets are usually considered in the context of *shareholder value* (that is, how much money they can help to make for people who invest in the company). For public sector organisations a host of stakeholders exist whom the organisation must consider, as well as the need to manage externally-imposed targets.

Targets can be set as:

✔ **Absolute:** Such as 'increase by seven'

✔ **Proportional or percentage:** Such as 'increase by 4%'

Targets should be defined:

✔ **Relative to internal benchmarks:** Such as 'Surpass last year's results'

✔ **Relative to external benchmarks:** Such as 'Surpass competitor X'

✔ **Relative to global best practice:** Such as 'Become as good as X'

KPIs vs. targets

People often ask me what the difference is between a target and a KPI and whether or not they are the same thing. They are not the same thing – even though when people speak about KPIs and targets they might use the terms interchangeably, which is not helping.

So to be clear – you start with a strategic objective (for example, to improve quality), you then decide how to measure it (for example, by reducing waste), and then define a target for your KPI, (for example, reduce waste by 10 per cent). You set your target once you have chosen the KPI you want to use.

Making targets specific

Considerable goal setting research and target setting practice shows very clearly that your targets need to be specific and time-bound. This specificity helps to define your desired target performance level and put a timeframe around the target to focus attention.

When the target is specific, you remove any confusion or ambiguity and allow the people involved to know exactly where they are and where they are heading.

Examples of some good and bad targets

To give you a little more context I've included a few samples of good and bad targets.

First, the good ones:

- ✔ Increase profit margins by 3 per cent over the next 12 months

- ✔ Decrease the number of defects on our production line from 6 to 2 per hour, by the end of the year

- ✔ Grow our relative market share in ice-cream sales so that we become the number one by 2020.

. . . and now the not-so-good to downright bad:

- ✔ Improve customer satisfaction

- ✔ Increase sales

- ✔ Improve quality

A good target gives you something very specific to aim at. It's very clear to everyone involved what "success" looks like and it's not open to interpretation. A bad target is the opposite – it is almost always vague, easy to fudge and open to interpretation.

Making targets realistic and achievable

Your targets should also present a challenge or 'stretch' when compared to current performance. But not too much of a stretch. If the people doing the work that is being monitored feel that the target is unrealistic – either too easy or too hard – then they won't like the KPI, they won't engage with it and they won't strive to achieve it.

KPIs should be used as a mechanism for learning and delivering break-through, or at least continuous performance improvement, and setting the right targets can help to facilitate that outcome.

Additional tips for setting the right targets:

✔ **Use existing and relevant information to review trends and history**. A good starting point is to look at performance over time to detect trends and patterns.

✔ **Where appropriate, consider seasonal or other variations in performance.** There is no point creating a target that is only ever possible for 3 months of the year! For example, don't set the same sales targets for ice-cream, if you know sales peak in the summer and tail off in the winter.

✔ **If applicable, take national targets, best practice benchmarks into account.** In other words, if you are not sure what a stretch target may be in your context have a look at performance levels of other companies in your industry or beyond.

✔ **Take the cause and effect relationships in the business into account**. For example there is no point setting top level outcome targets if you don't then set appropriate operational targets for the people charged with delivering on that target. After all, you can't expect to deliver better financial performance tomorrow unless you hit the right KPIs on customer satisfaction, efficiency and employee engagement today.

✔ **Remember to take time lags into account.** Sometimes it takes time for leading indicators (such as improved brand awareness) to translate into lagging indicators (such as increased sales).

Knowing Where People Go Wrong with KPIs

Before wrapping up this chapter and the basics of KPIs, I want to alert you to some of the most common pitfalls associated with them.

KPIs are incredibly powerful tools in modern business and most people have heard about them, which means that many businesses have sought to implement KPIs in some form or another. As a result, there is a danger that you could dismiss KPIs thinking, 'Oh I've tried KPIs. They don't work in my business,' or 'KPIs are not relevant in my business'.

KPIs do work and they are relevant in every business, from small family-run organisations to global multi-nationals. If you've tried to use them or you know someone who's tried to use them and they didn't deliver on their promise, then my guess is you or your acquaintance sprung one or more of the three common KPI booby traps.

Measuring everything that walks and moves

One of the biggest errors people make when seeking to implement KPIs is that they try to measure everything that walks and moves within the business. They ferret out every single metric, data point or information hot spot.

The assumption is that lots of information is better than no information, but actually it's not. Too much information is as useless as too little, so seeking to squeeze every drop of data from every corner of the business without any regard for what you actually need and how you will actually use the vast amount of data you plan to collect is just as damaging as doing nothing.

In fact you could argue it's more damaging, because you are wasting time and money collecting data you will never use: Not only pointless but very frustrating for the people who do the collecting!

Collecting the same measures as everyone else

The other big error people make is working out what KPIs to measure by looking at what everyone else is measuring. So a business leader may decide that KPIs are something she really needs to take seriously. However, rather than work out what information she needs and what critical business questions she needs the data to answer, she will look at competitor businesses or discuss KPIs with other senior executives inside or outside the business and gather a list of KPIs that everyone else is measuring.

Measuring what everyone else measures is inefficient and distracting. Unless you know what your competitor's strategy is and your strategy is identical you are going to be collecting information that is irrelevant to *your* business. We are all busy enough without measuring stuff that doesn't need to be measured. Your goal is to work out exactly what you need to measure to maintain performance and achieve your strategy and only measure that.

The tendency to jump on a specific KPI bandwagon can also arise if a particular KPI or metric gains popularity in leadership journals. Just because everyone is talking about customer satisfaction questionnaires or employee engagement surveys doesn't automatically mean you need those KPIs. Whether you invest in these types of measure should only depend on your strategy and what you are trying to achieve, and not on perceived popularity.

Not choosing the relevant KPIs

The final clanger people make when implementing KPIs is they don't choose the right ones. There are loads of KPIs to choose from, so many in fact that many business people are already completely overwhelmed by KPIs. If you also consider that the amount and type of data we have access to is constantly increasing, and with it number and type of KPIs, then it's easy to see why people panic and just grab the easy, obvious or common KPIs. At least that way they can say, 'KPIs – yeah, sure I have some of them!'

It really doesn't need to be that hard. KPIs are only useful if they are meaningful and deliver mission-critical information. It follows that your strategy, and nothing else, should drive the KPI selection process.

Chapter 3

Creating a Culture of Fact-Based Decision-Making

In This Chapter

▶ Initiating the right culture

▶ Getting senior management buy-in

▶ Introducing the right meetings

*I*mplementing useful KPIs that improve decision making and performance requires cultural change. Problem is, no-one likes change. And culture change is considered especially gnarly!

If designed properly and used intelligently, however, KPIs can transform performance and drive you towards greater and greater success. KPIs can push the culture of your business toward evidence-based action and decision making. Over time this evidence will replace opinion, guesswork, finger-crossing and *command-and-control* decision making. You know the sort of thing 'Just do it – I'm the boss so get on with it'! Implementing KPIs means that it will no longer be acceptable for anyone in your business to make decisions purely on their experience or assumptions without having evidence to back up their hypotheses or choices.

Unfortunately many people's understanding and personal experience of KPIs in the workplace is fairly negative – backward-looking only measurements that are collected, reported on and then used to whip employees into meeting ever-increasing targets. Apart from anything else that type of KPI is counterproductive and pointless. We need to move away from this interpretation. Instead we need to use them properly – as vital navigation tools that can act as the catalyst for learning, growth and constant improvement.

KPIs are just the tools. The only way to extract real value from the tools is through human interaction. And people won't use KPIs if they feel threatened by them, confused as to why they have been introduced or scared that they will be used against them. Getting the mindset and culture right is therefore an essential part of the effective use of KPIs.

But don't panic – I'm not suggesting you need to launch some lavish culture change programme. Instead, just employ a few simple techniques and approaches that will support a subtle culture shift. Essentially your culture represents the shared beliefs, norms, values, assumptions and expectations of your business. Often the component parts of culture are unconscious and unspoken but they still influence behaviour, attitudes and performance. That said, creating a fact-based culture is actually easier than you might imagine. After all, every business has a culture, but no one person created it. In most businesses the culture just emerged by accident, evolving over time. No-one ever designed it. If, however you know how to design a culture, and what building blocks to put in place to shift perception and defuse tension, then change is possible and it can often be seen in a very positive light.

Implementing the Key Components of Fact-Based Management

There are a number of building blocks that are especially useful when it comes to implementing a culture of fact-based management. Like with so many other initiatives, it is vital that fact-based management is lead from the top in order to create wide-spread buy-in across the business.

In order to foster a culture of fact-based management businesses need to focus on the right behaviours and processes. It is vital that KPIs are used for the right reasons, that they don't become targets in their own right, and that the right meetings take place to discuss the insights generated from KPIs.

Establishing senior management buy-in

Senior executives and the leader of the business always set the tone for everything that happens in that business. Your business will never be able to implement and use KPIs effectively if the people at the top don't take them seriously or don't buy into the need for fact-based management.

It's unrealistic to assume that people further down the business will take KPIs seriously and use them to inform decision making if the people at the top don't. You must lead by example if you want to shift the culture of the business. Employees engage in 'boss-watching' to see what the boss does in the same way children watch their parents to see what they do. If you have children you will know that they copy what you do, not what you say. Regardless of how irritating it is.

If you want to create senior management buy-in to the value of KPIs then involve senior managers in the design of the KPI framework. The key elements they need to be closely connected to are:

- **Developing the strategy map or strategic performance framework.** This will be discussed in more detail in Chapter 4 but essentially the strategy map describes the key business objectives on a single page.
- **Developing the key performance questions (KPQs).** In my experience senior executives are frequently left out of this process, which is a big mistake. They can become very engaged in identifying KPQs because it is so closely linked to strategy and often requires 'big picture', thinking which they tend to enjoy.
- **Reviewing and commenting on the KPIs**

You need to foster the idea of senior leaders as change agents who must embrace their responsibility to communicate the importance of fact-based decision-making throughout the organisation. Senior leaders and key influencers in the business must also set the right tone – with a focus on KPIs as improvement tools rather than command-and-control or simply external reporting tools.

The right management behaviour to foster cultural change toward fact-based decision making

If you are a senior figure in your organisation you need to behave in the following ways, and you need to encourage all the other senior employees and influential individuals to do the same:

- **Show visible commitment to KPIs:** Senior executives must show that they value KPIs as a way of keeping score and improving performance. When KPIs are discussed and written about at a senior level it sends important signals to the rest of the workforce.

- **Explain the role of performance management:** Leaders at every level need to explain why the KPIs are important to the business. Help the people around you to understand the key benefits KPIs bring to them and the business. You will probably need to explain the relevance and benefits of KPIs repeatedly so you keep beating the KPI drum – especially in the initial weeks and months.

- **Get actively involved in the KPI process:** Senior executives across the business need to be actively involved in the creation, implementation and on-going use of the KPIs.

- **Move from inspector to supporter:** Leaders throughout the organisation need to embody the fact-driven culture and lead by example. One of the best shifts you can make to facilitate cultural change is move from a 'performance inspector' to a 'performance improvement supporter'. You need to commit to personal improvement for yourself and help others to improve too. That means helping them with guidance, coaching and advice where necessary.

Introducing KPIs for the right reasons

Many different reasons exist for introducing KPIs into a business. But the only valid reasons are to develop learning, growth and empowerment which will, in turn, facilitate improved performance.

KPIs often meet with resistance from employees and management alike because those employees have past experience of KPIs which have been implemented as a tool to control, cajole and intimidate them. As a result there is often a residual hostility toward KPIs or any type of performance measurement system.

Employees panic because they immediately assume that KPIs are going to be used to monitor and control their behaviour and actions. After all, they've usually been told often enough that 'what gets measured gets done'. They fear that KPIs will become targets, goals or rules that are then used to mea- sure success or failure. In this context staff may quickly come to view KPIs as a management weapon for controlling behaviour, imposing conformity and dishing out reward and punishment. This approach is outdated and fuels a counter-productive 'them and us' mentality within the business.

Management panic because they immediately assume that they are going to have to spend their days creating bulky internal reports that no one ever reads! But it's not just internal reporting – traditionally, KPIs have also been used for external reporting and compliance – especially in public limited companies that must report to shareholders and the market regularly. The fear for managers when KPIs are mentioned is that more and more will be added until they do nothing but measure and report. Whilst some reporting, especially for a public company, is compulsory and necessary it is still not the best reason to introduce KPIs.

Introducing KPIs for reporting and compliance purposes only can often get in the way of real performance improvements. Both actually encourage people to find creative ways to fix or fudge the KPI rather than focus on genuine improvement.

Introducing KPIs as a way to develop learning, growth and empowerment will revolutionise your corporate culture. The right KPIs used in the right way provide vital real time performance information that, if explained and intro- duced properly, can empower employees and management to make better decisions and improve performance. The vast majority of employees want to do a good job. They want to feel as though what they do matters and they want to be able to improve and feel more and more valued. That outcome is made possible by the right KPIs. If an employee can appreciate the connec- tion between what they do on a daily basis and the corporate strategy, they are likely to be more engaged. If they have access to information about how well they are performing and whether they are on or off track then they can self-correct. In this context KPIs are no longer a management weapon, they are an evidence-based tool for continuous improvement and better decision making – at every level. Plus objective evidence via KPIs allow employees and management alike to legitimately challenge and potentially improve strategic assumptions and direction.

For example, one of my clients used to have KPIs to micro-manage their people by measuring how many sales calls they had made or meetings they attended. This approach led to a lot of 'gaming' where sales staff would make sales calls and set up meetings with people that are not likely to buy – simply to boost their KPIs. Today, the same company has changed their culture and now focuses on high level KPIs like revenue growth and leaves it up to the sales people to monitor the finer details of their job. Many of the sales staff still monitor meetings but not in a way that was done before, there is no longer the incentive to cheat. This way, people use KPIs to improve performance.

How many times has an employee spotted a flaw in a system or a process but seen their comments ignored by management? How many times has a manager or employee felt sure a strategic objective was faulty because they were in daily contact with customers or suppliers but couldn't raise the issue because they thought they wouldn't be taken seriously? The right KPIs give everyone in the business access to vital information that can help to direct and shape the company as a collective rather than 'them and us'.

Measuring for learning and empowerment is the only really valid way of using KPIs and this approach will always lead to the biggest performance improvements.

Establishing the processes and culture

If you are committed to creating the right culture, in which KPIs are seen as non-threatening learning and empowerment tools, you can help that cultural shift along by implementing the following initiatives.

Appointing a team to facilitate performance management activities

The idea of appointing a team was formalised by Dr Robert Kaplan and Dr David Norton, the creators of the Balanced Scorecard (more on that in Chapter 4) -. Often referred to as the *Office of Strategy Management* or OSM this performance management team integrates and coordinates activities across functions and business units to align strategy with operations.

By doing so the performance management team help to keep the strategy alive and kicking inside the business. Often, strategy is decided on high, dis-seminated to mid management and then promptly forgotten about for at least a year. This doesn't happen deliberately or with malicious intent, but it's just that the day-to-day operational challenges of the business take priority, and often the strategy becomes divorced from those activities. Appointing a performance management team to facilitate performance management activities helps to stop that disconnect from happening.

Initiating the right rewards and incentives

Another way to stimulate a culture of learning and fact-based decision making is through the right rewards and incentives. The key word in that sentence however is *right*.

Financial compensation is clearly a powerful motivator but it's not nearly as powerful as we have been led to believe. The fact that money does not improve results and can actually cause a drop in performance is actually one of the most robustly proven findings in social science.

Thirty years of research assessing 128 experiments on motivation concluded that, 'tangible rewards tend to have a substantially negative effect on intrinsic motivation.' In a separate study the Federal Reserve Bank in the US commissioned four economists from MIT, Carnegie Mellon and the University of Chicago to study the effectiveness of rewards on performance. In 2005 they reported, 'In eight of the nine tasks we examined across three experiments, higher incentives led to worse performance.' In a separate study again, the London School of Economics analyzed fifty-one studies of corporate reward schemes and confirmed, "We find that financial incentives . . . can result in negative impact on overall performance.'

Individual KPIs should never be directly hard-wired to someone's pay or bonus schedule. KPIs are not a target to hit, they are a navigation tool and performance should always be looked at across a number of financial and non financial factors. Plus linking KPIs to incentives invites cheating!

Look to initiate non-financial rewards and incentives. Apart from being cheaper for the business they are also much more motivational. I've seen many powerful examples such as:

- ✔ A senior executive who regularly sent handwritten notes to employees who deserved recognition.
- ✔ A CEO who gave everyone an extra day's holiday as a thank you for significant performance improvements.
- ✔ A CEO who sent flowers to high performing employees.
- ✔ A government agency who regularly holds 'performance parties' with free coffee and doughnuts to the team who performed well.

The list is endless and you should choose to say thank you in a way that is meaningful to the individual or group involved. That said, one of the most under used and undervalued ways to say thank you is to just say 'Thank you'!

Don't ever underestimate the power of a sincere 'Thank you.'

Incentive and reward suggestions

Below are a few incentive and reward ideas for promoting a fact-based performance culture:

✔ **Celebrate wins:** Most organisations – whether for-profit or otherwise – are not very good at celebrating success. Often they are so focused on the future and the next thing that they forget to take a moment to enjoy the achievements they do make. Make a point of celebrating your wins – even if it's just bringing a tray of cupcakes into the office one morning as a thank you.

✔ **Reward effort, not just results:** It's really important to recognise and acknowledge effort as well as outcome. This is especially relevant when major outcomes may take several months or even years to come to fruition. When people feel that their contribution is noted and appreciated then they are far more likely to remain engaged over the term of the project.

✔ **Reward immediately:** Studies show that if someone does a good job or achieves a significant milestone the quicker they are rewarded or acknowledged the better they will feel. Don't think, 'Oh I really need to say something to Sheila' or, 'Oh that reminds me I need to thank Roger next time I see him.' Stop what you are doing and go and see the person or pick up the phone and tell them what a good job they have done.

✔ **Don't create habits or expectations:** Social science has shown that once something becomes common it becomes expected and loses all its incentivising power, so

don't become predictable. Avoid using the same rewards and reward for different things to keep your people guessing!

✔ **Don't 'hard-wire' KPIs to compensation:** This turns a navigation tool into a target and invites dysfunctional behaviours.

✔ **Balance rewards for individual and corporate performance:** A business is more than the sum of its parts, and yet constantly rewarding individual performance encourages internal competition and reduces teamwork, which is essential for success. You need to balance individual performance with the performance of the team, groups, department and business as a whole. Individual performance, departmental or group performance, and corporate performance should all contribute equally to the success of the business.

✔ **Be creative with *rewards and recognitions*:** Many ways exist to show appreciation that don't cost the earth but which end up having a far better and longer-term impact than financial incentive. Remember to just say thank you and for extra oomph - match the reward to the recipient(s) so that it is especially meaningful to them. For example if you know one of your teams happen to love musicals you could get them all tickets to the Lion King. Not only would it be an excellent incentive, but it demonstrates that you know more about them than they might imagine. And that you care.

Eliminating the fear of measurement

In order for you to create a fact-based culture you need to eliminate the fear of measurement. The performance information that flows from KPIs should never be used negatively to punish, blame or in extreme cases force people out of the business.

If you use performance information in this way then people become scared of KPIs and either cheat, blame others or find novel ways to hide poor results. Accountability should not be synonymous with reward-and-punish or name-and-shame. You need to encourage a different mindset.

If, for example, you use a traffic light system of red, amber, green to indicate progress against objectives you need to help people to reposition their instinctive reactions that red is bad and green is good. Red may not be what you are aiming for but the information that things are off track is incredibly useful and simply allows everyone to re-engage, re-focus and nudge performance in a different direction. Your people need to know that red against real stretch targets, or targets that are going to be hard to achieve but represent real progress, is always preferable to green against easy targets that don't represent improvement.

Dealing with poor performance

So if you are not to link incentives and bonuses to KPIs and you are to eliminate fear of measurement so that people are not afraid of failure, does that mean you should allow poor performance? No, absolutely not.

Creating the right culture demands that you deal with poor performers, because if you don't they can become very demoralising for those who are seeking to improve.

Traditionally, this has been especially true in public sector organisations where underperformance rarely has any real consequences. Such organisation end up carrying *dead wood*, people who have no commitment to their job or their organisation or any interest in performing. This sort of problem does however also occur in commercial businesses. I have seen the incredible lengths people will go to to avoid dealing with poor performers, including creating new jobs with no responsibility or purpose just so they can put that person somewhere 'out the way'.

Look, let's stop beating around the bush . . . If you have poor performers, and I mean repeat or consistent poor performers not those that are having an off day or week, you have two choices – help them to improve or fire them.

If you are seeking to change the culture of your business you must understand that there is nothing more demoralising than seeing incompetent and blatantly lazy colleagues get away with doing nothing! Getting rid of the dead wood lifts morale, sends a very clear and powerful message and helps to rejuvenate a business around a shared vision.

Ideally, find ways to help the individual to improve, whether that is through training, mentoring or changing roles. But if they don't come to the party then show them the door.

Creating Improvement and Performance Preview Meetings

Cultural change doesn't happen overnight and it won't happen if you leave it to chance. You need to create improvement or performance preview meetings that look into the future, rather than the past. They should allow you to monitor progress and speed up the shift toward a culture of fact-based decision making.

To do this, consider creating four different and distinct types of meetings to discuss performance in an organisation:

- ✔ Strategic revision meetings
- ✔ Strategic performance preview meetings
- ✔ Operational performance improvement meetings
- ✔ Personal performance improvement meetings

The content and outputs of these meetings influence each other and are therefore interdependent. However, each has its own clear purpose with different time horizons, frequencies, outputs, focus and supporting performance information, as explained in the following sections.

Introducing strategy revision meetings

A strategy describes the high level objectives an organization needs to achieve in order to be successful.

As the name would suggest, strategy revision meetings are used to revise and renew the strategy! They provide a specific platform to question and challenge the strategy in light of new information that may emerge from the KPIs. This is also the forum in which to challenge any assumptions that underpin the strategy. For example, a strategic objective may be to increase brand awareness. The assumption underpinning that objective may be that greater brand awareness will increase sales. If you have run various brand campaigns, but sales have remained constant then the information is suggesting that the initial assumption that drove the strategic objective is incorrect, or at least needs further analysis.

For most organisations (government, not-for-profit or commercial) one strategy revision meeting per year is enough. If your market is particularly volatile or is experiencing rapid change, then you may want to schedule two per year.

Strategy revision meetings provide a much needed opportunity for you to get together with your executive team and directors to only discuss strategy and nothing else. The objective of these meetings is to agree on, or create a new strategy map (more on this in Chapter 4). This time horizon encourages everyone involved to consider whether the current strategy is still valid *and* will remain valid one to three years from the meeting date. Obviously, these discussions would be shaped and influenced by the KPIs and resulting analysis to ensure that any choices made are grounded in evidence, not speculation.

Make sure that the leader of your corporate performance management team and relevant performance management analysts are also in the meeting. These individuals can provide answers to any data or analysis queries.

It is always better to hold the strategy revision meetings off-site to avoid interruption. Getting away from the work environment can also open up thinking and invigorate the discussion. These meetings are focused on decision making and reaching strategic agreement, and usually last one or two days.

Establishing strategic performance preview meetings

Having a strategy is one thing, knowing whether or not it's working is another. Strategic performance preview meetings ensure that you know whether the agreed strategy is being executed or not.

The purpose of this meeting is not to question the overall strategic assumptions but to fine-tune elements of the strategy and to revise plans for its successful execution. Strategic performance preview meetings are essential for revising operational activities, including re-allocating resources and refocusing on various projects. The strategy map and key performance questions (more on them in Chapter 5) set the agenda and KPIs are used to guide the decision making.

The time horizon of these meetings is medium term – looking between one and six months ahead. Your strategic performance preview meetings should happen once a month and be attended by the executive team, directors and all the heads of department. It is also wise to include members of your corporate performance management team and relevant performance management analysts to provide answers to any data or analysis queries.

Strategic performance preview meetings are great for modelling and testing assumed causal relationships between different strategic objectives.

From my experience, strategic performance preview meetings are the rarest type of meeting in most organisations. They are however essential in creating a fact-based culture and delivering on strategy, so don't ignore them!

Putting in place operational performance improvement meetings

Operational performance improvement meetings provide a regular opportunity for department heads, functional supervisors and personnel to discuss and respond to short-term operational concerns or 'burning issues'.

These meetings usually take place on a daily, weekly or twice weekly basis depending on the nature of the business. The time horizon for discussion is short – looking at operational performance a week to a month ahead.

Operational performance improvement meetings either focus on specific operational performance issues or project performance. KPIs are an essential component of these meetings as they help to illuminate problems which can you can then discuss and resolve quickly.

Aligning personal performance discussions

Many of the annual chores that masquerade as personal performance and development reviews are actually administrative human resources (HR) tick-box exercises that change very little.

Real personal performance discussions should be one-to-one meetings where your employees and line managers can discuss their strategic priorities for the next year. Aligning personal performance to strategic objectives is the last missing element of a fact-based culture. This alignment is essential to help employees personalise the strategy to their daily tasks. When people understand how what they do matters, and how their cog fits into the machine, then they usually become more engaged with their work.

The time horizon for these meetings is between six and twelve months, and they usually take place on an annual basis. Once you have successfully aligned strategy to personal performance it is possible, and potentially beneficial, to hold these meetings every six months.

Personal performance discussions are a great opportunity to engage everybody in the business in a strategic discussion and ensure any personal objectives, performance plans and development plans are aligned with the overall priorities of the organisation. Plus these type of open discussions are more likely to yield innovation and ideas that can further help the business to achieve its objectives.

Guidelines for Productive Performance Meetings in a Fact-Based Culture

While each of the the four meeting types has its own purpose, some shared guidelines exist to help you to move away from dysfunctional behaviour towards a fact-based culture. Successful performance meetings will take time and effort but they are worth it. To smooth the transition:

✔ **Give the meeting an appropriate name**: Be clear and unambiguous and ensure the name reflects the purpose of the meeting. Don't use jargon and don't ever call a meeting a 'review' – people just get nervous. The purpose of all four meetings is to improve performance in the future. It is therefore necessary to look at the past but it's not the primary focus. You don't drive a car looking in the rear view mirror all the time.

✔ **Ensure key people always attend**: When used properly, these meetings are where critical decisions about future performance will be made, so it's important that all the key decision makers attend. As long as you involve those same key decision makers in the design and development of the KPI framework and schedule the meetings at sensible times this shouldn't be a problem

✔ **Foster discipline**: People are busy and meetings are not always popular. But you need to make the distinction between disciplined and undisciplined meetings. Make sure the agenda for each of the meetings is circulated in advance, always start and finish on time, follow the agenda and only discuss what is on the agenda. Expect people to apologise if they can't attend and make sure you reach agreement on action points and next steps so that you make progress. Finally, circulate minutes quickly so everyone involved knows they can rely on these meetings to do what they say on the tin.

✔ **Create an environment of trust, action and respect**. If you foster discipline, trust and respect will flourish: If you don't, they won't. The meetings should be relaxed yet purposeful and action-orientated. Meeting regularly or semi-regularly also helps to strengthen bonds of mutual respect and increases personal commitment, joint decision-making and learning. Blame gives way to solution-focused dialogue and action steps.

✔ **Encourage open dialogue**: Open communication, discussion, and even disagreement facilitate learning and improvement. But real dialogue does require everyone to suspend the notion of right and wrong, pull down their defences and listen. Seek to understand other perspectives, share your thoughts and reservations, and table complex issues. By doing so you are much more likely to uncover faulty logic and unconscious assumptions, and make real progress. This approach also allows everyone to get to know each other better, which will speed up the meetings.

✔ **Stay focused on strategy**: All your performance meetings should link back to strategy. They each represent an opportunity to reiterate what the business is seeking to achieve and assess progress from a number of different perspectives. As such the strategy map provides the structure and agenda for the various meetings.

✔ **Use your KPIs:** Identifying the right KPIs is obviously important, but creating an environment that constantly uses them is *more* important. KPIs provide much of the information in these meetings, and ultimately it is the constant and constructive use of KPIs that creates a fact-based decision making culture. Participants need to take responsibility for analysing the available data and KPIs before the meeting so they can get straight into tackling issues, answering questions and making decisions.

✔ **Aim for collaborative decision making and learning:** People need to feel heard. When they do they are much more responsive, innovative and collaborative, so aim to capture everyone's opinion and to openly discuss different points of view. This facilitates a better-informed debate, reduces conflict and enables collaborative decision-making and mutual agreement on next steps and actions. In these meetings it is absolutely necessary that people feel able to say, 'I don't know the answer', instead of winging it and hoping they don't get rumbled.

Chapter 4

Organising Your KPIs

In This Chapter

▶ Identifying KPI frameworks and their relevance

▶ Exploring the most popular framework – the Balanced Scorecard

▶ Exploring alternative frameworks

*B*usiness leaders and senior executives usually understand the importance of KPIs as navigation tools. They appreciate the value of relevant and timely information and yet most of the focus is on indentifying and designing the KPIs themselves with little regard for how they are organised. This is a mistake.

To help rectify this situation this chapter is about performance measurement frameworks and how best to organise your KPIs for maximum effect.

Understanding the Need for KPI Frameworks

Information is everywhere. Every business holds a vast amount of information. The business may hold it in different places or in different formats, but it is there. If anything, we now have access to too much information and data. Without some type of framework around which to organise that data we simply end up with a huge list of KPIs that we could, should or may measure.

Ultimately KPIs are only really commercially relevant and useful decision-making and navigation tools if they are used, and they will only be used if they are organised clearly and constructively around critical business areas.

Weighing the options

Like the number of potential KPIs that exist there are also many possible frameworks that you could use to organise your KPIs.

KPIs are equally relevant to government and not-for-profit organisations as they are for commercial businesses. But the focus and goals of each organisational type are very different and need to be considered when deciding the best framework for your KPIs.

If you run or are involved in a commercial organisation then there are a number of important areas to consider that are consistent across all for-profit businesses. Those areas may be called different things in different businesses but they cover finance, operations, staff and customers. It follows, therefore, that you , need a framework that includes those areas so that you can measure performance across them all.

If you run a government department or are involved in a not-for-profit organisation then you may still be interested in those areas, but the relative importance within different organisations may be very different and the framework you choose needs to reflect those altered priorities. A government department, for example, will be more focused on delivering services to the community than on financial performance. Financial performance is still vitally important to any government or not-for-profit organisation, but it is not the ultimate goal.

It's therefore important that you weigh up the options of potential KPI frameworks from the perspective of what your business already looks at and pays attention to. There is no point re-inventing the wheel and making additional work for yourself by deciding on a KPI framework that bears no resemblance to the way your business is organised.

Selecting the right framework

Selecting the right framework is crucial in achieving buy-in and acceptance for KPIs in your business. And that means selecting the right framework for *your* business or organisation, not just the first one you come across that looks like it might do the job.

The framework you choose needs to represent your organisation, so the people you want to use it will understand it and resonate with it. For example, you may like the Balanced Scorecard (BSC) – which we'll explore in more detail in the next section – but find your business doesn't call 'Internal Processes', by that name, instead referring to that perspective as 'Operational Excellence'. If that's the case, then change the terminology to match what your business already uses and is comfortable with.

The last thing you want to do is introduce *another* framework, process or methodology that people have to learn and use. The idea is to make the transition into regular KPI reporting as easy and painless as possible so that the KPIs become useful immediately.

So if you are already using a particular framework, or running a quality framework like the EFQM, for example, and that methodology is happily embedded into your business, then use that framework. It will probably already cover all the key areas or considerations that you will need KPIs to measure, so just piggy-back on what's already working in the business.

If the framework doesn't quite cover everything then adding a couple of additional KPI perspectives that the business and the employees are already familiar with is much more likely to succeed than introducing a completely new framework with new perspectives and new terminology.

The KPI framework is really just a way to organise your KPIs around areas that your business already considers important. Those areas will already be present in your business. The trick is to choose a framework that essentially wraps a KPI reporting structure around those areas to provide a meaningful way to present the KPIs and deliver only the information that is relevant to those important areas. Designing and creating the right framework for your business very much depends on the nature of the organisation.

Data-overload at Purolator

Purolator, one of Canada's leading courier companies, understands the importance of organising KPIs better than many. By getting this critical element right they were able to transform their culture from 'KPI scorekeeper' to business partner. Prior to the transformation, Purolator's division managers would each receive a fat ring-binder containing every possible measure, analysis, table and graph that might be relevant to them. The vice-president of finance and administration at the time said, 'We were trying to give them data to address every potential question'.

Only, the ring binder was so big and so daunting that the managers didn't use it. It thumped on their desk every month but the managers were overwhelmed by the sheer volume of data it contained and didn't know what to do with it.

You could argue that these KPIs were organised – they were, after all, in a large, neatly partitioned ring binder, but that's not the type of organisation that's required.

Once Purolator realised that what the managers really needed was KPIs that were organised around their strategic objectives and data that was interpreted and action-orientated, then change became possible. This change resulted in Purolator being voted as having one of Canada's ten best corporate cultures. Not only did the data become much more useful and aid corporate transformation, but it took less time to collate and reduced everyone's stress levels. The fat ring binders became a thing of the past.

Introducing the Balanced Scorecard

The Balanced Scorecard (BSC) is a widely used strategic performance management framework that allows organisations to identify, manage and measure their strategic objectives.

Business leaders need real-time, relevant information about the past and present in order to predict and manage the future successfully. The BSC provides a brilliant, simple and logical solution to that challenge.

Like most great ideas, the BSC is conceptually simple. Its inventors, Kaplan and Norton (see the nearby sidebar 'Finding the point of balance' for more on them and their brainchild) identified four generic perspectives that cover the main strategic focus areas of any company. The idea is to use this model as a template for designing strategic objectives, measures, targets and initiatives within each of the four perspectives, thus providing a more balanced scorecard - hence the name of the tool.

Finding the point of balance

Although the idea of the balanced scorecard was originally developed by Art Schneiderman, it was taken to the world by Dr Robert Kaplan, of the Harvard Business School, and management consultant Dr David Norton. Following a research study into business performance measurement, in which Schneiderman was one of the participants, Kaplan and Norton noticed that most companies measured their performance through a series of solely financial measures. Even in the early 1990s it was clear that whilst financial bias may have worked in the past it was losing its relevance. Clearly business success is not just about how much money a business is making today, but also about the non-financial objectives that will ensure good financial performance in the future.

In addition, financial performance only relates to what has already happened in the past. By their very nature financial measures are lagging indicators and *only* tell the business where it's been. As a result, while they're necessary and important, financial measures do not tell a business leader much about where the business is heading. As such, they're not particularly balanced or insightful when it comes to directing strategy and meeting corporate objectives.

In 1992 Kaplan and Norton published their findings, including the need for a Balanced Scorecard, in the prestigious Harvard Business Review (HBR). The article proved to be hugely popular and clearly hit a business nerve. The pair went on to write a landmark book on the subject, cementing their place as the creators of the concept. Since then the BSC has been chosen by HBR as one of the most influential business ideas in the magazine's then-75-year history (from 1925 to 2000).

In a Balanced Scorecard approach you first define your most important business objectives across 4 perspectives, which are depicted in a strategy map that shows the interdependencies between the objectives. You then define the performance measures and targets for each objective before you finally create an action plan that outlines the initiatives you need to perform to deliver the objectives (see Figure 4-1 below).

The four perspectives explored by the BCS are:

✔ **Financial:** Focuses on performance from the financial perspective. It covers the financial objectives of an organisation and enables managers to track financial success and shareholder value.

✔ **Customer:** Focuses on performance from your customers' perspective. It covers the customer objectives such as customer satisfaction, brand experience and product and service attributes.

✔ **Internal Process:** Focuses on performance from the perspective of the internal processes required to deliver your product or service. It covers internal operational goals and outlines the key systems and processes necessary to deliver the customer objectives.

✔ **Learning and Growth:** Focuses on performance from your employee's perspective. It covers the intangible drivers of future success such as human capital, organisational capital and information capital including skills, training, organisational culture and leadership

Getting a grasp of the four BSC perspectives

Most business leaders, senior executives or managers are and perhaps always have been acutely aware that running a successful business is not just about income and expenses. But it wasn't until the BSC gained popularity that these insights and understandings were formalised in a meaningful framework that allowed those same business leaders to guide their businesses from a variety of business perspectives.

Even if business leaders appreciate their strategy and performance targets are skewed around the financials, the drive to deliver shareholder value and the constant pressure to perform in that numbers-driven environment can make the task much harder than it may, at first, appear.

As a result many businesses still end up measuring performance in an unbalanced way. You need to think of the four perspectives of the BSC like the legs of a table. Most businesses have a strong working knowledge of their financials and a thorough knowledge of their internal processes. But two legs won't support a table _ at least not without a bit of luck. The table may stay upright for a while, but it will not be strong and it certainly won't survive any commercial knocks or bumps.

The balanced scorecard encourages you to measure, analyse and improve all four legs together so as to create a very stable platform. Like a table with four legs, a business that focuses on, and measures around all four BSC perspectives is considerably stronger and much more stable. Ironically, the only way to really deliver financial performance is to extend your focus beyond financial performance to include the other three BSC perspectives.

Tackling the financial perspective

One of the reasons that the BCS is so popular is that it is very easy to understand and is applicable to almost all organisations.

If you consider a commercial business, for example, then clearly making money is a primary goal of that business. But finance is also a very important area for not-for-profit companies or government departments. Their strategy may not be focused around how to make more money, increase shareholder value or initiate growth into new markets, but that doesn't mean that money isn't important. Far from it: Not-for-profit organisations or charities must be extremely vigilant and transparent around how they spend money – constantly seeking to make what they have go further. Government departments or organisations must also be fully aware of their financial performance and measures so they can control costs and be accountable to taxpayers for the money they receive or generate. And this is especially true in times of cutbacks and austerity.

Regardless of the type of organisation in which you are involved, you have to know how much money you make, where the revenue comes from and how much you spend to achieve those results. In the commercial world, it's important that you know the level of shareholder returns your company will deliver as well as revenue growth, profit margins and cash flow positions. But taking a financial perspective alone can be dangerous and short-sighted. It can lead to decisions that are not in the best interests of the business, the community it serves or the wider economy. If, for example, you brush away the rhetoric and scratch the surface of the global financial crisis you will see individuals and businesses hell-bent on the financial perspective and *only* the financial perspective.

Lots of different financial metrics exist, including cost of goods sold, market share, price-to-earnings ratio (PE) and return on equity, that are used by stock market analysts to measure performance and predict future share price movement. In fact the number of potential financial metrics alone can be utterly overwhelming.

It makes sense therefore for you to seek to organise your financial KPIs around your financial objectives. Consider what you are trying to achieve financially:

- ✔ Are you seeking revenue growth?
- ✔ Do you plan to improve profit margins?
- ✔ Are you aiming to be number 1 in term of total shareholder returns in your sector?
- ✔ Do you plan to maximise shareholder value?
- ✔ Are you aiming for long-term sustainable income?

Once you know what you are trying to achieve you can then ask yourself what information or data is going to help you know where you are in relation to that objective? At this stage, don't worry whether you have the data or could get the data - just think about what you would like to know in an ideal world.

The ultimate outcomes

Some say business exists to make money. Certainly making money is crucial to business success, so it's hardly surprising that much of the focus of commercial organisations is on the financial perspective.

This is especially true of publicly-listed companies that have to measure and report their performance to the stock market every quarter. This information can and does have a profound effect on the share price of the organisation, so it's easy to see why CEOs, CFOs and Financial Directors are so consumed by the financials of a business. In many respects their careers depend on being able to demonstrate positive and upwardly trending financial performance.

How do you look to your shareholders

The critical question that financial measures should help you answer is 'How good does your business look to your shareholders?'

Analysts and investors will be poring over your financial statements to decipher whether you are growing, stagnating or contracting, and they will use that information to decide whether to buy, hold or sell your stock.

Often you have no choice about your financial KPIs or priorities because you are being judged purely on financial performance. As a result you are in competition with every other company on the stock market.

Making sure you're delivering to your customers

Although traditionally business has focused on financial performance and has been pretty good at organising and reporting KPIs from this perspective, without an equally sharp eye on customers, the financial performance of any company can very quickly deteriorate.

After all, if your customers are not happy with the quality of your product or service, or the way you treat them or market to them then they won't buy from you or they certainly won't buy from you again. And if you can't find and keep customers then it won't matter how creative you get with your financial KPIs, you won't make money.

You need to know what your customers really want. You need to know whether you are delivering to meet their expectations. You need to listen to what they are telling you – either verbally through feedback or via their buying behaviour. You need to know what they are happy about and what they are unhappy about. And you need to access this information so that you can better anticipate what they are going to want tomorrow.

And yet, the reality is that most business don't really know. Senior executives may sit in round table discussion and make assumptions about what their customers want, but they rarely involve the people in their business who may actually know. Customer service employees, for example, are rarely asked about their insights, and yet they are the ones on the coal face of the business who are probably best placed to provide information about customer needs.

The information locked up in a business about customers is often significant, but unfortunately it is often stored in different places, departments or databases that never speak to each other. And yet this data when unlocked can transform performance.

For example if you know exactly who your customers are, where they live, where they shop and what they read you can tailor your message to them and find more customers who will also like your product. If you know what they want and what they expect then you have a far better chance of delivering loyalty-generating service and creating raving fans who will happily recommend you to others.

The customer perspective of the BSC ensures that you stay focused on this critical area of performance and organising KPIs around your customers will ensure that you really know what's going on from your customer's perspective.

Understanding how your customers see you

The critical question you are seeking to answer with customer focused KPIs is how do your customers see you? Not how do you think they see you, or suppose they may see you but how they actually see you.

And there is no way of getting this information without interacting with your customers and measuring what they actually do.

In the customer perspective you define and measure your customer objectives, which can relate to your market position (e.g. your market share or industry performance), your product or service attributes (e.g. are you delivering in terms of price, quality, availability or functionality), the relationships you have with customers (e.g. customer loyalty) as well as the brand image (e.g. brand perception).

Assessing the impact of the internet and social media

There is little doubt that the customer perspective has taken on new and increased importance since the advent of social media and smart technology.

It is now likely that a great many of your customers are almost constantly connected to the internet via their computer or mobile phone. Every whim, irritation, surprise, delight or frustration is a click, tweet or status update from being in the public domain.

Customers are increasingly asked to share their experiences and rate companies either by the company themselves or via blogs, specialist websites, or social media platforms. This presents both a serious opportunity and a serious threat depending on how well you look after your customers.

Your customers now have a clear and constant connection to the worldwide web which allows them to share every thought and experience with the world – including having a good rant about a perceived or real lack of service or quality.

Looking at your internal processes

Although called *internal processes* in the BSC, this perspective basically explores the operations of a business. How does what you do get done, created and delivered, and how well.

This perspective is probably ignored the most in business. The relevance of customers is obvious as is their impact on finance. But internal processes are often discounted from measurement and assessment because they are either non-core processes such as paperwork, database design, purchasing protocols, warehousing and distribution or they are just taken from granted as part of doing business. Plus they often just evolve over time as the business grows and develops. They need to get done so someone does them, but we rarely stop to consider whether the way we are doing something is the best way to do that thing and whether or not there is a better, cheaper, easier or more efficient way of doing it.

And yet because they have often evolved or been cobbled together when needed they are often ripe for improvement and can yield significant cost and time savings.

United Breaks Guitars

When Canadian musician David Carroll and his band decided to tour Nebraska in 2008 they chose United Airlines, which would take them from Halifax Nova Scotia to Omaha Nebraska — a flight that connected through Chicago O'Hare airport. Obviously they needed to take their guitars, so that they could woo their up-coming audiences, but were told they couldn't take them on board as hand luggage so reluctantly checked them in. While on the tarmac at Chicago, waiting to get off and change planes Dave and his fellow passengers watched, horrified as United's baggage-handling crew threw guitar cases onto the tarmac. Next day, after arriving at his destination and reclaiming his guitar he discovered what he feared to be true - his $3,500 Taylor guitar had been broken.

For almost a year Carroll tried to get United to accept liability for the break and pay him compensation but he was simply passed from one person to another, each denying liability and citing a variety of reasons why it wasn't their fault. Eventually Carroll realised he was fighting a losing battle and in his last email exchange to the company told them that he was going to write three songs about United and post them online.

No doubt the recipient of the email laughed, and may have shared the joke with his or her colleagues. Only Dave *did* write his songs. The first, a remarkably catchy song called *United Breaks Guitars*, was uploaded to YouTube on 6th July 2009. Within 24 hours it had been viewed by 150,000 people. This prompted United to sit up and take notice, but it was too late. Within three days half a million people had seen it. As of January 2014 the clip had been viewed over 13 million times! Plus Carroll also wrote songs two and three. Collectively over 15 million people watched the songs and learned all about how terrible United are at handling complaints!

The good news is that Bob Taylor, who owns Taylor Guitars, offered Carroll two new Taylor guitars. And United use his video for internal training. Carroll got a personal apology from Rob Bradford, United's managing director of customer solutions who told Carroll that United would learn from the incident and change its customer service policy to ensure that it never happens again.

This is a great example of how the balance of power has shifted away from business to customers. The odd unhappy customer didn't used to matter because they really couldn't do that much damage. Now they can. No one can afford to deliver bad service or ignore an irate customer. Your business is always 'on' so you need to know what's happening for your customers through customer focused KPIs which enable you to fix problems or rectify issues before a disgruntled customer whips out his camera and shares his discontent with untold millions.

It is so important to take the automatic pilot off when it comes to internal processes and operational efficiency. And in order to do that you need to incorporate a suite of operational KPIs that can help you to work out what's really going on inside your business – including policies, procedures and quality protocols. Internal process KPIs can allow you to identify where the gaps and opportunities are for increased efficiency, which can in turn increase value inside the business.

Implementing KPIs around internal processes can also allow you to anticipate the future so that the operational part of your business is best equipped to meet the changing needs of your customer.

Knowing what you should be best at

The critical question you are seeking to answer with KPIs focused on internal processes is 'What should we be best at?'

Just as customers are connected to finance, internal processes are also con-nected to both customers and finance. Armed with more customer insight from customer-focused KPIs you are better equipped to know what you need to be best at – according to your customers. And if your internal processes are robust and efficient, able to flex and adapt to changing market conditions, then your financial KPIs will also indicate a strong healthy business.

Paying particular attention to quality

Quality is obviously very important in business but it is relative. What makes the BSC such a powerful KPI framework are the interconnections and balance that it provides between the different perspectives cover in the earlier sections in this chapter. For example, unless you know what your customer actually wants then you could be wasting time and money perfecting quality that the customer doesn't even care about. You need to match your quality needs to what the customer wants, not what you think they want.

There is little doubt that poor quality can be costly not just financially but to your brand as well. But so can excessively high quality or seeking to raise the bar for a particular part of the offering that the customer doesn't appreciate.

If for example you run a hotel, you might decide that you are going to change all the sheets in the hotel to 100 per cent Egyptian cotton. That may cost you a lot of money, but was anyone complaining about the sheet quality in the first place? And even if they love the new sheets are lovely sheets really enough to entice that customer to tell others about the hotel or book again? Unlikely! It would probably be a better use of money to employ more restau-rant staff or a better chef.

Improving and driving future value

The final perspective of the BSC is learning and growth, which seeks to ensure that your business maintains focused on how you are developing and improving. This perspective is critical in modern business because the status quo is rarely the status quo for very long. Business is much, much more competitive than it used to be – even a couple of decades ago – so paying attention to how your business will grow and develop over time is essential. Again the links between this perspective and the other three are obvious with each impacting on the other – either negatively or positively.

Shining the light of KPIs, measurement and assessment into learning and growth will allow you to flag potential areas for concern. For example, do you have long serving employees who are critical to your business?If you do, have you downloaded what they know to others in their team, or is it all still stored between their ears? What happens when that person retires, or if they leave the business?

But it's not just about people.

The 1992 HBR article that introduced the BSC to the world actually labelled this perspective as 'Learning and Innovation'. By the time the first book was published in 1996 this perspective had been renamed 'Learning and Growth'. Early implementation demonstrated that innovation was a better fit in the internal process perspective, but organizational experience has found that even the term *Learning and Growth* has proven problematic and open to various interpretations. For instance, it is not unusual for companies to call this perspective a 'Human' or 'People' Perspective, to only focus on staff satisfaction, training, turnover or other 'employee' objectives and measures. The danger in just focusing on people is that companies miss out other important enablers of future performance, which is what the Learning and Growth perspective is really about.

To address this problem, Kaplan and Norton have articulated what they consider to be the principal components of the Learning and Growth perspective, namely:

- ✔ **Human Capital**
- ✔ **Information Capital**
- ✔ **Organisation Capital**

The following sections cover each of these components.

Looking at people and their skills

Assessing your people is the most obvious component to consider from the learning and growth perspective. Here you might want to assess staff satisfaction and engagement as well as what's actually happening with your employees, what skills, knowledge and experience they have and whether or not those skills are hardwired into the business or remain in the individuals who posses them.

Developing KPIs around the people side of learning and growth will help ensure that you are not held to ransom by individuals who know a lot about your business. It will also allow you to work out how engaged your people are in their work and the strategic objectives of the business. Do they even know what they are? These people focused metrics can help to identify knowledge gaps, identify training needs and help to foster and develop talent within the business. All of which is essential to ensure you deliver what you need to deliver, keep customers happy and make money.

Looking at information and systems

The less obvious component of learning and growth is information and systems.

Developing KPIs around this increasingly important area will help you to work out whether your information systems, databases, networks and technology infrastructure are sufficient to meet your strategic objectives now and into the future.

Looking at leadership and culture

The final component of learning and growth seeks to deliver answers around leadership and culture.

Developing KPIs in this area help you to work out how aligned people inside the business are to each other and the corporate objectives. Plus they can help to shine a light on organisational culture, leadership style, teamwork, productivity and knowledge management.

Putting it on paper and mapping it out

It's worth nothing that the BSC has evolved significantly since its original presentation in 1992 and this has been well documented in a number of further Harvard Business Review articles and five books by Kaplan and Norton. These additional resources do not, however, represent a step-by-step approach to implementation but rather an evolution of the authors' thinking based on experiential learning. As a result there is still a great deal of confusion around the BSC and the term is now used to describe several different things!

Some executives and even management consultants are still using the old terminology and see it as just a measurement and reporting tool. It's not. It's much more than a measurement tool. Kaplan and Norton's updated thinking very clearly positions the BSC as a strategic performance management framework that puts strategy front and centre, in effect wrapping the four perspectives around the corporate strategy so that the business stays aligned to the strategy and measures only what is relevant to that strategy.

Today a typical Balanced Scorecard framework has three key components:

- ✔ A strategy map
- ✔ Strategic KPIs with targets
- ✔ Strategic initiatives in the format of an action plan.

Each component is laid out according to the performance perspectives that the organisation uses. So, for example, objectives that appear on the Strategy Map, such as excellent relationships with key stakeholders, will be supported by appropriate initiatives, KPIs and targets.

Kaplan and Norton suggest that the process of strategic performance management consists of four critical processes:

- ✔ Clarifying and translating the vision and strategy
- ✔ Communicating and linking the strategic objectives and measures
- ✔ Planning and setting targets, and aligning strategic initiatives
- ✔ Enhancing strategic feedback and learning

Whatever KPI framework you decide to use organising your KPIs effectively absolutely must start with your strategy. It is imperative that you articulate your strategy clearly, put it on paper and map it out, ideally in form of a strategy map.

Strategy maps and cause and effect maps

The creation of a strategy map is the most important element of a modern BSC. It describes the key business objectives on a single page. All too often business executives feel compelled to create long strategy documents. While they may look impressive, few people read them and even if they are read in the business the strategic objectives are often hidden or lost in extraneous information.

Strategy maps solve this problem by identifying the few (usually 2 to 5) key objectives for each BSC perspective that if achieved, will result in the successful implementation of the strategy. The BSC strategy map therefore makes the definition and communication of the strategy easier by creating a visual representation of the key objectives boiled down to a single page diagram. This one page map outlines the strategic aims and priorities of an organisation and is the central element of a modern Balanced Scorecard that helps to ensure everyone is pulling in the same direction. Figure 4-1 shows a sample strategy map.

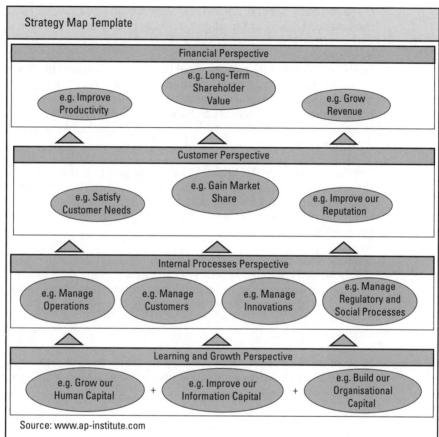

Source: www.ap-institute.com

Figure 4-1:
Sample
strategy
map for a
commercial
organisation

The capitalisation of 'Balanced Scorecard' and Strategy Map is currently inconsistent. Is there a key reason why either should have initial caps?What the strategy map does is put all four perspectives on a single page, which encourages everyone involved to see the cause and effect relationship between them. Otherwise the danger is that the perspectives are seen in isolation, so the Sales and Marketing Director owns the customer KPIs, the Finance Director owns the financial KPIs, the Operations Director owns the internal process KPIs and the HR Director owning the learning and growth KPIs, and they often compete with each other. The strategy map helps to prevent this because it allows all these people to really appreciate the relationship between the four perspectives and their role in them. A strategy map is a brilliant, easy to digest tool for breaking down competitive inter-departmental politics and avoiding the temptation to see the perspectives as boxes that need to be populated with metrics. Instead it's clear that all are linked, and that everyone can see what the business is trying to achieve and how everyone is connected to that objective.

Once you have defined, agreed and understood the strategy, you can use the Balanced Scorecard to align the whole organisation with the strategy and ensure it gets executed. The scorecard helps organisations define and prioritise the activities, projects and programmes necessary to deliver the strategy. Moreover by making sure that processes and activities are aligned to the strategy and the understanding of that strategy is cascaded down through the business the scorecard helps to ensure that everything the organisation does is focused on its agreed strategy. Plus when you add relevant metrics and KPIs you facilitate better decision making and performance improvements.

Get the map right and it becomes much simpler to select meaningful initiatives, measures and targets. The Strategy Map describes the performance enablers and drivers from learning and growth and internal process perspectives that will deliver successful outcomes within the customer and financial perspectives.

Strategy Maps therefore outline what an organisation wishes to accomplish (financial and customer objectives) and how it plans their accomplishment (internal process and learning and growth objectives). This cause-and-effect logic is one of the most important elements of modern best-practice Balanced Scorecards. It allows companies to create a truly integrated set of strategic objectives.

Figure 4-2 shows an example strategy map for a commercial company while Figure 4-3 shows an example strategy map for a not-for-profit or government organisation.

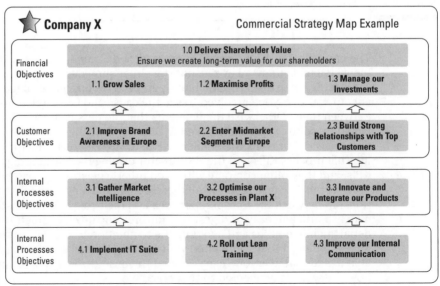

Figure 4-2: An example strategy map for a commercial company.

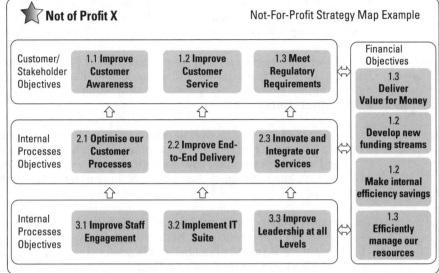

Figure 4-3:
An example
strategy
map for
a not-for-
profit or
government
organisation.

Customising your BSC and Strategy Map for maximum impact

When implementing the BSC, strategy map and KPI framework you need to customise them to fit your business. That means changing the labels to ones that better fit your internal terminology and also shuffling the hierarchy of the strategy map to fit your organisation. As you can see from Figure 4-1 each strategy map is presented as a hierarchy. For a commercial organisation finance is often at the top, but not always.

If, for example, a business has a very strong customer culture then the strategy map may position the customer perspective at the top. Obviously most businesses exist to make money and deliver returns to their shareholders, but without their customers they can't usually achieve that. More and more of my clients now want to represent the importance of their customers by placing them at the top of the map. This not only sends a strong message to the outside world but also speaks to employees who are usually more excited about delivering to customers (who they deal with every day) than delivering returns to shareholders. Actually, most of those put customers and finance next to each other at the top. This way, you can still make the point that both are vital but one feeds into the other.

The strategy map for a public sector organisation is almost always different from that for a commercial organisation because finance is not the driver, so customers or stakeholders are often assigned the top position. For most not-for-profit or government organisations it makes sense to have the finance perspective running along the side (as shown in Figure 4-4).

Feel free to move the perspectives around, add new perspectives that are important to your business and change the terminology that describes the various perspectives to resonate more authentically with your business.

When I was working with a pharmaceutical company to help them create a KPI framework that was appropriate and meaningful to them it became clear very quickly that they were very conscious of not wanting to put finance at the top of their strategy map.

Far from just not wanting to look too mercenary or commercial, the executive team felt very strongly that it was not an accurate representation of their focus and would not resonate with their employees – many of whom were with the company because of their strong and focused research into cancer treatments.

Their strategy map therefore put finance alongside the other three perspectives – in the same way that government or not-for-profit organisations would do. The difference was that the content of this perspective was much more commercial, with a focus on revenue growth and sales margins. This felt much more authentic to the senior executive team and their employees. As such it was much more likely to get traction and engagement moving forward.

Looking at Alternative KPI Frameworks

BSC is not the only potential framework around which you could organise your KPIs. It's well known and used largely because it comes ready-made and is already relevant to every organisation. All organisations whether commercial, not-for-profit or government departments share the four perspectives of finance, customers, internal processes and learning and growth. They may call them different things or prioritise them differently but the elements are always present.

That said, you can create your own or find a framework that is already used or familiar to your business.

What you want is a framework that supports what you already do and are already using. Don't go re-inventing the wheel.

Using Quality or Lean Frameworks

If your business is already running a quality or efficiency initiative such as the European Foundation for Quality Management (EFQM), Baldridge Award in the USA, Lean or Six Sigma, then these frameworks already cover the critical areas of business that you need to measure.

For example if you look at the EFQM model in Figure 4-4. you will see the framework identifies five areas referred to as *enablers* including:

- ✔ Leadership
- ✔ People
- ✔ Policy and strategy
- ✔ Partnerships and resources
- ✔ Processes

There are also four results areas:

- ✔ People
- ✔ Customers
- ✔ Society
- ✔ Key performance results

Innovation and learning run parallel to both enablers and results.

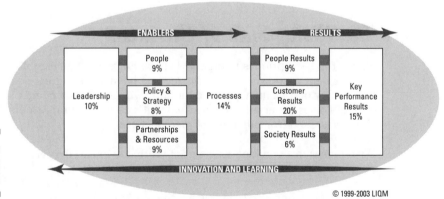

Figure 4-4:
The EFQM
model

If your business is already using the EFQM framework then it makes sense to organise your KPIs around this already familiar framework. The same is true for other existing frameworks as they might already cover, in one form or another, all the main business areas that need to be measured, monitored and analysed in order to improve performance and hit strategic targets.

Using Project Management Frameworks

Although it's very important to design and identify KPIs that will allow you to monitor where you are in relation to where you want to be, often it's also necessary to design KPIs on a project level to ensure that the strategy is executed.

So again, if your company already uses a project management framework like PRINCE2, that framework already allows for the project owner to identify milestones and outcomes and connects the dots about how that project fits into a bigger strategic picture. So organising KPIs around this type of framework can also be very beneficial, not only because it's familiar to the business but also because it sits one level below the strategic level and that can often help in delivering that strategy. When the KPIs are clustered around what actually needs to get done it's easier for people to see the connections.

So while a business may have a BSC approach at the top of the organisation if you were to look inside that business you would see that lots of the actual deliverables of the organisation, or the way the strategy is delivered is in projects. So if you are already using a project management methodology then it would make sense to organise KPIs around that.

The Risky Side of Business

Finally the last option is to organise your KPIs around an established risk management framework. Some businesses have spent a great deal of time and money on risk management and they will know what could or may go wrong. This is especially powerful when it's complimentary to the BSC and risk is assessed from all four BSC perspectives.

What makes this combination so useful is that if you assess risk from a strategic perspective it too could potentially offer a familiar way to organise your KPIs.

KPIs can be daunting, so finding a framework that is not too much of a stretch from what the people in the company already know and use will always improve implementation and use.

Part II
Implementing and Using KPIs Effectively

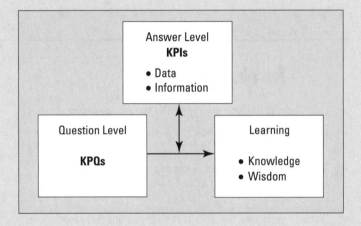

In this part . . .

✔ Learn how to develop the right KPIs for your business.

✔ Understand the importance of translating KPIs into business-relevant insights.

✔ Test the assumptions you've made about your business, and understand how without KPIs, every strategy can only be an assumption.

✔ Come to grips with the datafication of our business world, and learn how to pick and choose the data you need.

✔ Spread the word effectively by making sure your KPIs reach the right people in the right way.

Chapter 5

Developing a KPI

In This Chapter

▶ Identifying the critical questions that need answered

▶ Identifying the right KPIs for your needs

▶ Assessing data collection techniques

*T*he vast majority of executives fully acknowledge the need to measure performance in real time, so they can work out if they are on track toward their objectives or not. However, they don't always know how to develop the right KPIs. How do you distil the mountains of data into meaningful action-orientated information that can direct decision making? How do you find the necessary needles in the ever-expanding haystacks?

This chapter helps you to answer those questions so you can develop the right KPIs for your business needs.

My working life is spent helping organisations define and articulate their strategy, develop dashboards or scorecards around that strategy and developing the right KPIs that will help them to monitor and manage their business successfully and deliver those strategic objectives. What I find time and time again is that any prior effort to achieve this result has been thwarted by a back-to-front approach to the process. Too often organisations fall into the trap of retro-fitting objectives to existing and established measurement protocols. An objective is not necessarily a good objective just because you can already measure it!

KPI development must *start*, not finish with strategy.

The Question is The Answer: Developing Key Performance Questions (KPQs)

The nature of KPIs is to provide answers. But answers to what?

There is no point wasting time and energy sourcing answers to questions you didn't ask or couldn't care less about. To ensure that you don't I developed a concept called Key Performance Questions (KPQs). When it comes to developing KPIs the question is actually more important than the answer – at least it is at the start of the KPI development process. You need to know what questions you need answers to *before* you develop your KPIs. And those questions are KPQs. Essentially a KPQ is a management question that captures exactly what you need to know when it comes to each of your strategic objectives.

The rationale for KPQs is that they trigger a search for meaningful answers and focus your attention on what actually matters – what you need to discuss to improve performance. More importantly, they provide guidance for choosing the right performance indicators. For example, you may be able to work out the average age of your customer but does that information help you achieve your objectives? If it doesn't, you don't need to know it!

Business is tough enough without making it tougher with unnecessary KPIs.

Harnessing the power of questions

The main reason for strategic performance management is to improve future performance. Improvement in anything depends on learning. Real learning is only possible when you take the time to reflect on past results and reflection is facilitated by questions. Just think about it for a moment: When I ask you a question it triggers a search mechanism in your brain. This is the start of a thinking and reflection process which constitutes the beginning of learning. KPQs are therefore essential components of good performance management because they help to put the data into context and turn it into actionable knowledge (see Figure 5-1).

KPQs help you to identify your information needs and ask yourself: 'What is the best data and management information we need to collect to help us answer our key performance questions?' As a result the KPQs ensure that, by default, all your subsequently designed performance indicators are relevant to your business.

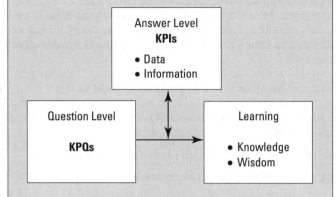

Figure 5-1:
Relationship
between
KPIs,
KPQs and
Learning

KPQs help you and your executive team to:

✔ See the wood from the trees regarding what's important and what's not.

✔ Identify the most important unanswered questions in your business.

✔ Understand the relevance of the data sought because KPQs indicate to everyone what your company's biggest concerns are.

✔ Open communication and guide discussion.

✔ Make better evidence-based decisions.

KPQs help everyone to appreciate and stay focused on the key concerns of the business.

Google, one of the most successful and admired companies on the planet run their company by questions. In considering their strategic performance management process, Google have formulated about 30 KPQs that they need to answer in order to ensure that they stay successful. Google executives recognise that asking questions stimulates conversation and debate, and that innovation emerges from this dialogue. Innovation is essential for many companies, especially companies like Google, yet they recognise that innovation is not something that they can just add to a bucket list of strategic objectives. Innovation is something that they need to facilitate, and questions make that possible.

Creating good key performance questions (KPQs)

There is a right and wrong way to go about creating your KPQs. For a start you need to get comfortable with asking questions! As children we ask questions constantly, irritating our parents with endless curiosity and 'But why's'.

Then we grow up and we stop because we don't want to look like we don't know the answer. After a few years in business we can almost be afraid of questions because the pressure to have all the answers is so acute. And yet businesses that facilitate a very open, questioning culture always out-perform those that don't.

There are ten steps to ensure that you create good KPQs:

- ✔ Identify one to three high level KPQs for each strategic objective on your strategy map.
- ✔ Make sure that your KPQs are performance related.
- ✔ Engage your colleagues in the creation of the KPQs.
- ✔ Make your KPQs clear, short and punchy.
- ✔ Phrase your KPQs as open questions.
- ✔ Make sure you KPQs focus on the present and future.
- ✔ Seek to refine and improve your KPQs over time.
- ✔ Use your KPQs to guide your KPIs so they deliver relevant and meaningful information that answers your KPQs.
- ✔ Use your KPQs to challenge and where necessary refine your existing performance indicators.
- ✔ Include your KPQs in the reports you communicate within the business to review performance.

A few years ago a large blue chip company approached me to audit their performance management approach. As part of their strategy, they had moved to a business model that focused on building and maintaining close partnerships with their suppliers and so it was clearly important to manage those partnerships effectively. In their drive to assess the health of their partnerships, they designed a generic questionnaire which they outsourced to a data collection agency, who reported back with detailed assessments – including graphs, charts and trend analysis – on the questions from the survey. When I spoke to the partners, however, it was clear they were less than thrilled by the survey. It contained about 50 questions that took about three days to complete every six months. Ironically the partners were happy with the relationship but irritated by the data collection!

When I pressed my client about what they were using the information for, it transpired that all of the data they were collecting was 'interesting to know', but that they hadn't made a single decision based on the information collected from those surveys in over three years. They were creating unnecessary work for themselves, and more importantly their partners, for no discernible benefit – not to mention the cost of conducting the survey and getting the results.

Together we went back to the drawing board to really ascertain the key performance questions to which they were actually seeking answers via the survey. And it turned out there was only one: 'How well are our partnerships progressing?' With that as the target we were then able to design a system that automatically e-mailed a very simple form to the account managers with just two questions: 'How would you assess the relationship with our company?' and 'How well is the partnership progressing?' In response to the first question recipients could choose from three options: problematic, indifferent and positive. The second again offered three options: Worse than before, same as before, better than before. There was also space to write additional comments if the recipient wanted to. The simplified survey was sent out monthly because it was much easier for the recipients to complete, and more importantly it flagged potential issues early enough so they could be rectified before they escalated into an big problem. The company now has a very simple monthly data collection system in place, which allows them to get all the information they need to answer their KPQ. It saves them time, money and effort while giving them the real time information they need to manage the partnership relationship effectively, improve performance *and* they've stopped irritating their partners with lengthy unnecessary surveys. That's the power of KPQs.

If you are ever tempted to collect and distribute information in your organisation first ask yourself, 'What is the KPQ I am trying to answer with this data?' If the data does answer relevant questions then send it out and make sure you also circulate the KPQs to help put the information in context for the recipient.

Examples of KPQs

Some powerful KPQs might be:

- To what degree are our customers likely to recommend us to others?

- To what extent are we growing profit margins among our new customers?

- How well do we facilitate innovation in our culture?

- To what extent are we raising customer lifetime value?

- How engaged are our employees?

- To what extent do our project teams trust each other?

- How well are we communicating our strategy internally?

- To what extent are we improving customer loyalty in segment X?

- How well are we promoting our products and services in China?

- To what extent are we growing market share in the South West region?

Deciding on the Right KPIs

Your ideal KPIs will consist of a customised suite of indicators that deliver exactly the information you need but no more. That means KPIs that help you and your team to make better decisions, improve performance and guide strategy.

In order to help you decide on the right KPIs for your business I have designed a ten-step performance indicator decision framework. This framework ensures that you apply a rigorous thought process to every potential KPI that you identify or design. Make sure you work through this ten-step process for every new KPI you want to add to your regular measurement agenda, and apply the process retrospectively to any existing KPIs that your business currently uses.

I'll explain the process below and then provide an example so you can appreciate its usefulness in action.

Step 1: Linking KPIs to strategic objectives

Ask yourself, 'Does this KPI link to our strategic objectives?'

KPIs need to be clearly and directly linked to the strategic objectives of your business, division or project i.e. what matters the most. When KPIs are tightly linked to objectives they provide relevant information that can then be used to monitor progress and stay on track.

Don't make the mistake of assuming that it's impossible to measure some of the more intangible or complex aspects of strategy. Everything can be measured – as long as you get really clear about exactly what you *want* to measure.

Step 2: Identifying the unanswered questions

Ask yourself, 'Does this KPI help to answer specific, important unanswered questions that will help our business?'

The only reason you should include a new KPI or keep an existing KPI is if it helps to answer important and relevant questions that are currently unanswered. And this is where the KPQs come in. Take a step back and identify a key performance question (KPQ) you want answered.

The KPQ further defines the context of the KPI and narrows the area of interest still further from a 'big picture' strategic objective to a much more specific key question. The KPQ puts a manageable boundary around exactly what information is needed and why. If you can't identify the KPQ you are seeking an answer to then it's unlikely you need the indicator.

Step 3: Isolating the decisions to take

Ask yourself, 'Will this KPI enable us to make specific decisions better?'

Once you have identified a pertinent KPQ, there are still likely to be several KPIs to choose from. In order to further filter the KPIs so you can chose the right one for your needs, seek to isolate the decisions you could take as a result of the KPI information.

By articulating the KPQ and the possible decisions a potential indicator will help to address, you can reduce the shortlist still further. Again, if you'll make no decisions as a result of the KPI then you probably shouldn't collect it. Discard that KPI and find another more suitable one.

Step 4: Checking for existing data and methods

Ask yourself, 'What existing data and data collection methods already exist in the business?

Assuming your potential KPI has passed the test of the first three steps then you need to check for existing data and data collection methods to ensure you don't waste time designing something that already exists or could exist very easily.

It may be that someone in a different part of your business is already measuring the KPI you are interested in. Or perhaps someone has already used your proposed data collection method. Alternatively, a simple Internet search could reveal a variety of potential collection methods that you could easily adapt rather than starting from scratch.

Step 5: Collecting meaningful data in time

Ask yourself, 'Can we collect meaningful data of the right quality, at the right time for this KPI?'

Assuming you can identify a pertinent data collection method, you need to ensure that you can actually collect meaningful data when it's needed. You need to make sure that your source data is available, that it's in the right format, is of the right quality and that it's possible to collect the data at the required frequency.

If you discover that you can't collect meaningful data for the KPI then you need to go back to step four and identify another way to collect the data that *will* be feasible.

Step 6: Assessing the usefulness to answering the question

Ask yourself again, 'Does this data help us answer the KPQ?'

Even if you can collect meaningful data for your KPI, and data can be collected in the right format, quality and frequency it's important to double check against the KPQ. Is this potential KPI still actually helping to answer the key performance questions?

Once you start this ten-step KPI decision framework it's easy to shift your focus from identification to design. Make sure you double check that the KPI and data collection method you are assessing still help you to answer your KPQs. If not, then go back to step four again and re-assess existing and alternative data collection methods.

Step 7: Assessing the usefulness to decision-making

Ask yourself again, 'Does this KPI data help us make better decisions?

Step 7 is another sense check to make sure you can act on the data you are about to collect. You want to be sure that you are only developing KPIs that help you to make better informed decisions. If the data you collect is ambiguous then you may need to interpret it so you can act upon it.

If you are not going to make any decisions as a result of the data, or the interpretations of the data are too difficult, then the KPI is pretty worthless and you should find an alternative.

Step 8: Creating awareness of cheating

Ask yourself, 'How easy will it be for people to hit the benchmark or target for this KPI without actually improving performance?'

You need to consider whether or not it's going to be easy for people to manipulate the KPI. Normally KPIs have targets, and these targets can invite people to cheat or at least get very creative in how they collect and report on data.

The best way to avoid this scenario is to create an awareness of cheating and the potential for manipulation, so you pre-empt the problem and ensure your KPIs are hard to fudge. If it's too easy to cheat or there are too many ways to cheat, consider going back to step four and finding a data collection method that is less susceptible to manipulation.

Step 9: Are the costs and effort justified?

Ask yourself, 'Is the insight derived from this KPI worth the cost and effort required to get it?

Once you've identified and developed your KPIs and you know what you could gain from the KPI, but also know what's involved in terms of data collection and interpretation, you will be in a much better position to ascertain whether the costs and effort associated with each KPI are justified. Implementing and using KPIs can be very expensive. For example, estimates suggest that the 'Best Value' measurement initiative introduced by the UK Government added £29 million (almost US$50 million) a year to the running costs of the police force due to the increase in data collection and reporting.

If the KPI is expensive, time-consuming or you're having trouble justifying it, then go back to stage four and consider whether you can get the same information more efficiently.

Step 10: Collecting the data

Ask yourself, 'OK, what are we waiting for?'

If your KPI has reached step ten intact and the KPI benefits are clear, start collecting the data and use the KPI.

Following this ten-step process every time you are considering a KPI or want to review your existing KPIs ensures that you can rest easy knowing that you have designed a suite of relevant and meaningful KPIs.

Making it work: the ten-step template in action

I was working with a major hotel chain when we applied the KPI decision template to improve existing ways to measure performance, and they had one 'Aha!' moment after the other.

Let's look at the measurement of staff as an example. In the past, the company happily conducted an annual staff survey. Here are the various steps and some key learning points:

✔ **Step 1: Linking KPIs to strategic objectives.**

The management team acknowledged that staff were absolutely vital to the success of the business, but the various questions on the staff survey were not tightly liked to any strategic objectives. The biggest staff-related strategic objective for this hotel group was: To have engaged staff that are proud to work there.

✔ **Step 2: Identifying the unanswered questions.**

Again, the team realised that the findings from the staff survey would often throw up new questions, but rarely systematically provide answers to the key business questions. The key questions were: 'To what extent to our staff feel engaged and proud?' as well as 'What do employees particularly like and dislike about working here?'

✔ **Step 3: Isolating the decisions to take.**

What the team realised was that they had lot of data and numbers but little actionable insights, especially around the things staff particularly liked or disliked. The aim was to create metrics that could lead to corrective actions.

✔ **Step 4: Checking for existing data and methods.**

The existing staff survey was very comprehensive but was lacking the information on the things employees particularly liked and disliked.

✔ **Step 5: Collecting meaningful data in time.**

The company only conducted the staff survey once a year, leaving a lot of time to pass between any measurements. We changed this to quarterly surveys (of a quarter of the workforce each time). The traditional survey was replaced with a three-question survey:

- Would you recommend this company as an employer to a friend?

- What do you particularly like about being employed here?

- What do you think the company could improve to become a better employer?

✔ **Step 6: Assessing the usefulness to answering the questions.**

The new set of questions was now tightly linked to the KPQs and was providing the answers to the most critical staff-related business questions.

✔ **Step 7: Assessing the usefulness to decision-making.**

The balance between the numeric input from the first question and the open-ended feedback from the second and third questionS provided rich insights that could easily be turned into corrective actions.

✔ **Step 8: Creating awareness of cheating.**

The management team had few concerns about cheating when it came to the staff feedback, but felt that the new approach improved accuracy and eliminated some of the dangers around bias – for example, where the data is collected only once a year and might coincide with unusually positive or negative headlines or events.

✔ **Step 9: Are the costs and efforts justified?**

The new approach reduced the costs significantly because the company was able to bring the data collection back in-house, instead of paying an external survey company a lot of money each year to collect and analyse the data. In addition, the time staff spend completing the survey has gone down, and so has the time it takes to analyse and interpret the data.

✔ **Step 10: Collecting the data.**

The hotel group has now been running the new survey for a number of years and is very happy with the insights it is getting. Each quarter, a new set of initiatives is launched to improve staff engagement and overall the survey is showing increasing levels of staff satisfaction.

Deciding on How to Collect the Data

Once you have identified suitable KPIs and applied the decision-making framework to ensure they are the right KPIs for your needs, you need to decide how you will collect the data.

Deciding how to extract actionable insights and knowledge depends on your answers to three interdependent questions:

1. **What data do you need to meet your information needs?**

2. **Does the data exist in the right format?**

3. **If you have not got the data in the right format then what is the best way to obtain that data?**

You need to ensure that you collect the right data and the right quality of data so that you can answer you KPQs accurately. An effective data-driven strategy is built on your ability to collect, analyse, and turn data into meaningful information and insights. Poor quality or inappropriate data will compromise your ability to make important decisions, implement the right strategies for your business and improve performance.

Identifying types of data

When it comes to data collection the two main types are usually called *quantitative* (numeric) and *qualitative* (non-numeric).

As a general rule qualitative data is particularly useful for establishing theories and gaining a deeper understanding of specific issues, while quantitative data is particularly useful for testing theories and assumptions.

Applying quantitative methods

The most common assumption about KPIs is that they are numerical. If you were to ask 100 executives for an example of a KPI, my guess is that all of them would immediately name a quantitative KPI such as Return On Investment. Quantitative data is by far the most commonly collected in business, because it is easier to collect. Plus it's also easier to translate and interpret. It's much more black-and-white.

If your KPQ requires that you classify features, count them, and then construct a statistical model to explain what you observed, then you probably need to collect quantitative data. Quantitative data is usually collected automatically via normal operations such as customer service conversations, or through a well-designed survey.

Creating good surveys

Questionnaires and surveys are popular methods for collecting valuable performance data. Although they can be extremely expensive, they don't need to be. Once you have designed the survey, technology can distribute it electronically to thousands of employees or customers around the world, at minimal cost.

There are, however, some rules to follow when designing your survey to ensure that you collect meaningful data that you can then use to improve results:

✔ **Explain the purpose and potential benefit of the survey.** If recipients understand why they are being asked to complete the survey and what difference the results might make to their lives then they are more inclined to take it seriously, engage with the questions and provide useful information.

✔ **Make the purpose of each question clear so it's obvious why you're asking it.** Most people are responsive to questions when they appreciate why it's being asked and can appreciate the relevance and importance of the question.

✔ **Use clear, simple language.** That means no overly complex 'business-speak' or jargon.

✔ **Ask one question at a time.** Don't roll questions together – this can be irritating if the recipient wants to answer them differently. For example I saw an HR survey that asked recipients to score from 1–5 'How successful are we are linking competency assessment to business strategy and the evaluation of individual performance.' They are two different questions.

✔ **Make it as short and easy to complete as possible.** Only ask questions that you genuinely need the answers to.

✔ **Have your survey professionally designed so that it looks attractive and includes plenty of white space.** If the survey looks unprofessional or cluttered then it will actively deter people from completing it.

The weaknesses of quantitative data

The biggest weakness of quantitative data is that it can often lack detail and context.

For example a section of your staff may indicate they are disengaged but the survey won't reveal why. And without the why, you don't have the insight necessary to change the situation.

Understanding qualitative methods

You often need to collect qualitative data after completing the initial survey to dig deeper into the quantitative responses. If, for example, your staff survey identified disengaged employees, a further qualitative approach would help to shed light on why they were disengaged. By analysing this additional, richer data in context you will understand how these employees feel and what is driving their behaviour. And it is those insights that can help identify a solution.

In the following sections, I discuss the most popular methods for collecting qualitative date.

Conducing qualitative surveys

Instead of asking recipients for quantitative data – such as rating their level of agreement with a specific statement, for example – a qualitative survey asks open questions to collect more detailed, albeit less structured, information. For example, you might ask your customers to describe their last purchasing experience with your company.

To save time, money and potential survey overkill, many companies are now incorporating both quantitative and qualitative elements into their surveys. Allow recipients to provide additional feedback should they want to, so they have the opportunity to raise issues that are important to them but do not appear on the survey.

Focusing on focus groups

Focus groups are facilitated group discussions of between five and 20 participants who are asked to share their ideas, experiences and opinions.

Focus groups offer an interactive element which can result in better data. When people get together and share their experiences, this debate can often trigger additional insights and information that may be missed in a survey. As a result this approach is particularly useful for assessing highly subjective indicators such as customer experience, customer or staff engagement, team-working, organisational culture, or trust. They can, however, be quite expensive and time-consuming so you'd better make sure you really need the data, and that it will drive decisions and improve performance.

The mystery of mystery shopping

First used in the mid-1980s by the more pioneering retail organisations to assess customer experience, mystery shoppers are now used extensively in the service sector, for example in the hospitality, banking and financial services industries.

As the name would suggest, a company employs or outsources 'secret shoppers', posing as genuine clients or customers, who then buy a product or service and report back to HQ about the experience. This approach is useful because you don't have to impose on your real customers to get an idea of the customer experience. Plus you can control what you are trying to assess more easily. For example, you could ask your mystery shoppers to focus on a particular area of the customer experience, such as complaint handling. You can also use this approach for other internal performance assessments, such as organisational culture or atmosphere.

Conducing peer-to-peer assessments

Gathering information via peer-to-peer assessment can be very insightful because you are effectively getting people who work closely together to assess each other – either openly or anonymously. Done well, it allows people to learn from each other and to consider their own performance from the perspective of their colleagues. However, peer-to-peer assessment is a recipe for disaster if done badly. It's imperative that the process is put in the right context so that the people involved do not get defensive.

Peer-to-peer assessment is particularly useful for gauging things like:

- ✔ Trust
- ✔ Knowledge and experience
- ✔ Teamwork
- ✔ Relationships

Observing situations

Observing situations or activities without interfering in or manipulating the environment can also provide a great deal of qualitative data. The benefit of this approach is that you don't disturb or interrupt anyone. It can also provide additional, more subtle, insights because the person observing can take in and make sense of the entire experience through all the senses. As a result, observation can provide a more holistic understanding of what's being observed than other data collection methods.

Observation outputs can be score sheets, checklists, reports or video or audio recording. This approach can be particularly useful when assessing organisational culture, employee skill and experience, emotional intelligence, and creativity.

Putting bullets on a board

Many of the methods above have been around for a long time. Changes in technology, however have also created addition methods for data collection.

For example, online bulletin boards allow a discussion (or *thread*) to develop over time and can be a rich source of qualitative data. By regularly interacting with participants on the bulletin board you can assess how an idea, concept or sentiment grows and changes over many weeks or even months. This is also true for blogs and social media. In a world where just about everything is shared there is, by definition, a wealth of qualitative data online if you know where to look.

The weaknesses of qualitative data

A biggest challenge with qualitative data is that it's not neat, formulaic or structured. As a result it can be much harder to collect, analyse and interpret.

It is also more susceptible to bias than quantitative data, because it is much easier for a person to put a particular spin on the collection of perceptions or observations than it is on hard numbers. Numbers are more definitive and objective: They are what they are. Qualitative data is subjective and open to interpretation.

To minimise bias make sure you challenge the data and the person collating the data to understand the assumptions that sit behind their findings.

Combining data to improve insights

Both qualitative and quantitative methods are important. Using one without the other can obscure facts and introduce bias and assumption rendering the whole data collection process useless.

You need to accept that KPIs will not capture the whole truth about your business. They are indicators, not necessarily facts. After all, if they were facts then we would be talking about KPFs and not KPIs! KPIs indicate a certain level of performance, but they don't measure that performance. For example, a customer service indicator will give you an indication of how your customers feel about you but it won't measure total customer satisfaction or provide a complete picture. If you were to take the Mensa I.Q. test, it would give you an indication of a particular type of intelligence but it doesn't completely measure all dimensions of that intelligence.

The more data points you get – quantitative and qualitative – the more complete your picture will be. A data point is just an item of factual information gained from measurement or research. For example there are many data points around a financial transaction including how much was transferred, when it was transferred, who sent the money, who received it and what currency it was received in. Each item or piece of factual information is known as a data point.

When you also vary the data collection methods you use, you can *triangulate* the information. This simply means that you collect data from different data sources, use different methodologies or use different people to collect the data so you can contrast and compare what you find, helping to validate the reliability and accuracy of the information.

It is incredibly easy to unwittingly introduce bias into data collection. Ultimately the process is managed by people and people come with a whole bunch of expectations, judgments, beliefs, values and assumptions that can colour the data.

Abraham Wald was a WWII statistician who helped the air force to assess aircraft vulnerability. The strategy was – find out the areas on the aircraft that were most vulnerable to enemy fire and reinforce those areas. Makes sense! Every airplane was then examined for bullet holes to establish what parts of the plane were hit the most. Based on the data the air force then concluded those areas most hit should be reinforced. Again, makes sense . . . until Wald pointed out that the data was flawed. The only planes that could be examined were the planes that made it back to base. The fact that the aircraft made it home proved that the bullet holes, regardless of how many, were not fatal in those locations. It therefore probably made more sense to reinforce all the areas where there were *no* bullet holes because those planes never made it home!

The big data challenge

In the last two decades two things have changed the game when it comes to data collection. The first is that computer storage and processing power has increased exponentially. If you think back to your first desktop computer – go on, it's not that long ago – the smartphone in your pocket is now more powerful. You can buy a portable hard drive with a terabyte of storage for under $100. You could write books 24 hours a day seven days a week for the rest of your life and never come close to filling a terabyte of storage! Plus technology has also made it possible to process and analyse all that data for the first time.

The second game changer is the amount, type and quality of data being generated. Consider the explosion of social media and our love of sharing (and over-sharing) information. Data is everywhere, in words, numbers, images, video, audio, status updates, tweets and so on. The amount of data we now produce is genuinely staggering, hence the term *big data*.

Potentially, this messy, unstructured data offers you many more data points from which to draw your evidence. The challenge, however, is that the sheer volume of the data now available makes the task of finding the right bits even more daunting. It is now more important than ever that you develop the right KPIs, so that you can pluck the useful information from the ever-expanding sea of irrelevant data.

Finalising Your KPIs: Applying the KPI Design Template

To help you design your KPIs I've developed a KPI design template. Ideally you should use this in conjunction with the KPI decision framework described earlier. The template helps you to eradicate the ambiguity, ambivalence, and inconsistency that can so often creep into data collection and KPI reporting.

If your KPIs are to become the basis for strategic execution, growth, learning and evidence based decision-making everyone must understand what the KPIs mean, why they are needed, how reliable they are, where the data comes from, how it's collected while also identifying the KPI targets.

Use this design template to develop completely new KPIs that deliver the answers you need or improve the effectiveness of your existing

The basics

The first four elements of the KPI design template address the basics of each KPI and help to put it in context.

Strategic Objective

It's always best to clearly specify to which strategic objective the KPI relates, so that everyone looking at the KPI immediately appreciates its relevance.

If appropriate you can also identify the person(s) or function(s) responsible for the management and delivery of the strategic objective that the KPI is assessing. This may be an individual executive or employee, or a team of people. Clarifying ownership in this way allows you to know who to call in the future should you need to discuss performance, or fine-tune the KPI.

Audience and Access Rights

Here you define the primary audience for this KPI – basically, who will see the data and who will have access to it.

Sometimes it is possible to define a primary and a number of secondary audiences. For example, the primary audience for financial information might be the senior leadership team, and secondary audiences might include shareholders, analysts and other functional managers within the business.

Key Performance Question (KPQ)

For each KPI, state the KPQ that the indicator is helping you to answer.

Again this helps to provide context around why this particular indicator is being introduced and on which specific issue it is going to shed more light. It puts the KPI in context and helps keep people engaged in its on-going measurement.

How will and won't the data be used?

Specify how the KPI will be used; for example, share the decision(s) the KPI is helping you make. This provides even greater context, so that everyone who uses the KPI or comes across the KPI is clear about how you plan to use the information and evidence it provides.

This is especially important if you are introducing a suite of new KPIs, because it helps to reassure everyone involved that every one of the KPIs has a very specific purpose and is not just added to make the initiator look good!

Another part of this section is to define how the KPI will *not* be used. Sometimes, people are scared to report on measures because they fear negative results could be used against them. Here, you can say that the KPI won't be used to determine the performance of individuals and won't be linked to bonus payments.

Completing your KPI Template

The rest of the KPI template covers the more technical aspects of the data collection. It's essential that you consider the strengths and weaknesses of the different data collection methods and how appropriate they are for you and your business.

As designer of the KPI you should include the elements in the following sections.

Indicator name

Every KPI needs a name so that you can discuss it collectively and everyone knows exactly what is being discussed. Choose a name that clearly explains what the indicator is about.

If the KPI you have chosen to measure already has a name, make a special effort to ensure that everyone is on the same page. Too often in business we use language or jargon that means something different to different people. This can cause problems, so double check that everyone is talking about the same thing.

Data collection method

Identify and describe the data collection method you are going to use for each KPI. It's important to keep the strategic objective and KPQ in mind when you do this. Too often the decision about which data collection method to use is an automatic response based on traditional methods, past experience or plucking the latest one discussed in management journals. It is far better to really engage with the challenge and consider the strengths, weaknesses and appropriateness of different data collection methods.

Data collection methods include surveys, questionnaires, interviews, focus groups and collection of archival data.

Targets and Performance Thresholds

Define a target or benchmark for each indicator – for example, grow our revenues by 20 per cent over the next 12 months. Here you can also outline the performance thresholds, that is, when performance levels are judged to be good or bad. A common way to do this is to institute a traffic light system where red represents bad performance or target missed, amber (or yellow) is flagging up minor issues and green is good performance or on target. Some companies prefer to add another one – usually blue – to indicate target exceeded, which in most cases is a good thing but could indicate too much effort is put into one area maybe to the expense of another.

Scale Types

Many different types of scale exist:

- **Nominal:** Differentiates between items based on names or categories such as gender, nationality or language.

- **Ordinal:** Differentiates between items based on rank order such as determination of more or less, star ratings etc.

- **Interval:** Differentiates between items based on intervals, where the steps of the interval are the same, but you can't claim that 10 is half of 20 such as temperature in Fahrenheit or Celsius.

- **Ratio:** Is the highest form of measurement scale, where we look at an interval scale that has a true zero, so that you can claim that 10 is half of 20. Example include length, time, or temperature in Kelvin.

- **Likert scale:** Determines the extent to which the respondent agrees or disagrees with a statement. A typical Likert scale is:

  1 = Strongly disagree

  2 = Disagree

  3 = Neither agree nor disagree

  4 = Agree

  5 = Strongly agree

The scale you choose is very important because it has implications on how you can use the data. For example, a nominal scale just tells you if something is one thing or the other – it doesn't reveal any order or relative size. An ordinal scale adds more depth by telling you whether something is bigger or better than another although it won't tell you how much bigger or better. The Likert scale can be used to determine how much bigger or better.

Different options exist to extend the classic 5-point Likert scale and to change between odd-numbered and even-numbered scales. The danger with odd-numbered scales is that there is, by definition, a middle value which represents a neutral, undecided or neither agree or disagree response. This can become an easy option or cop-out for respondents. Even-numbered scales avoid this scenario because they don't provide a neutral response. As a result, even-numbered scales are often called forced-choice response scales because they force the respondent to get off the fence one way or the other. Forced-choice questions are useful tools if respondents are reluctant to state their preferences.

Formula, scales and assessment criteria

It's important to specify the formula, scale or assessment criteria that will be used for the KPI so that you create uniformity around the data, and so that everyone is talking the same language. Is it possible to create a formula? Is it an *aggregated KPI* (where for example overall sales revenue is aggregated by adding all the sales revenues from the business units) or index that is composed of other indicators (for example, a quality index could be composed of waste levels and rework levels)? Are you using a scale?

Source of the data

Your KPI template should specify where the data is coming from so that people using the KPI can be assured of its reliability and validity.

For example, if you decide that the best way to collect customer sentiment is through interviews, questions may arise about how reliable that data is. People are not always as honest as they could be in that environment, so interviews in this context are likely to give a distorted picture of what's really going on.

Data Collection Frequency

You need to specify how often the data for the KPI will be collected and coordinate the dates when data is collected.

Some KPIs require data to be collected continuously. Others specify hourly, daily, monthly, quarterly or annual collection. It's important to know why you are choosing the frequency so you can make sure the data is only collected as often as it's actually needed. If you wanted to lose weight you would make the best decisions if you knew what you weighed every day; you wouldn't gain anything if you chose to weigh yourself every hour. It would just waste time and energy.

The reporting requirements for each KPI will also influence frequency of collection. If, for example, the data has to be reported at the end of each month, then it makes sense to schedule collection so that there is enough time to collect the data, chase people where necessary, analyse it, aggregate it, solve any issues and deliver the report while still ensuring the data it contains is as recent as possible.

It also makes sense to coordinate collection dates. Too much data collection is *ad hoc* and uncoordinated. The result is it either doesn't get done, is the first thing to get bumped off the to-do list when someone gets busy, or it wastes too much time. Wherever possible, coordinate and schedule the data collection so as much of it as possible gets done at the same specified time. This is much more efficient than scattering collection over a longer period, and if all departments are collecting data at the same time it is much easier to get a valid snapshot of performance across different areas of the business. This is much harder if data is collected at different times from different departments.

One of the biggest mistakes companies make in performance assessments is in not collecting data frequently enough. For example, most large companies conduct staff surveys once a year, which provides a single snapshot of staff sentiment. A far more insightful way to collect that data would be to survey 10 per cent of the workforce every month. Everyone is still only surveyed once a year but this approach allows you to plot trends because there are 10 data points (10 per cent for 10 months) instead of 1 data point.

Data Reporting Frequency

You need to specify when and how often the data for the KPI will be reported. It might go into the weekly or monthly performance report or be updated on the performance dashboard on a bi-weekly basis.

It makes sense to coordinate the data collection and reporting frequency to ensure the data you are reporting is as current and up-to-date as possible. For example, you don't want to end up in a situation where data is collected in January and reported at the end of the year.

Who measures and reviews the data

Your KPI framework should also specify the individual or job title of the person responsible for the data collection and data updates. It is always preferable to name a specific individual because the job is more likely to get done that way.

The owner of the KPI can be a named employee or business function, or, increasingly, an external agency; many businesses are outsourcing data collection for some KPIs. This is especially common for KPIs connected to qualitative issues such as customer satisfaction, reputation, brand awareness and employee engagement.

Make sure you also clarify whether there are any review or sign-off cycles. Often one person will be responsible for collecting the data, including data input, and another person will be responsible for cross-checking or signing-off the data before it is released.

Expiry and revision dates

Your KPI template should always include an expiry date or revision date. KPIs are sometimes only needed for a specific period of time, perhaps during a particular project or restructuring process. Without an expiry or review date these KPIs can continue indefinitely, causing unnecessary work.

Even if indicators are not time- or project-specific they should be assigned a review date which is in the diary of everyone involved. When that date rolls around you re-visit the KPI to ensure it remains relevant and useful. If it's no longer relevant then delete the KPI.

How good is the indicator?

Following the KPI decision framework allows you to develop the right KPIs and *only* the right KPIs. The final part of the process establishes how good your KPI is in terms of cost, completeness and ability to manipulate.

How much will it cost?

Introducing and maintaining a KPI can be expensive. It follows, therefore, that you need to estimate the costs involved so you can make sure it's all worth it. That estimate should also be included in your template to remind you of that assumption should anything change that would require you to re-evaluate the validity of the KPI.

Costs can include the administrative costs or outsourcing costs for collecting the data, as well as the efforts needed to analyse and report on the performance.

How complete is this indicator?

By now you will have worked through all the key aspects of the KPI and will be able to determine how confident you are that the KPI will help you answer your KPQs and support your decision making.

For financial KPIs, your confidence is probably high, since long-established and widely used KPIs are used to measure performance in this area. However you may not be as confident measuring intangibles such as organisational culture, employee competencies or brand image and reputation. It's important to acknowledge this and assess your confidence level, because doing so forces you to think about how confident you are that the KPI will actually measure what it was designed to measure.

You can express your confidence in the KPI in a variety of different ways:

- ✔ As a percentage from 0 to 100 per cent
- ✔ As a grade from 1 to 5
- ✔ As a colour code such as red, amber and green
- ✔ As symbols such as smiley faces or frowns.

In whatever way you choose to express your confidence level, include a brief written comment to clarify the level of confidence and explain the limitations of the KPI.

Being aware of any unintended consequences

In the development process you will already have thought about the various ways the KPI can potentially be manipulated or how people can cheat. Make a note of these. If you discover new ways, add them to the list. Reflecting on possible KPI dysfunctions allows you and the people using the KPI to consider even better ways of collecting and assessing performance. Calling these behaviours out at the start can help to stop people from trying them and alert everyone to monitor for those behaviours.

Together, the KPI decision template and the KPI design template provide powerful tools to make any KPI development project a success. In the sample KPI template you can find two practical examples of how the template could be completed for the NPS (Net Promoter Score) and profit margin KPI. The KPI design template is shown in tabular form in Table 5-1.

Table 5-1	Sample KPI Design Template	
	Example 1	*Example 2*
Strategic Goal: *Name the strategic objective (from the strategy map), which is being assessed with this indicator.*	Grow Customer Satisfaction (Customer Perspective)	Grow Our Profits (Finance Perspective)
Audience / Access Name the key audience for this indicator and clarify who will have access rights to it	Board of Directors and Marketing Team	Board of Directors and Finance Team
Key Performance Question(s): *Name the performance question(s) this indicator is helping to answer.*	To what extent are our customers satisfied with our service?	To what extent are we generating bottom-line results?
How will and won't this indicator be used? *Describe how the insights this indicator generates will be used and outline how this indicator will not be used.*	The indicator will be used to assess and report on our customer success internally. It will not be used to assess performance of individuals or to determine bonus payments.	The indicator will be used to assess and report financial performance internally and externally. It will also be a key indicator to determine executive pay.
Indicator Name: *Pick a short and clear indicator name.*	**Net Promoter Score**	**Net Profit**
Data Collection Method: *Describe how the data will be collected*	The data will be collected using a mail-based survey.	The data for the net profit metric is collected from the income statement (or the finance and accounting system).

	Example 1	*Example 2*
Assessment / Formula / Scale *Describe how performance levels will be determined. This can be qualitative, in which case the assessment criteria need to be identified, or it can be numerical or using a scale, in which case the formula or scales with categories need to be identified.*	Using a 0-10 scale (Not at all likely to extremely likely) participants answer: How likely are you to recommend us to a friend? NPS = pecentage of Promoters (score 9–10) – 5 of Detractors (score 0–6)	Net Profit ($) = Sales revenue ($) – Total Sales ($)
Targets and Performance Thresholds *Identification of targets, benchmarks, and thresholds for traffic lighting.*	55 per cent by the end of 2020	$1,250,000 by the end of 2020
Source of Data *Describe where the data will come from.*	Survey of existing customers	Finance and accounting system
Data Collection Frequency *Describe how frequently is this indicator will be collected. If possible, include a forward schedule.*	Monthly data collection – sampled 10 per cent of our customer data base	Weekly
Reporting Frequency *Outline how frequently this indicator will be reported to the different audiences (if applicable).*	Monthly	Weekly

(continued)

Table 5-1 *(continued)*

	Example 1	*Example 2*
Data Entry *Name the person or role responsible for collecting and updating the data?*	Ian Miller – Marketing Assistant	Joe Blox (Finance Clerk)
Expiry / Revision Date *Identify the date until when this indicator will be valid to or when it will have to be revised.*	24 months	Target to be revised annually
Validate your KPI		
How much will it cost? *Estimate the costs incurred by introducing and maintaining this indicator.*	Costs are significant, but cheaper than a traditional customer satisfaction survey.	The costs of producing the net profit measure are low because the data is readily available.
How complete is this indicator? *Briefly assess how well this indicator is helping to answer the associated key performance question and identify possible limitations.*	It provides us with a nice simple number, but the data should be supplemented with unstructured feedback about: What is particularly good? What could be improved?	Net Profit is one of a range of profitability metrics. However, on its own it will not give us the full picture and can lead to short term thinking. It will need to be seen over time and in the context of other measures such as revenue, profit margin, operating profit, return on assets and return on equity.
Possible unintended consequences *Briefly describe how this indicator could influence the wrong behaviors or how people could cheat on this KPI.*	People could possibly influence customers before they take the survey or they could select customers who are likely to respond positively.	The danger with net profit is that people could cut costs to the detriment of long-term performance but deliver positive shot term results.

Chapter 6

Use it or Lose it: Turning KPIs into Insights

. . . .

In This Chapter

▶ Understanding how to analyse KPIs to produce insights and guide decision-making

▶ Combining KPIs with other datasets to enable more sophisticated performance analytics

▶ Using KPIs to test your strategy, run business experiments and gain competitive advantage

. . . .

*M*ost people have heard of the term 'use it or lose it' although usually it is used in relation to brain function or physical fitness. We learn that if we don't keep our brains active and stretch our intellectual capacity we will lose the advantage active, healthy minds can give us. Having a brain is not enough – we need to use it. We are also encouraged to use our muscles to stay healthy and active, or risk losing the advantages a strong body can give us. The same is true of KPIs. Having KPIs, even understanding them and implementing them, is not enough – we have to use them.

KPIs are only really useful when you turn them into insights that help to steer your business and influence your decision-making. They are just pieces of information that help you to know more about your business and whether you are on or off course against your strategic and operational objectives. Unless you use the information they provide it's just data, and data alone will not alter outcomes or improve your business.

KPIs become truly useful when you apply them to really understand your business. In this chapter I show you how to do this, and I also discuss how the best-run companies turn their KPIs into insights by combining the KPIs discussed in this book with other data they hold to extract new and more comprehensive insights. Smart companies also use their KPIs to challenge their strategic assumptions by running experiments. For example, rather than just assuming that happy customers are more loyal and loyal customers are more profitable, smart businesses run experiments to test the theory before investing in customer loyalty programs.

The chocolate cake analogy

If you want to bake a chocolate cake that baking queen Mary Berry would be proud of, you need the right amount of the right ingredients, mixed together in the right way, cooked at the right heat for the right amount of time. When you know what you are trying to achieve the disparate pieces of information and numbers begin to make sense and you learn how to bake the perfect chocolate cake.

Without the right information, success is largely down to skill and good fortune. And the same is true in business.

KPIs are the business equivalent of the chocolate cake ingredients; measurements, instructions and timings that allow a business leader to create stakeholder delight instead of stakeholder disaster. KPIs provide the raw data or ingredients, which when combined in the right way transform into meaningful business insights capable of delivering *consistent* success and elevated performance.

Testing Cause and Effect Relationships

Successful organisations in the modern business environment are those that create clear and comprehensive strategy roadmaps, and use performance data in order to extract management insights for learning and decision-making.

If you know about the scientific method you will be familiar with the importance of knowing what you are looking for before you start looking.

The scientific method states that you start by defining the question you want to explore and collect enough information to form a *hypothesis,* a proposition or theory which can be tested. Then you decide on the most appropriate research method and collect more data which you analyse and interpret to prove or disprove that hypothesis.

The right KPIs allow you to test the hypothesis to establish whether the cause and effect relationship you think exists between two features or variables really actually exists before you take action and make mission critical decisions based on that hypothesis. For example, one of my clients is a major retail bank and they believed that happy customers would be more loyal and that more loyal customers would drive growth and profit margins. When they started to test these assumed relationships using KPI data from the past 10 years, the company realised that happy customers were more loyal but that only 20 per cent of the loyal customers were profitable. These insights let the company to reconsider its strategy. Instead of delivering a 'gold standard' service to all customers, even the unprofitable ones, the company started to segregate service offerings in order to provide the 'gold standard' service only to the customers who were profitable. The unprofitable ones still receive a good service, just a more automated and streamlined one.

Why strategies are just assumptions

As I discuss in Chapter 4, many companies create *strategy maps*, single page documents that depict the various cause and effect relationships that exist between the various strategic objectives of the business. In its simplest form, strategy is a road map for the company that determines where the business is going, why it's going there, and how it's going to get there. Whilst strategy is usually created by experienced individuals they are almost always making certain assumptions about what their business, the market and the economy is going to do over the coming years. And yet those assumptions are rarely articulated in the strategy creation process and almost never documented. As a result they are never questioned or scrutinized to establish whether they are valid or not.

Your strategy may be created out of an educated guess based on your leadership skill and years of experience, but it is an assumption nonetheless. For example, one of your strategic objectives may be to increase your customer loyalty. But what is the definition of loyal? Has anyone actually checked whether customers that currently fit that definition of loyalty make more money for the business than any other customer?

Whether we like it or not, human beings run businesses and human beings come with a whole bunch of preconceived thoughts, beliefs and values that always influence opinion and outcome. Those creating strategy are not immune from these challenges. You have to accept or at least acknowledge that your strategy may be little more than collective 'group think' or the single decision of a forceful leader.

The only way to elevate strategy beyond assumption is to inject consistent standards and rigour into the strategy creation process that forces everyone involved to question and validate those assumptions. So it's crucial that you appreciate that assumptions *will* have been made, deliberately seek them out, and test them before formulating and executing the strategy. If you don't, the assumptions are likely to doom the strategy before it ever gets off the ground.

Tackling assumptions also allows you to increase your credibility and build a stronger platform for consensus and strategic alignment. If you as the business leader are seen by your executive team to question your own opinions and demand that even your own assumptions be validated rather than just demanding your strategy is implemented then you have a far greater chance of building consensus and aligning everyone around a shared goal. KPIs act as the crucial data-points that can be used to test strategic assumptions.

Testing your assumptions

Fewer than 20 per cent of businesses consistently identify and test the cause-and-effect relationships between drivers of strategic success (such as product quality or customer service) and outcomes (for example, financial results). Yet the companies who do test these relationships outperform their rivals financially. Any practical and useful strategic analysis hinges on your ability to collect valid data, and to analyse and interpret that data while constantly testing the assumptions that underpin it and the assumptions that you draw from it. Robust strategy should always be able to stand up to critical questioning.

In business it is very easy and convenient to presume that there is a direct correlation between customer loyalty and profitability or employee engagement and productivity, but you must test those assumptions to ensure they are valid in your business. It may be that there is a relationship in some organisations operating within certain markets for certain products, but to assume there is a causal relationship that applies to all businesses is a mistake.

Insights that reveal that your strategic assumptions are wrong can be even more valuable. For example, one of my customers – a major airline – assumed that on-time departure would be a key factor in customer satisfaction and loyalty. However, when the airline used its KPIs to test this assumption they found that it wasn't actually the case. The data was showing that when the planes left late, customer satisfaction was often higher than when the planes left on time. The company had evidence for what is often referred to as the *service recovery effect*, meaning that when something goes wrong and the service provider makes up for it with exceptional service; they can turn a slightly disgruntled customer into an advocate. Obviously the company didn't want to initiate late flights just so they could benefit from the service recovery effect but instead of focusing time and effort on on-time departure they invested in some extra training to ensure all aircrew were aware of the service recovery effect and how should a plane be delayed this created a significant opportunity for increased customer satisfaction.

Once you get used to using KPIs to test assumptions so that you can consistently differentiate between verifiable fact and supposition, you will probably find that there are only a few 'bundles' of business drivers influencing your business. Identifying those and then verifying them using fact-based analysis will provide you with the credibility necessary to 'sell' the resulting strategy into all parts of the organisation. Often the people charged with executing the strategy can resist it, especially if they feel it's just another knee-jerk reaction to external forces. However if the data verifies the strategy then people, even those not involved in the creation of the strategy, can get behind it because they appreciate the logic and facts that lie behind it. Testing your assumptions is therefore crucial if you are to successfully turn KPIs into useful business insights.

Treat all your business beliefs and any resulting strategic objectives as assumptions that you have to verify and test. Use your KPIs like flashlights - able to prove or disprove any theory by shining the light of fact into any corner of your business.

Testing Business Assumptions at Google, Inc.

Google, one of the most successful companies on the planet, know that their future business success depends on their employees, or Googlers, as they call them. Google's corporate mission is organise the world's information and make it universally accessible and useful. Clearly, Google recognise the transformative power of information, so it's no surprise that the company uses data and information to test their business assumptions.

One of the assumptions Google set out to test was: 'Good managers make a difference.' They wanted to know whether employees really were happier, more loyal and more productive if they had a good manager. To test this hypothesis Google collected existing KPIs such as staff satisfaction and staff turnover rates as well as productivity by department. These KPIs were then compared to the 360-degree review data that rates every manager. A 360-degree review, as I'm sure you are aware, is the feedback that comes from an individual's entire work group not just their boss. The results were stark: The departments with the best managers had the highest levels of productivity, lowest levels of staff turnover, and the highest levels of staff satisfaction.

However, Google didn't stop there. They wanted to identify what made a good manager in Google. Introducing a 'Best Manager Award', Google asked employees to write a short description of why their nominated manager should win the award, and what made him or her such a great person to work for. Google also interviewed 25 per cent of managers perceived to be the best and 25 per cent of managers perceived to be the worst, so they could extract key distinctions between the two groups. Based on an analysis of the interview data and best manager award nominations, Google was able to identify eight behaviours that mark out a great manager in Google. For Google, a great manager:

- ✔ Is a good coach
- ✔ Empowers the team and doesn't micromanage
- ✔ Expresses interest, concern and care for team members' success and personal wellbeing
- ✔ Is productive and results-orientated
- ✔ Is a good communicator able to listen and share information
- ✔ Helps with career development
- ✔ Has a clear vision and strategy for the team
- ✔ Has important technical skills that help him or her advise the team

Google is actively using these insights. For example, they now measure their managers against these behaviours through twice-yearly feedback surveys. This has allowed them to put in place early warning systems to detect both great and struggling managers. Google has also revised its management training in the light of these findings.

Learning from Business Experiments

You can also use KPIs to run business experiments.

After all, performance analysis of any type simply involves looking at a problem or opportunity from as many different perspectives as possible. When you gather subjective and objective information in this way you can analyse performance and propose a solution based on what you've discovered.

Evidence over experience

The story of how Bill James changed baseball is a brilliant demonstration of the difference between observation, reflection and experimentation.

Prior to James, baseball talent was spotted by experts and talent scouts who believed that the best way to find the next star was to watch that individual play. They would then use what they saw as 'evidence' of ability and clubs would then engage in expensive bidding wars to secure those players.

James argued that simple observation, even expert observation was not evidence and was not sufficient to differentiate a good player from a brilliant player, especially when the difference in actual on-field performance was almost impossible to gauge just by watching the players. To test his hypothesis James created a scientific evidence-based formula that looked at elements of the player's game that could be broken down and quantified.

Billy Beane, general manager of the baseball team the Oakland Athletics (better known as the Oakland A's) heard about James' theory and decided to work with him. Beane had the third lowest payroll in the league and he couldn't afford to compete with deep-pocketed baseball franchises like the New York Yankees. James' formula offered him the opportunity to track new talent that was otherwise missed by the big team talent scouts – and it worked. Observation still played a role once the formula identified potential star players, but it was no longer the sole methodology. Beane was able to buy undervalued talent which took the club all the way to the playoffs in 2002 and 2003.

The same principle now applies to business. Using KPIs and smart data analysis allows any business to level the playing field. Like Billy Beane, smaller businesses that don't have access to limitless reserves – like those enjoyed by the New York Yankees – can use the insights gleaned from their performance data to make better decisions and gain a competitive advantage without the massive price tag.

This need for experimentation is really important especially in modern business, where the pressure to act, take a position and execute strategy is relentless. Experimentation alone however isn't enough. You need to observe the facts, reflect on the outcomes and use experimentation to verify the results *before* making the decision. Too often the decision is retro-fitted to the data after the fact. In other words, leaders and managers jump to conclusions or convince themselves that they have the skill and experience to make the call without the evidence. Then, when it doesn't work out, they find supporting – albeit flawed – data to back up the faulty decision making the data the convenient scapegoat.

Removing Bias through Business Experiments

The whole purpose of business experimentation, where you make a change in one place and compare the results with other where the changes has not been made, is to learn something you didn't know before you did the experiment. You may have formed a hypothesis about what you think will happen but until you conduct the experiment you won't know for sure.

However, you have to remove bias if you want to be sure the results are valid and accurate, and that isn't always easy. Say that one of your employees came to you with an idea for a new product line. You might like the idea and ask him to present his findings more formally. That employee wants to be proven right – it's just human nature. The more work he does on the idea and the more he finds out the more invested he becomes in the idea and the more likely he is to try to find evidence that supports his theory rather than designing an experiment that will objectively test it. The more invested he becomes the less able he is to see the faults and the pitfalls and the more likely he is to focus blindly on the upside. There is always a danger that people looking to prove their hypothesis, might use tools such as modelling to simply 'confirm' their assumptions – rather than put them to a scientific test.

This is equally true for negative or positive bias. For example, if you think something is a bad idea you are similarly much more likely to find supporting information that it won't work rather than designing an experiment that would objectively test it.

Human beings are biased. We might not always be aware of the bias but it is always present. So removing as much bias as possible from the experimentation process is essential to preserve the integrity of the results.

To remove bias:

- ✔ **Ensure representative sampling to make sure any data collection doesn't exclude any people.** Phone surveys at 11 a.m. might exclude most of the working population, while data collection on specific social media sites might introduce an age bias.

- ✔ **Collect data more regularly.** Collecting staff satisfaction data only once a year can expose a company to potential bias where particularly positive or negative events around the time of the data collection can bias the findings.

- ✔ **Triangulate data from different data sources so that you look at the same issue through different lenses, using different data sets and measurement approaches.** For example, a hotel might compare the findings from their own customer satisfaction data with the reviews it is getting on travel review sites and social media mentions.

- ✔ **Look through different lenses at the same issue:** Balancing qualitative and quantitative measures is another way of triangulating data. For example, companies could ask people to rate their customer experience on a numeric scale and then also analyse written feedback and social media mentions using sentiment and text analysis. Sentiment and text analytics allows a company to look at the words used to ascertain if the communication is positive, negative or neutral.

- ✔ **Measure actual behaviours rather than opinions.** Asking people their opinion can often introduce bias, and where possible it is better to monitor actual behaviours. For example, one of my clients is a leading telecom company, which learned that customers who were regularly reported in surveys to be extremely satisfied and likely to be loyal, then defected to the competition as soon as a better or cheaper contract offer came along. In these cases it is much better to monitor actual churn behaviour than what the customer says they intend to do.

When you use data and KPIs in your organisation to test or challenge assumptions, create a control group that allows you to remove any bias and approach the data analysis with an open mind.

The pharmaceutical industry can teach us a lot about removing bias from. In a medical trial, the effectiveness of a new drug is tested scientifically in so-called *double-blind tests*. The new drug is administered to one group of patients suffering from the condition. Another group of sufferers known as the *control group* receives a placebo – usually an inert sugar pill that looks exactly like the drug.

Only a handful of people who created the medical trial know who gets the real drug versus the placebo. None of the participants in either group or the people administering the drugs know who has received the real drug or the placebo. As a result, the experiment provides an unbiased view of the drug's benefits and side effects.

Homepage experiments at Yahoo!

Online search engine Yahoo! Inc is a great example of best practice experimentation and its impact on revenue and profit. Millions of people use the Yahoo! search engines every hour. As a result, the volume of data they are privy to is phenomenal, and this allows them to test new hypotheses or assumptions very quickly. For example, Yahoo! wanted to know whether certain alterations to their website — e.g. the positioning of advertising, the phrasing of headlines, etc. would change visitor behaviour, and if so how.

They devised an experiment where they randomly assigned several hundred thousand users to an experimental group, leaving the other several million visitors as the control group. By running this simple experiment they were able to ascertain whether or not the changes to the home page resulted in the anticipated or desired behaviour change or not. The insights gained from this experiment allowed them to optimise their offerings to all users and therefore enhance revenues and profits. Plus the results of these experiments were often visible within minutes, making them an extremely dynamic tool for shaping company strategy and direction. The speed of accurate feedback, together with minimal disruption and low cost mean Yahoo! typically runs about 20 experiments of this type at any given time.

In addition to learning from these business experiments Yahoo! are able to cut out all the lengthy discussions about website design and layout while also removing bias because it's the evidence-based results that drive behaviour and strategic direction and not personal preference, consensus or even a dominant leader!

Freestyle experiments at Coca-Cola

The Coca-Cola Company is the world's largest beverage company, with nearly 500 brands. Along with Coca-Cola®, recognised as the world's most valuable brand, the Company's portfolio includes 12 other billion dollar brands, including Diet Coke®, Fanta®, Sprite®, Coca-Cola Zero® and POWERADE®.

In 2009, Coca-Cola announced its new Freestyle fountain vending machine that allows consumers to mix their own combination of flavors, with or without calories and/or caffeine. Clearly, while Coca-Cola may talk about providing consumer choice the Freestyle fountain, which links back to database at HQ, is also a very powerful experimentation devise that will provide the company with detailed real-time data on consumer preferences and local trends. The machine therefore eliminates guesswork and tells the company exactly what people actually like and want to drink. This in turn will provide fact-based insights that will help bring new products to market and allow Coke to exploit regional preferences.

Such experimentation can lead to surprising findings. For example, the drug Buproprion (marketed under several names including Zyban) was originally developed as an anti-depressant. However, medical trials found that some of the patients who had taken the real drug were able to stop smoking. This evidence was then used to guide commercial decision making and the drug was later certified for sale as an aid for those who wished to stop smoking, as well as an anti-depressant.

Business Intelligence and Analytics

Your traditional KPIs sit very well with other data-driven initiatives such as your business intelligence and analytics programs and efforts. One the one hand, you can use the additional data to support the insights from your KPIs and on the other side, you can use KPIs to provide meaning to your business intelligence and analytics activities.

Business intelligence and *analytics* (in other words, technology, applications and practices for the collection, integration, analysis and presentation of business information) can be used to further support insights from traditional KPIs. For example, a company might have customer KPIs that measure market penetration and customer satisfaction levels, but it might also hold a lot more market intelligence and customer information in their customer relationship management database, which it could use to provide additional insights.

Leading companies combine their traditional business KPIs with data-sets that were previously inaccessible and impossible to collect and use. For example, one of the biggest challenges business leaders face is that they know that there is a huge amount of information inside their business and the amount of data is growing constantly. They are also acutely aware that the data is in various places, owned by different departments, stored in different databases or archive files and also held in different formats (numerical values, percentages, statistics, reports, surveys, questionnaires, performance reviews etc.) That challenge used to mean that the data was virtually impossible to use without a limitless budget. But not anymore! Computer processing capacity and technology has improved significantly which means that it is now possible to analyse huge, messy data sets and still extract useful insights. As a result we are seeing a global explosion of internal and external data available to businesses. This datafication of the world – where data is being captured and stored on all aspects of our lives – presents a serious opportunity, but only if we can learn how to turn it into insight.

Datafication

Data comes in multiple forms including words, numbers, sounds or pictures and it is being produced as we record, track, share and analyse virtually every aspect of our life. Consider:

✔ **Electronic communications such as email are stored in corporate databases and back-ups.** Social media updates are filed, and telephone conversations are digitized and stored as audio files.

✔ **Companies and organisations are creating vast repositories of data.** These repositories exist inside financial systems, stock control systems, ordering systems, sales transaction systems and HR systems. And these data depots are growing by the minute.

✔ **Our activities are constantly tracked.** Most things we do in the digital world leave a data trail. Online, our browser logs what we are searching for and what websites we visit, websites log how we navigate through the site, how long we stay, what we click on, as well as what and when we buy, share or like something. When we read digital magazines, newspapers or books or listen to digital music the devices we use will collect and share data on what we are reading or listening to, how often and for how long.

✔ **We are now surrounded by an increasing number of sensors – all generating data.** Our smart phones track our location and how fast we are moving, sensors exist in our oceans to track temperatures and currents, in our cars to monitor how well we drive, and on packaging and pallets to track goods as they are shipped along supply chains.

✔ **Wearable devices such as Smart Watches, Google Glass and pedometers collect data.** I wear an 'Up band' that tells me how many steps I have taken each day, how many calories I've burned, and how well I've slept each night.

✔ **The proliferation of smart phones has meant that photographs and videos are now almost exclusively captured digitally.** Around 100 hours of video footage is being up-loaded to YouTube every minute and something like 200,000 photos are added to Facebook every 60 seconds. When you add Twitter, Instagram, and include the millions of hours of CCTV footage captured every day around the world the volume becomes unfathomable.

✔ **Internet-enabled devices such as smart TVs automatically generate data and share it.** A smart TV is able to track what you are watching, how long you are watching, how often you change channel and they can even detect how many people are watching TV at any given time!

✔ **Data, previously held in specific organisations or government departments is now being made public.** For example, weather data is now shared by the Met Offices and governments are releasing census data and land registry data. Also, think of all the data Google collects and makes accessible through tools such as Google Trends or Google Maps.

Tesco Analytics

British multinational grocery and retail giant Tesco is a classic example of the power of analytics. A laser-like focus on data analysis has helped Tesco to become the second largest retailer in the world as measured by profits. In the UK £1 in every £7 of UK retail sales is spent at Tesco and it enjoys a 31 per cent market share, significantly more than its nearest rival at 17 per cent. Much of Tesco's success has been attributed to its use of analytics to morph from a company that *thinks* it knows what customers want to a company that *knows* what customers want and how those preferences shift over time.

Amassing this customer knowledge took a major step forward in 1995, when Tesco introduced the Tesco Clubcard. Like many competitor initiatives Clubcard was initially introduced as a loyalty scheme. However, it was the data that would be collected via Clubcard that convinced senior Tesco leaders to endorse the Clubcard and push it way beyond rewarding customers for repeat business. It is the volume of data collected through Clubcard and Tesco's dedication to understanding, analysing and using that data that has financially transformed the business.

Tesco's data analysts are seen geographers and statisticians who apply their skills in order to understand how customers will behave. By crunching thought the data that comes from Clubcard they are able to see the patterns which in turn helps management to understand what's going on and what should be done about it. Analytics therefore allows Tesco to find the data that matters, present it in a way that makes sense so that decisions become stark, and clear.

Today, Tesco operates one of the most successful loyalty programmes in the world. With over 14 million users, the Clubcard scheme allows Tesco to collect detailed transaction information on two thirds of all shopping baskets processed at their tills. According to an article in the *Wall Street Journal* it was the business intelligence and analytics made possible by the Clubcard that allowed Tesco to thwart Wal-Mart in the UK.

A fuller case study on Tesco can be found within the library resources section of the website of the Advanced Performance Institute (API) www.ap-institute.com

Analytics

Analytics refers to the ability to *use* the data, evidence statistical, quantitative and qualitative analysis, explanatory and predictive models to drive business strategy and improved fact-based decision-making. For example:

> ✔ **Many companies now identify marketing opportunities by applying analytics to their sales data.** Loyalty card or credit card information can be used to identify patterns of behaviour. For example, supermarkets can now tell when a woman is pregnant and even what trimester she is in based on her changing buying patterns. This information can then be used to target that customer with relevant offers.

✔ **Retailers can also use analytics to optimise their stock levels.**
Traditionally, shops would analyze which items sell the most and stock
them. Modern analytics can go far beyond that. For example, one of my
clients identified that a particular stock item didn't sell very often but
the people that bought it were big spenders. Therefore it was important
to always have this item in stock. Looking at the stock item in isolation
it would have been easy to assume it wasn't worth stocking the item,
however analytics is also to look at multiple data sets that can provide a
clearer picture of reality on which to make business decisions.

✔ **Companies can also optimise their supply chain performance using
analytics.** Data from sensors on their trucks or pallets allows them to
identify the most optimal delivery route (also taking into account traffic
predictions and weather conditions).

We can now analyse huge volumes of fast moving data from different data
sources to gain commercially relevant insights that were never possible
before. Analyzing large and messy data sets is often referred to as 'Big Data'
and the 'Data scientists' or people able to accurate analyse these large messy
data sets are already being hailed as the business heroes of the 21st Century.

Chapter 7

Spreading the Word: Reporting and Communicating KPIs Effectively

. . . .

In This Chapter

▶ Making sure the people who need the information get the information

▶ Displaying the KPIs for maximum impact and understanding

▶ Creating performance dashboards

. . . .

Creating the right culture, organising your KPIs, developing the right set of KPIs for your business and extracting meaningful insights from the data won't count for anything unless your organization reports and communicates the KPIs to others effectively.

Often the focus on KPIs can concentrate on data collection and creating reports rather than really communicating the findings to the right people.

KPIs are rarely reported and communicated in a way that gives people enough information and puts it in context. The resulting ambiguity and confusion creates doubt which makes decision-making and learning almost impossible.

According to a global research study conducted by the Advanced Performance Institute, of which I am the founder, the most popular format for communicating performance information is with tables and spreadsheets, complemented by graphs and charts. The second most popular was purely numeric without the graphs and charts. The least popular way to communicate KPIs was through narrative commentary with supporting numeric data, and verbal communications of performance information. Over one-third of respondents felt that their current communication formats were not appropriate for the audience. Finding a more appropriate way to convey information is clearly important for the success of any performance improvement initiative.

Ultimately your KPIs are just signposts on the way to your stated destination and markers on the road to confirm your current location. What really matters is the picture of reality that the KPIs allow you to create so you can make better evidence based decisions. This reality is always more complete when words, numbers and pictures are used to paint that picture and they are put in the proper context.

Getting the Attention of the Decision Maker

Most business leaders, executives and decision makers are already drowning in a daily Tsunami of important, useful or potentially meaningful data. Only for the most part the nuggets of really important information that could genuinely impact the business and make the decisions easier and more accurate are lost in 30-page reports.

The best way to get the decision maker's attention is to make sure the KPI data is easily accessible. Don't make managers and executives wade through reams of needless information to get to what they need in order to make better decisions and improve performance.

Make the KPI reports short, to-the-point, accessible and visually compelling. Blocks of dense text are off-putting so mix narrative with visual representations of the data to make the report more engaging. The report must also put the information in context at the very start and remind the reader what questions the data is seeking to address.

A picture paints a thousand words.

The importance of communicating

Reporting and communicating performance findings is obviously a critical component of any effective performance management strategy. It doesn't matter how mission critical the outputs and data turn out to be if the right decision makers don't have access to that information. The whole point of KPIs as a performance management tool is to provide executives with evidence that allows them to fine-tune the way they and the people around them operate.

Disseminating the right information, in the right format to the right people is therefore extremely important. Manager and staff deserve to understand the "so what" implications of the KPIs they are involved in monitoring.

KPIs will only come to life and become a permanent part of their decision making repertoire when everyone involved can answer the questions, 'How does this affect me?', 'What unanswered question does this help me answer?' and 'What do I/we need to do differently in the future as a result of this information?'

How losing sight of key facts cost lives

When NASA was planning to launch the Challenger space shuttle, some of the engineers at base had some serious concerns. Their calculations and tests showed that there was a serious problem with one of the components (an O-ring), which could potentially fail. Prior to the launch, the engineers reported all the detailed results of their tests to decision-makers in NASA with the assumption that they would take one look at the data and abandon the launch. The problem was that the messages were not clear: Key facts were hidden in the detail and long reports, and as a consequence the Challenger was launched, leading to a devastating disaster and the death of seven crew members.

Keeping in mind the target audience

Making sure the KPI reports get the attention of the decision makers also comes down to target audience. One report does not fit all.

For KPI reports to be used as intended and used by the decision makers that receive them they must be customised to meet the specific requirements of each decision maker. It is therefore essential that whoever creates the report considers each recipient in turn and asks themselves five key questions:

1. **Who is going to read this report?**
2. **What do they know about the issues in the report?**
3. **What do they expect to see?**
4. **What do they want to know?**
5. **What will they do with the information?**

The answers to these five questions should then guide the customisation of the report so that each recipient gets exactly what he or she needs, not exactly what the analyst wants to provide, or what is most convenient or easiest to create.

When you create a single report that seeks to be all things to all decision makers it immediately loses its impact and usefulness. The result is always a longer report which is off-putting to time-pressed managers. In addition, this approach increases the chance of key distinctions and insights for one group being lost or missed amongst data that is useful for another group.

Using best practice performance reports

KPI reporting and communication can't be left to chance. It's unrealistic to expect busy executives to sift through mountains of data, umpteen email attachments and screeds of spreadsheets in order to figure out the key messages. In addition, this approach leaves the interpretation to the individual, so the data is open to misunderstanding or 'spin', where the person looking at the information can effectively pick and choose the bits that confirm his or her preferred decision. This, of course, negates the whole purpose of KPIs as evidence-based decision making tools.

Best practise performance reports create context and impose uniform interpretation, which helps to prevent this type of data hijacking. They also provide strategically relevant insights presented through a mix of visual displays and written narrative.

To make sure your KPI reports are engaging and useful follow the following five step process:

1. **Include the strategy map at the start of the report to re-iterate the connection between the subsequent data and the stated strategy.** This helps to put the KPIs in a big picture context.

2. **Frame the report with a key performance question (KPQ) to remind the reader which of their unanswered question(s) the data is seeking to answer.** Again, this helps to put the KPIs in even greater context, increase the relevance and turn 'interesting' into 'valuable' and therefore engaging the target audience.

3. **Support the KPQ with appropriate and meaningful graphs and charts.** Placing a visual representation of the data directly after a KPQ is a great way of quickly illustrating KPQ progress.

4. **Use headings to capture the salient points or key insights of the report.** This allows the reader to scan the document and get the crux of the information very quickly.

5. **Explain the data in words to add depth to the story and contextualise the graphics.** Numbers and charts will only give a snapshot – add narrative to embellish on key points, observations or implications.

Publishing analogy

When it comes to ensuring reports get and keep decision makers' attention, we can learn a lot from the publishing industry. Although we are encouraged not to 'judge a book by its cover', we do! In magazine publishing, for example, the cover is critical. Publishers spend a huge amount of time and energy deciding on the cover and arranging the content for maximum impact, interest and engagement.

Go into any newsagent or hop online to look at magazine subscription sites, and you will probably be overwhelmed at the choice – even in the same subject category or genre. The way the magazines look has a profound and instant influence on what your eye is drawn to and therefore what you are most likely to buy.

To grab would-be readers' attention, the publisher will use bright and vivid colour, high-resolution, attractive photographs or graphics and smart, interesting or curious headings to encourage the browser to look inside and hopefully buy the magazine. Only when a customer quickly flicks through the magazine to confirm that the inside lives up to the cover's promise are they likely to buy.

In the same way, creating a key performance indicator report that people will pick up and read requires the smart combination of presentation, aesthetics and meaningful, useful content.

Great content is as useless as terrible content if the reader never reaches it!

You need to ensure your information is presented in an attractive and visually compelling way. A bunch of spreadsheets, the odd black and white chart and a blank cover page titled, 'Quarterly Sales Forecast' isn't very appealing. And it's certainly not going to stand out in a sea of equally uninspiring data dumps currently stacked on the decision maker's desk!

The data does not speak for itself. The report needs to speak – clearly, succinctly and loudly, if necessary, so that executives can use what the report tells them in order to improve performance.

Headline, photo and narrative

Use some of the tricks of the publishing trade to communicate your KPI reports effectively and get the decision makers' attention.

Getting the headline right

If you think of any front page newspaper story or major magazine article, you'll understand that they follow a similar format that includes a headline, a photo or graphic and narrative. If you use this approach as your standard KPI reporting methodology, you'll increase engagement and maintain interest.

Create a report title or headline that grabs the reader's attention from the start. Obviously if the report is the Quarterly Sales Forecast then you need to say exactly what the report is but you could also add a subheading to increase interest and/or curiosity.

Business reporting doesn't have to be drab or dull, or put readers to sleep. Follow the lead of publishing and use more creative and inventive headlines to initiate early interest.

Using arresting images

A high-quality colour photograph or graphic is also a staple in publishing because an image can convey a lot of information very quickly. Pictures don't tell the whole story, but they are a brilliant way to increase interest and put the report in context. The whole story is then expanded with a short executive summary and additional, more in-depth narrative to provide as much or as little information as the reader wants.

Organising your material effectively

Don't be tempted to miss out the narrative either. A picture or graphic can improve and speed up understanding but is not a total substitute for words. Looking pretty but incomprehensible is as futile as looking terrible and easy to understand.

To maintain engagement throughout the report, make continuous use of both headings and visual displays. Headings break up blocks of text and make the page much more inviting, and they help the reader to navigate the report easily and find the nuggets of information they need most. This type of layout also allows the reader to go back to the report and find what they need easily without having to read through information in which they are not that interested.

Never disseminate parts of the report to different people. It's not uncommon, for example, for one large report to be created and certain pages pulled out and sent to different managers. This is unacceptable. Customise the reports to the recipients and only include what they need to know, putting the information into a context that is relevant or meaningful to them.

Visualising KPIs: Using Graphs and Charts

The ultimate aim of a KPI report is to disseminate valuable information that looks great and is easy to understand and use. Using graphs and charts can certainly facilitate that outcome.

The most common visual display tools for reporting purposes are graphs and charts. There are many different types of graphs and charts to choose from, each with a different purpose – and some are more effective than others.

Bar graph

Bar graphs, also known as bar charts, display rectangular bars (hence the name) of varying lengths representing different values. The bars are positioned either vertically or horizontally, with one axis showing the specific category being compared and the other representing the discrete value each bar represents. Because the information is displayed side by side, this type of graph makes comparison between adjacent values particularly easy.

In Figure 7-1 the example is of customer satisfaction with different products. Satisfaction here can take any number between 0 = not satisfied at all to 100 = completely satisfied.

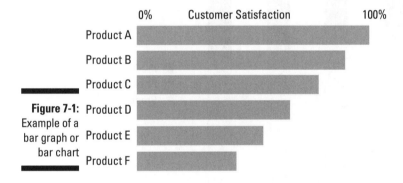

Figure 7-1: Example of a bar graph or bar chart

The bar graph is particularly useful for nominal (a categorisation e.g. men, or women) or ordinal (ordered or ranked) scales. Stick with horizontal bar graphs, where the data is presented left to right because the labels are easier to read (they can be as long as you want and still be readable, while in vertical bar graphs there is a space limit) and order them in size for easy interpretation (instead of a random order, put the longest bar either at the top or bottom and put the rest in descending order).

Some bar graphs, known as grouped bar graphs, can illustrate more than one category being measured (see Figure 7-2, which shows profit margins of different products across four regions). A stacked bar graph shows the bars divided into sections to illustrate cumulative effect (see Figure 7-3, which shows the relative proportion of three different products across four regions)

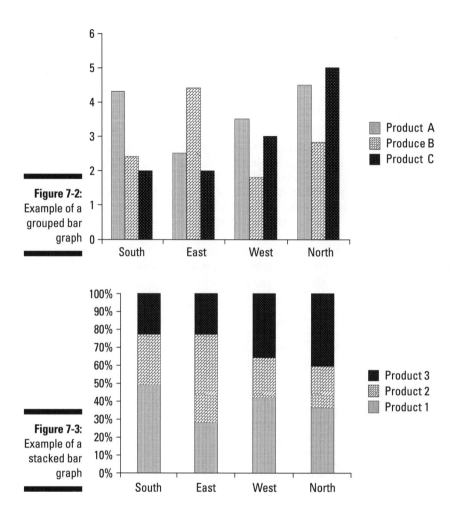

Figure 7-2:
Example of a grouped bar graph

Figure 7-3:
Example of a stacked bar graph

Line graph

Line graphs are ideal for displaying time-related data, such as variations in share price over time or sales made over a certain time period.

What a line graph does well is illustrate trends, fluctuations, cycles, rates of change, and the comparison of two data sets over time. For example, Figure 7-4 illustrates how orders of one product fluctuate across the year, with sales peaking in the winter and summer months, showing seasonal dips in spring and autumn.

Figure 7-4: Example of a line graph

Pie chart

Pie charts display various segments that represent the data as a percentage of the total data. In business, pie charts are overused. In most cases, bar graphs are the better choice. Pie charts are best when there are fewer than six segments to illustrate, otherwise it can become too difficult to distinguish between the values. For example, Figure 7-5 illustrates that one quarter (25 per cent) of all votes were 'no' votes, while 75 per cent were 'yes' votes.

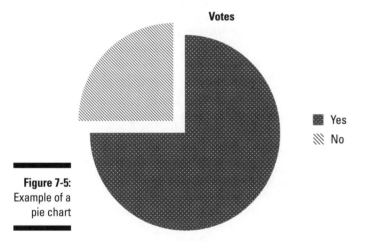

Figure 7-5: Example of a pie chart

Scatter chart

Scatter charts, also known as scatter plots, are particularly useful for showing or indicating the correlation between two sets of data and illustrating the strength and direction of that relationship. For example, Figure 7-6 illustrates the positive correlation between income and spending – that is, that people with more income tend to spend more. Each data point here represents an individual that is placed across the income axis and the spend axis. Viewed together, the distribution shows a trend.

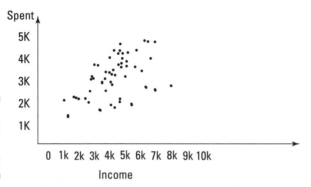

Figure 7-6:
Example of
a scatter
chart

Bullet graph

The bullet graph is better version of a speedometer dial (see the next section) that looks a little like a horizontal thermometer. It was developed by data visualisation expert Stephen Few, and is more space efficient, making it easier to read and compare across a number of graphs. However, it only displays a single measure in relation to target performance.

For example the bullet graph in Figure 7-7 illustrates revenue for the year 2014 (in millions). The black bar in the centre shows the current value, here $250m. This value sits relative to the colour coding (0–150m = red, 150–250m yellow, 250–300m = green) as well as a benchmark (the vertical line at 200m). This display can have multiple benchmarks and performance thresholds.

Figure 7-7:
Example of a
bullet graph

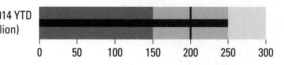

Speedometer dials or gauges

I often see speedometer dials in KPI reports and dashboards, but in most cases they have no place there, and are the wrong type of display. They have been designed to represent a dashboard on a car, where the needle is constantly moving round. That's fine in a car, because we can it helps us to monitor our speed at any given point in time. However, KPIs tend to be much more static and don't move up or down all the time. Speedometer dials are also not very space efficient and can be difficult to compare. Furthermore, they only provide a view of performance at a particular point in time, maybe in comparison to a target, but can't show trends. Overall, my advice would be to avoid them altogether wherever possible. Figure 7-8 shows a typical speedometer dial.

Figure 7-8:
Example of
a speedom-
eter dial

Using innovative ways to visualise data

Helping decision makers to read, understand and use the data that you report to them is just as important as providing the data in the first place. Seeking new and novel ways to present the data in an engaging and visually appealing way will always increase the likelihood of the data being used.

Graphs, charts, images and diagrams get the important facts across to the reader very quickly. A visual depiction of the data can often make it easier to understand and give a deeper and broader insight into the findings. Plus graphics are often easier to recall. The problem is that these significant benefits can result in their overuse. Most word processing packages come with graphic capabilities fully installed. Report writers no longer need to hire specialist graphic designers – they can just add the graphs and charts themselves. So they do so, often at the expense of the information the graphics are seeking to present.

The secret is knowing when and how to use graphics to visualise data appropriately. Here are some ideas to keep you on the right track:

✔ **Keep visuals simple and make sure they are relevant and deliver information that your target audience wants.** Just because it looks funky doesn't mean it should be added. And don't feel the need to fill every corner of the report – too much clutter makes it harder to find the important information.

✔ **The person reading the report should be drawn to the most important pieces of information first.** Make sure the key messages stand out.

✔ **Use colour sparingly and only when you want to highlight specific issues or when it's necessary to clearly differentiate between elements on a graph or chart.** Often business reports are only in black and white which can make differentiating between data sets very difficult especially if similar shades of grey or patterns are used.

✔ **Be mindful of the colours you use as they often come with unconscious meaning.** For example, red is considered a warning or danger colour. Also, 10 per cent of men and 1 per cent of women are colour-blind, so choose colours that are not affected by colour blindness.

✔ **Avoid three-dimensional graphs:** These can make a report look like a high school geography project and are harder to read!

✔ **Don't use too many different types of graph, chart or graphic.** If it's going to be useful to compare various graphs with each other then make sure you use the same type of graph to illustrate the data so that comparison is as easy as possible.

✔ **Avoid unnecessary decorations, background colours, fancy fonts, coloured paper and so on.** Aim for clean, attractive but functional reports.

✔ **Graphs are only useful if they show something meaningful.** Don't use them if there is so much data the visual is a mess, or too little data that the findings are statistically insignificant.

Developing Management Dashboards

A performance dashboard is simply the concise visual display of the most important information that decision makers need to help them achieve one or more stated objectives.

When you are driving your car, a single glance at the instruments, dials and gauges on your dashboard can tell you all you need to know about whether or not you are going to get to your destination on time and in one piece. For example, you can immediately tell whether you have enough fuel, how fast you are travelling and whether the engine is coping well with your driving. Most cars also come with warning lights that flash or turn red when your car is in trouble or needing a service. A performance dashboard should do the same for your business.

Management dashboards are best considered from an operational and strategic perspective. Your operational dashboard allows you to check the day-to-day processes and outputs of your business to make sure everything is running smoothly. They provide information that allows you to fix issues before they become problems and affect performance. Your strategic dashboard on the other hand looks to the future and seeks to identify obstacles and challenges that you may face on the way to your new strategic destination. Both are important to develop.

When properly developed management dashboards allow decision makers quick access to the critical indicators or instruments of the business, and help them to decide whether they are on track or not.

Seven dashboard design tips

In a frenetic, information-rich corporate environment, a management dashboard is an extremely useful tool. The dashboard clusters all the mission critical data in one place so that managers and decision makers can access it quickly and know exactly where they are and what they need to do. Here are seven tips for designing a dashboard that delivers on that promise:

1. **Keep your dashboard to a single screen or single page of paper.** The whole point of a dashboard is that you get a succinct overview of the business and potential red flags in a few minutes. It's a snapshot, so don't include excessive detail. If it takes you half a day to look through your dashboard then it's not a dashboard! Forcing yourself to rein in the dashboard to a single screen or page will also force you to really engage with the most important information your reader needs to know.

2. **Put the data in context by including the KPQ the metric seeks to answer.**

3. **Only include the most critical, insightful KPIs necessary for achieving your operational and strategic objectives.**

4. **Choose an appropriate and accessible way to display the dashboard.** For example if you use software make sure that everyone that needs to dashboard has access to the software.

5. **Make the dashboard easy to look at, navigate and understand.** Don't cram as much information onto one page as you possibly can – arrange the data aesthetically.

6. **Focus on information delivery and understanding.** Avoid excessive design, and don't introduce meaningless variety just to make the dashboard appear more interesting.

7. **Keep the dashboard clean and clear.** Don't include decoration or excessive use of colour – everything on the dashboard should serve a purpose, or it shouldn't be there.

Making use of software tools

Software tools can be a great performance management enabler and can greatly assist in the reporting and communication of performance data – including through the creation of automated dashboards.

However, the key word in that last sentence was *enabler*. Software is not a blanket solution. You still need to go through the process of executive discussion to work out what you want the software to tell you. You still need to design and develop the right KPIs for your business and you need to understand what information you need in order to answer specific unanswered questions that could improve performance. So you still need to do all the front-end work around creating a performance management framework in order to get the most out of any software tool you may then chose to buy.

That said, software can bring the data and information to life through powerful communication and collaboration features. Visually rich, colour coded, intuitive dashboards can be created in minutes, so users can understand information at a glance and update that information with a click of a button any time they want. In addition, most of the tools available today are web-based, which means you can access the information via your internet browser at any time. Software can therefore make the ongoing data crunching, reporting and communication much easier.

Some of the leading software products are sold by vendors including:

- ✔ ActiveStrategy
- ✔ Actuate
- ✔ Corporater
- ✔ Cubus
- ✔ Covalent
- ✔ Dundas
- ✔ IBM
- ✔ Infor
- ✔ Klipfolio
- ✔ KPIFix
- ✔ Microsoft
- ✔ Microstrategy
- ✔ Oracle

- ✔ Procos
- ✔ QlickTech
- ✔ QPR
- ✔ SAP
- ✔ SAS
- ✔ SpiderStrategies
- ✔ Rocket Software
- ✔ Tableau
- ✔ 4GHI

Part III
Developing Financial KPIs

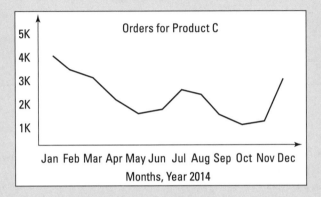

In this part . . .

✔ Learn how to measure the crucial financial KPIs, and then how to turn the data you uncover to the benefit of your business.

✔ Lift the lid on revenue and profit KPIs, put them in perspective, and get a handle on the overall financial health of your business.

✔ Make sure there's always enough money in your business by mastering liquidity and cashflow KPIs

✔ Keep the bosses onside with the shareholder and value-added KPIs which give an accurate picture of your business's value and growth.

✔ Measure the efficiency of your business: understand how well it makes money, and where and how it could improve.

Chapter 8

The Holy Grail of Business: Revenue and Profit KPIs

In This Chapter
▶ Putting profit in perspective
▶ Understanding margin
▶ Measuring revenue

*T*he most common or familiar types of KPI are financial KPIs. By their nature they are quantitative, usually expressed as a number, ratio or percentage. Their quantitative nature often makes them easier to measure than qualitative KPIs. Perhaps most importantly, they represent the Holy Grail of business KPIs because financial benchmarks are universally used as the yardstick of success.

Financial KPIs are the heartbeat of any business because they tell owners and stakeholders whether that business is making money, how much the business is spending and how much of the revenue is profit. And considering that the primary purpose of business is usually to make money and grow year on year, then it's easy to see why financial KPIs are considered so important.

The Bottom Line – Gauging Profit

There are two main financial perspectives driving any business – bottom line profit and top line growth. All businesses must keep an eye on both but profit is more important than growth because you need to have something left at the end to make your efforts worthwhile. Focusing on growth instead of profit can work – if you look at business success stories like Amazon, for example – but it's risky and usually requires deep-pocketed investors.

For most businesses re-invested profit is what makes business possible; besides, if you are not making any profit then what's the point? No commercial operation exists for long if it can't generate a profit.

The meaning behind top line and bottom line

The terms *top line* and *bottom line* refer to the location on the income statement where the information is reported. You will see from the simple income statement in the following figure that revenue (also known as turnover or sales) is always the first number recorded on the top line of the income statement.

Conversely net profit (also known as net income) is always the last number to appear on the bottom-line of the income statement. The term bottom-line has also become part of our everyday language – 'tell me the bottom-line' is a direct request for the key facts that the person needs to know, regardless of context.

In business the key fact that you need to know is 'Are we making money?'

Example Company
Income Statement
For the Year Ended December 31, 2014

Sales Revenue:		
Total Sales	$1,505,500	
– Sales Returns	– 2,000	
– Sales Discounts	– 3,500	
Net Sales Revenue		$1,500,000
Less: Cost of Goods Sold:		
Beginning Stock	$150,000	
+ Purchases	800,000	
+ Freight-In	10,000	
– Purchase Discounts	– 15,000	
– Purchase Returns	– 5,000	
– Ending Stock	– 140,000	
Cost of Goods Sold		– 800,000
Gross Profit		$700,000
Operating Expenses		
Selling Expenses:		
Freight-Out	$60,000	
Advertising Expense	55,000	
Sales Commissions Expense	40,000	
Administrative Expenses:		
Office Salaries Expense	150,000	
Office Rent Expense	120,000	
Office Supplies Expense	30,000	
Total Operating Expenses		– 455,000
Operating Income		$245,000
Other Incomes and Expenses:		
Gains on Sale Equipment	$20,000	
– Loss on Sales of investments	– 10,000	
– Interest Expense	– 12,000	
Net Other Incomes and Expenses		– 42,000
Net Profit		$203,000

Profit means prizes

Making a profit has considerable advantages that go way beyond simple survival. A profitable company:

- Can reward its shareholders by paying a dividend, which in turn can attract additional investors and increase the share price. Even if the business is not a public company profit makes it much easier to attract investors and customers.

- Finds it much easier to borrow money, and can negotiate a much lower interest rate on the money it secures.

- Can reinvest in the business to expand into new products, locations or markets.

- Has a buffer against changes in market conditions or economic downturns which can help the business survive during difficult times.

- Can hire more people and can often attract better quality ones.

- Is financially better equipped to experiment with new products or services.

Understanding the different perspectives on profit

You can look at profit in three main ways – each offering a different perspective on how well your business is performing.

Gross profit

Gross profit, also known as *sales profit* refers to the total amount of money made by a business (the *revenue*), minus the *cost of goods sold* (COGS). COGS consist of all the direct expenses necessary to create and supply that product or service. That means the cost of raw materials, electricity and labour costs of the people directly connected to making the goods. COGS doesn't include indirect expenses such as transport, distribution or advertising costs.

Gross profit is expressed as a number which can be compared between quarters or years. It is a very useful measure for management, because it indicates how efficiently your business uses various resources in the production of your product or service. Plus it is the source metric for many other important KPIs. Gross profit helps you to answer the KPQ 'How efficiently do we use labour and supplies in the production process?'

Types of profit – and what they mean

The easiest way to understand the various types of profit is to put them in context. This table shows the year-on-year details for a manufacturing company.

In $ millions	2013	2014
Revenue	4320	4800
Cost of Goods Sold	(1680)	(2160)
Gross Profit	2640	2640
Operating expenses	(600)	(960)
Operating Profit	2040	1680
Other income (expenses)	120	(240)
Extraordinary income (Expenses)	(240)	960
Interest costs	(360)	(480)
Net Profit before tax	1560	1920
Taxes	(480)	(600)
Net profit	1080	1320

If you just looked at the bottom line net profit of this company you could be forgiven for thinking that the business was doing well – profit has increased by $240 million. But a closer look at the other profit figures reveals some interesting information. Even though revenue increased in 2014, gross profit stayed the same. Cost of goods sold increased significantly. It may be that raw materials increased in price, but if you were a potential investor you would want to find out more before you invested. You would for example need to find out why COGS increased so significantly and whether it was an anomaly or likely to remain at the higher figure. Clearly, if the increase was likely to remain constant this would erode any future growth.

More troubling is that the operating profit also went down from 2013 to 2014. This drop could indicate that the company overheads (ongoing expenses of operating the business) are becoming bloated and perhaps that the business is not being run as efficiently as it could be, or was in the previous year. Although top and bottom line figures look impressive, closer inspection of the figures in between can reveal a very different story. In this case a little rudimentary investigation via the corporate website or company accounts might reveal that the extraordinary income of $960 million in 2014 was created when the company sold one of its manufacturing plants. Not only could this divestment potentially impact sales in future years as less inventory will be available to sell but as it is distorting the real picture regarding net profit. As it is a one-off revenue injection if we remove that $960 million from the accounts the net profit in 2014 was actually $360 million – a significant drop from the $1080 million of 2013. Clearly something fundamental is going wrong in this business despite the rosy accounts and this is why it's important to look at profit from many different perspectives.

Gross profit looks at total revenue, which can be misleading and present a distorted view of reality if your business earns additional revenue from other sources such as the one-off sale of a division or rent from buildings, for example. While the rent may be ongoing, the one-off sale of a division will distort the financial picture for the year of the transaction.

Operating profit

Another way of looking at profit is to examine *operating profit.* Operating profit, is gross profit (sales revenue minus COGS) minus operating expenses, depreciation and amortisation. Depreciation is the decrease in value of tangible assets over time. A tangible asset is a physical asset that can be touched such as machinery or premises. *Amortisation* is the same as depreciation only for intangible assets. An intangible asset is an asset that can't be touched such as Intellectual property, brand reputation or goodwill.

As such, many analysts believe that operating profit is a much more accurate indicator than gross profit because it looks specifically at the profitability of the business under normal or 'business as usual' circumstances.

This perspective focuses on how efficiently you produce and sell your product or service. Operating profit helps you to answer the KPQ: How efficiently do we manage our normal business operations?

Net profit

Net profit, also known as *net income* or *net earnings* is the amount of money left after paying all the expenses of the business. Unlike gross profit or operating profit, net profit looks at total revenue from all sources, not just sale of goods and services. This time, though, it also deducts *total* expenses including depreciation, interest, taxation and all other costs.

Net profit helps to shed light on business results, but looking at net profit alone can give a distorted picture of the business and it is a metric that is easy to manipulate. For example, if a business has sold off part of its operation, the income from that would be reflected in the net profit figure. This additional revenue could make the business look much more successful than it really was, and might indicate revenue growth instead of a one-off bonus that would not be repeated next year.

Why profit only matters in context

Profit, whether gross, operating or net, is only really important and only provides insight when it's put in context. The numbers that represent these various profit types are only useful when they are compared with previous quarters or previous years or similar companies in the industry.

It is also very important that you look behind the bottom line number to examine what's really going on. For example if your business has recently invested heavily to build a new factory then costs associated with that initiative can easily distort the profit metrics.

Measuring profit in practice

The most useful profit KPIs are net profit (which requires the calculation of gross and operating profit) and earnings before interest tax, depreciation and amortisation (EBITDA).

KPI: Net Profit

The key performance question net profit helps to answer is: 'To what extent are we generating healthy bottom-line results'? This metric (net profit) is usually collected every month as part of normal accounting practise in the creation of the income statement.

Net profit ($) = Sales revenue ($) – Total costs ($)

Net profit is reached on a profit and loss account (P&L) via the following process:

1. Sales revenue = [Price of your product or service] × [Quantity sold]
2. Gross profit = [Sales revenue] – [Cost of goods sold (COGS) and other direct costs]
3. Operating profit = [Gross profit] – [Overheads and other indirect costs]
4. Pre-tax profit = [Operating profit] – [One-off expenses such as redundancy payments – interest payments]
5. Net profit = [Pre-tax profit] – [Tax]

Net profit is easy and inexpensive to measure because the data already exists as part of standard accounting practise.

You can calculate net profit for a business, business unit, department or even a product or service. This directed focus can be very useful in identifying areas of weakness. That said, it's only valid if fixed costs and overheads are allocated appropriately, so that the resulting number is accurate.

KPI: EBITDA

The key performance question EBITDA seeks to answer is: 'To what extent are we operating our business efficiently to generate profits'? It is usually measured on a monthly or quarterly basis and is extracted from the income statement.

As the name would suggest EBITDA is calculated when you take sales revenue or earnings and subtract all expenses before interest, tax, depreciation and amortisation. As such this KPI measures a company's operational profitability over time by removing expenses that can easily distort performance such as the cost of capital.

Formula: EBITDA = Revenue – all expenses except interest payments, tax liabilities, depreciation and amortisation.

Like net profit EBITDA is an easy metric to collect because it is calculated from data already available through your normal accounting practise.

Although widely used EBITDA is not one of the Generally Accepted Accounting Principles (GAAP) which means that there is no definitive globally used distinction around what is and is not included in its calculation. As a result it's difficult to know if you are comparing like with like – even within the same company as companies often change what is included from on reporting period to the next. If you decide to use EBITDA then make sure you business defines what is and is not included and stick to that definition so meaningful comparisons can be made.

Measuring Profit Margins

Measuring gross, operating or net profit provides very important information. As these profit metrics are expressed as a single number they are easy to compare to past performance over the previous month, quarter or year. But as we've seen above the numbers alone can be deceptive and need to be compared with caution. Profit margins are earnings expressed as a ratio or percentage of total sales revenue, and this gives you a much deeper and more accurate picture of efficiency.

If for example a company becomes more efficient and reduces its production costs then it will increase its profit margin and therefore the money it makes without necessarily increasing its volume of sales or sales revenue.

Why margins are so vital

Measuring profit margins is particularly useful because they allow you to assess costs relative to profit and sales. Instead of exposing how much money is being earned from business in the way the straight profit metric does, profit margins measure how much money is being squeezed out of the revenue from sales.

Because margins create a standardised way of looking at the same thing they also allow for more accurate comparison across divisions within a company, or even companies within industries.

Knowing the different profit margins

Just as there are three different profit perspectives, there are three different types of profit margin.

Gross profit margin

Gross profit margin deducts the cost of goods sold or cost of sales. These are the direct production and distribution costs your business incurs for the supply and delivery of your goods or services. A company that buys in raw materials may have gross profit margin of, say, 40 per cent, which means that 60 per cent of its sales are made up of direct costs. To put it another way, for every dollar in sales, they spend 60 cents in direct costs to make that product. For a software developer with minimal production costs, the gross profit margin may be as high as 80 per cent, meaning that only 20 cents are spent for each dollar in sales.

Gross profit margin should be significantly higher than net profit margin, because overheads and other expenses are not accounted for in gross profit margin yet still need to be paid. It is particularly useful for shining a light into your production costs to help identify how you are becoming more or less efficient or how you compare to your competitors.

Operating profit margin

Also known as *operating margin* this KPI provides additional insight into your operating efficiency and pricing strategy, because it only includes revenue from normal business operations.

It provides a much clearer and unpolluted picture of how much money a company makes (before interest and taxes) on every dollar of sales. This is a particularly useful metric for working out whether operating costs are too high, especially if your competitors' costs are lower.

Net profit margin

This metric sheds light on how well your business is run. It helps to illustrate how efficient the business is and how adept it is at controlling costs. A low net profit means that your business has a lower tolerance to changes such as lower sales or increased costs.

Net profit margin is particularly useful when comparing performance over time. Plus it is often used by investors to assess the relative merits of a business. For example, say someone was looking to invest. They would look at profits. Suppose Company A had a net profit of $523 million on sales of $620 million and Company B earned $670 million on sales of $990 million. If the investor only looked at net profit alone Company B made $147 million more profit than Company B. But if they looked more closely they would see that Company A's net profit margin is 84.35 per cent ($523 m divided by $620 million multiplied by 100) and Company B's is 67.67 per cent ($670 m divided by $990 m multiplied by 100). In other words Company A generates 84 cents for each dollar of sales, while Company B only generates 68 cents for every dollar of sales. So company A is more profitable than company B.

Measuring profit margins in practice

If you want to include profit margin KPIs in your KPI mix then you can choose one or all of the following:

KPI: Net profit margin

The key performance question net profit margin helps to answer is: 'How much profit are we generating for each dollar in sales?' Net profit margin is calculated from data that appears on your income statement and it's usually measured once a month, or however often the income statement is prepared.

$$\text{Net profit margin} = \frac{\text{Net profit}}{\text{Revenues}} \times 100$$

Although net profit margin varies between industries, the higher the net profit margin the better, as this shows the business is run efficiently and has a safety net of financial reserves that can help the business deal with changing market conditions.

The average net profit margin for all S&P 500 companies is around 10 per cent. A net profit margin of between 20 per cent and 40 per cent is considered very good – regardless of industry.

You can apply the net profit margin metric to a business, division or product to gauge profitability. Using this metric in particular areas allows you to identify what part so the business or product range are profitable and which ones are not.

KPI: Gross profit margin

The key performance question gross profit margin seeks to answer is: How much profit are we generating for each dollar in sales? The data necessary to calculate gross profit margin is usually captured through normal monthly accounting for the profit and loss statement.

$$\text{Gross profit margin} = \left(\frac{[\text{Revenue} - \text{Cost of goods sold}]}{\text{Revenues}} \right) \times 100$$

Gross profit margin is a particularly useful KPI to use at the business unit, department or product level because it can highlight the real profit drivers in the business. For example if you analysed all your products from a gross profit margin perspective you could see which ones were the most profitable and use that data to consolidate your product offering and improve net profit margins.

Don't confuse *product mark up* with gross profit margin. Gross profit margin is a percentage of the *selling price* while mark up is a percentage of the *seller's costs*. Say for example you are a retailer and you buy goods at $87 and you are going to sell them for $149 (the selling price). Your mark up is $62 which, as a percentage of the cost is 71.26 per cent ($62 divided by $87 multiplied by 100). Gross profit margin, however, is 41.61% of the selling price ($62 divided by $149 multiplied by 100). Although margin and mark up are the same in dollar amount, $62, they represent two different concepts and many businesses have gone bust because they assume their mark up and margin is the same thing.

KPI: Operating profit margin

The key performance question operating profit margin helps to answer is: To what extent are we operating our business efficiently? The data needed to calculate this KPI is captured through the normal monthly accounting process and reported on the income statement.

$$\text{Operating Profit Margin} = \frac{\text{Operating profit (EBIT)}}{\text{Revenue}} \times 100$$

All the data needed to calculate the three profit margins are easily extracted from the accounting data.

You can use operating profit margin to compare your company to your competitors – even if they don't issue a separate disclosure of their cost of goods sold (which is necessary for calculating gross profit margin).

The Top-Line: Measuring Revenue Growth

Business success is not just a measure of bottom-line profit. Top-line revenue growth is also a key consideration and a yardstick of prosperity. Profit can be improved by cutting costs and becoming more efficient, but revenue growth or turnover depends on your ability to sell more products to more people.

When revenue isn't everything

Investors, analysts and stock market pundits are all keen to identify businesses that are growing. It is important, especially if your business is a publicly listed company that revenue is growing over time. Consistent top-line revenue growth is considered a pre-requisite for any company wishing to attract investors.

That said, revenue is not the be-all and end-all of business. Growth is important but only if it's married to profit. It is certainly possible to grow your business year on year and still go bust.

Why you should track revenue over time

Revenue is a single figure that represents how much your business makes through sales. Whilst interesting, it only really becomes insightful when you track and measure it over time, so you can appreciate the growth trend.

Revenue growth is a dynamic metric that needs to be compared with something else – a different time period, a different company or a different product – in order to be really meaningful.

Measuring revenue in practice

Two main KPIs exist to measure revenue and revenue growth rate so you can establish whether or not your business is growing or contracting.

KPI: Revenue

The key performance question revenue provides an answer to is: 'How much money are we making from sales?' The data needed to calculate this metric are collected in your general ledger or the main accounting record of your business, and the revenue figure is usually calculated and reported monthly.

> Revenue = Total number of goods or services sold × The price they were sold at.

For example, if you sold 764, 340 widgets at $12.50 each your revenue would be $9,554,250.

KPI: Revenue growth rate

The key performance question revenue growth rate helps to answer is: 'How much money are we making from sales compared to another time period?' Again, the data needed to calculate this metric is already available in your general ledger or the main accounting record of your business and is calculated and reported monthly.

> Revenue growth rate = Difference in revenue between two time periods/ Revenue in earlier time period × 100

For example if your company generated $5.7 million in revenue during the last quarter of 2013 and $4.9 million in the third quarter of 2013 the quarterly revenue growth rate would be 16.32 per cent from the third to the last quarter:

> $5.7 – $4.9 = $0.8/$4.9 × 100 = 16.32 per cent

If your revenues were $3.2 million for the last quarter of 2012 then your year-on-year revenue growth rate would be 78.12 per cent:

> $5.7 – 3.2 = 2.5/3.2 × 100 = 78.12 per cent

Chapter 9

The Ones You Can't Take Your Eyes Off: Liquidity and Cash Flow KPIs

In This Chapter

▶ Getting to grips with cash

▶ Understanding the critical nature of cash flow

▶ Appreciating the dangers of liquidity

*T*he most common cause of business failure is not lack of sales or too little profit – it's running out of money. To ensure this doesn't happen, you need to incorporate some cash flow and liquidity KPIs into your performance management schedule. Knowing how money is moving in and out of your business (*cash flow*) and knowing how easy it will be to convert your assets to cash should you need money quickly (*liquidity*) are essential measures to help you gauge the health, stability and longevity of your business.

Even if you have a brilliant business model and great products that sell well, every business is susceptible to money challenges from time to time. The best way to navigate these periods is to know they are coming before they arrive, and the KPIs detailed in this chapter will help you do just that.

Tracking Your Cash

Running a business day-to-day requires a certain amount of cash to keep things ticking along. Tracking your cash is vitally important in business because you need to know how much money is coming in from sales and any other sources and equally importantly, when that money is coming in. This income then becomes the reserve from which you can pay the bills and cover the overheads of the business. Making sure there is enough money in the reserve to cover those costs at all times is an ongoing challenge for most businesses.

Seasonal businesses, for example, may make all their income across a few months of the year, even though their bills arrive at regular intervals, even when money isn't coming in. Managing money in this type of environment is especially challenging.

One of the most popular cash flow KPIs is the *cash conversion cycle* (CCC) which calculates the number of days it takes for an organisation to convert resources into cash. It measures how long each dollar is tied up in the business before being converted into cash via a sale to a customer.

The CCC therefore reveals three important pieces of information:

- ✔ The amount of time it takes to sell the inventory or stock (goods the business holds for sale.)
- ✔ The amount of time it takes to collect the money after a sale is made (this money is called the *receivables*).
- ✔ The amount of time the company can take to pay its bills without incurring interest charges or other penalties.

Clearly, the longer it takes to convert money spent on creating the product into money in the bank, the greater the risk for the business. It is important to recognise that CCC is not the difference between when the money is spent and when the sale is made but actually the time between when the sale is made and when the money is received from the sale, which could be weeks or even months after the sale. I cover the detailed definition and use of CCC in the section 'Measuring cash flow in practice'.

Why cash is king

In business there's a saying: - Cash is king. The reason cash is held in such high regard in business is because it oils the wheels of growth. And cash doesn't cost anything: If you can manage cash flow properly and ensure that you collect your revenue quickly and efficiently and that revenue covers your costs then you don't need to borrow money.

Borrowing money costs money (in interest payments) and is a much more expensive way to cover any financial shortfall in a business.

Cash-rich companies have more options and much more flexibility about how they run their business and the decisions they make. They are not rocked or sent to the wall by unexpected expenses, because they have the surplus to cover the costs.

In addition cash in the business means by definition that the income has been received and is banked. In the same way that a bird in the hand is worth two in the bush, cash received today is always better than sales revenue sitting on the balance sheet which still needs to be collected tomorrow.

What cash flow tells you about your business

The cash flow of your business tells you (and your potential investors) three things about your business:

- ✔ **Operating activity:** How you are running the business. Is the business able to generate cash from normal business operation? A strong and efficient business will be able to generate a lot of cash from sales of its products and services, and this will make up the bulk of revenue.

- ✔ **Investment activity:** Cash flow can also tell us where money is being spent in the business. Is the business re-investing in equipment or is it just treading water? Ideally a business should be using its cash wisely to invest in new products, or to upgrade or maintain equipment so as to ensure future growth and profit.

- ✔ **Financing activity:** Cash flow also tells us where money is coming from and where it is going. How much was paid to shareholders? Was there any release of capital?

Measuring cash flow in practice

The cash flow KPIs that are most useful are Cash Conversion Cycle (CCC), Working Capital Ratio, Cash Flow Solvency Ratio, Cash Flow Margin and Cash Flow Return on Assets (ROA).

KPI: Cash Conversion Cycle

Cash conversion cycle (also known as cash cycle) helps to answer the key performance question 'How well are we doing at managing a healthy cash flow?' This metric is usually reported annually, but if cash flow is a concern it should be measured quarterly or even monthly.

Cash Conversion Cycle (CCC) = Days Inventory Outstanding (DIO) + Days Sales Outstanding (DSO) – Days Payable Outstanding (DPO)

To find the data necessary to calculate CCC you need to analyse sales records, stock or inventory records and accounts. So long as your business keeps complete and accurate account records and has a good handle on inventory, then this KPI should be relatively easy and inexpensive to measure. This metric is really useful for helping to open up discussions around improving efficiency all the way along the supply chain.

Calculating CCC: An example

To help to make CCC clearer I've included an example of how each section of the formula is calculated.

Calculate DIO like this:

- ✔ Divide the cost of sales from the income statement by 365 days to calculate a cost of sales per day figure. For example 5,600/365 = 15.34

- ✔ Calculate the average inventory figure for the period. For example if you want the average inventory for a year you would go to the balance sheet and add the inventory for the start of the year to the inventory at the end of the year and divide by two to get an average inventory for the period. For example 800 + 870 = 1670/2 = 835

- ✔ Divide the average inventory figure by the cost of sales per day figure to give your DIO figure. For example, 835/15.34 = DIO of 54.43

In this example therefore it takes 54 days for the company's inventory to turn into cash.

Work out DSO like this:

- ✔ Divide net sales from the income statement by 365 days to get a net sales per day figure. For example 4,600/365 = 12.60

- ✔ Calculate the average accounts receivable figure by looking at the balance sheet and adding how much was sold (although not necessarily paid for yet) at the start of the year to how much was sold at the end of the year and dividing by two to get the average accounts receivable for the year. For example 760 + 680 = 1440 / 2 = 720

- ✔ Divide the average accounts receivable figure by the net sales per day figure. For example 720/12.60 = DSO of 57.14

In this example it takes 57 days for the company to collect on sales that go into accounts receivable. In many businesses, sales are not cash sales. Instead an invoice is issued to the buyer to settle the account DSO measures how long it takes for the company to collect that money.

Calculate DPO as follows:

- ✔ Divide the cost of sales from the income statement by 365 days to get a cost of sales per day figure. For example 5,600/365 = 15.34

- ✔ Calculate the average accounts payable figure by looking at the balance sheet and adding the accounts payable at the start of the year to the accounts payable at the end of the year and dividing by two to get an average accounts payable amount for any given year or period. For example 450 + 540 = 990/2 = 495

- ✔ Divide the average accounts payable figure by the cost of sales per day figure to get the DPO figure. For example 495/15.34 = DPO of 32.27

In this example it takes 32 days for this company to pay its suppliers.

Armed with these figures it's now possible to calculate CCC

CCC = DIO (54.43) + DSO (57.14) – DPO (32.27) = 79.3. Meaning in this example it takes the company 79 days to convert their resources into cash.

Do not assume that reducing your CCC is always a good thing. Business is about fostering relationships with customers and suppliers. Insisting on immediate payment by customers and delaying payment to suppliers can easily backfire and damage long-term business relationships.

KPI: Working Capital Ratio

The key performance question working capital ratio helps to answer is: To what extent do we hold enough short-term assets to cover our short-term debt?'

Working capital, also known as *current position* is a measure of current assets minus current liabilities. This metric therefore measures how much you have available in liquid assets to build and maintain your business.

Like so many financial metrics, this one becomes especially useful when it's converted into a ratio, so that you can compare it to equivalent measurements from other time periods or companies. The working capital ratio indicates whether a company has enough short-term assets to cover its short-term debt. You can extract he data needed to calculate working capital and working capital ratio from the accounting data and balance sheet. It's wise to measure your working capital once every quarter.

Working Capital Ratio = Current Assets/Current Liabilities

For example, say Company A has current assets of $460,000 ($140,000 in cash, $120,000 in inventory, $80,000 in securities and $120,000 in inventory) and current liabilities of $210,000 ($130,000 in accounts payable, $30,000 in accrued expenses and $50,000 in current debt).

Working capital = $460,000 – $210,000= $250,000

Working Capital Ratio = $460,000/$210,000= 2.19

Company A's working capital ratio of 2.19 means that for every dollar in liabilities it has $2.19 in assets.

In general, companies with strong, positive working capital are more successful, since they have the financial resources to expand and improve their operations. Companies with negative working capital will probably lack the funds for growth or be forced to borrow money for expansion, and this can put additional pressure on the cash position.

Working capital ratio is often closely followed by investors because it is a measure of an organisation's overall health and liquidity. A negative working capital position makes your business unattractive to potential investors and can negatively impact your share price.

Working capital ratios vary by industry, although a ratio of between 1.2 and 2.0 is widely considered sufficient.

Explanation of Important Data Locations

The key locations for the data you need to carry out the calculations in this chapter area as follows:

✔ **The Balance Sheet:** This financial document summarises what your company currently owns (assets), what it owes (liabilities) and what it is worth to its shareholders (shareholder equity).

✔ **The Income Statement:** This financial document lists all your company's revenues over a certain period such as a quarter or year. It is this document that details what profit was made.

✔ **The Statement of Cash Flow:** This financial document lists your company's cash position including inflows and outflows of cash. This document is focused on whether the company generated cash.

KPI: Cash flow solvency ratio

The key performance question cash flow solvency ratio helps to answer is: 'How easily are we going to meet our debts?' The data you will need to calculate the cash flow solvency ratio can be found from your balance sheet and statement of cash flows.

Cash flow solvency ratio = Cash Flow from Operations/Total Liabilities

If you were to decide to seek funding, this metric would be of particular interest to decision makers at the funding organisation because it indicates how easily you can pay your current debts.

The higher the ratio, the better as it indicates that there is plenty of money in the pot to pay the debts. A lower cash flow solvency ratio means you have less financial flexibility and are more likely to run into problems.

Looking Out for Liquidity

Although closely connected to cash flow, *liquidity* is slightly different. Whereas cash flow is the actual movement or flow of cash around the business, liquidity is a measure of where that money is located and how quickly it can be accessed. When a business is *liquid* it either has a lot of cash in the bank or it can *liquidate* short-term investments or assets quickly to convert those assets to cash when needed.

A business may own a huge warehouse worth millions of dollars, but that asset is not a liquid asset as it may take many months or years to sell. A portfolio of shares would be much easier to liquidate and gives the company much more flexibility and room to move and grow.

The often unseen danger

Often when businesses are focused on profit and growth they will want to use all their resources and assets to push growth forward. The danger in that strategy however is the unforeseen. Even the smartest leaders and executives will get it wrong some of the time. Markets and economies change – often rapidly – and if you don't have enough money in the bank or assets you can convert into cash you can easily land in hot water.

You need to strike a balance between maximising your reserves and making your money work for you, and maintain a safety net – or at least quick access to a safety net – should the need arise.

Measuring liquidity in practice

The liquidity KPIs that are most useful are Current Ratio, Quick Ratio, Cash Ratio and Days of Working Capital. These metrics help you to measure how well your business can use its short-term assets to meet its short-term liabilities. Liquidity KPIs help determine business health and offer insight into your exposure to risk and therefore give you the opportunity to reduce that risk if necessary.

KPI: Current Ratio

The key performance question that current ratio helps to answer is: 'Do we have the money to meet our short term obligations?' This metric measures the amount of current assets you have to pay for every $1 of current liabilities. The data you will need to calculate this KPI is located on the balance sheet.

Current Ratio = Current Assets/Current Liabilities

Current assets include cash, inventory and accounts receivable. Current liabilities include accounts payable, current debt and tax liabilities.

Your company is in good health if your current ratio is 2 or more. This means that you assets are twice as high as your liabilities and you have more than enough assets to pay what you owe.

A ratio of 1 or less indicates concern, because your assets are worth either the same or less than your liabilities. This means that you may not be able to pay all your debts. Although not a great sign, it doesn't automatically spell disaster, but you will need to access more funds or improve efficiency to increase assets.

The current ratio will give you a sense of how efficiently your business is run and how easy or otherwise it is to turn your goods and services into cash. Companies that take too long to be paid or have a long lead time for their product can easily run into liquidity problems because they can't get the money in fast enough to pay their debts.

That said, what is perceived as a good or bad current ratio does vary between industries. In order to get a better sense of how acceptable your current ratio really is then compare it to other companies in your sector.

KPI: Quick Ratio

The key performance question that the quick ratio, also known as the *acid test ratio* helps to answer is: 'To what extent are we able to meet our short-term obligations with our most liquid assets?' This metric is a more conservative look at liquidity than current ratio, because it only takes cash and account receivables into account, not inventory.

Quick Ratio = (Current Assets – Inventory)/Current Liabilities

By excluding inventory from current assets you get a much more realistic picture of how quickly you can meet your business liabilities, especially if it wouldn't be easy or even possible to convert the inventory into cash quickly. If, for example, you sell aircraft, they may be worth a great deal but the market is very small and the sales process may take months if not years.

If you have a quick ratio of 1 or more the business is healthy and able to meet its liabilities from existing sales already made, plus cash. A lower quick ratio indicates that your business may not be able to pay for its current debts. This metric can alert you to potential challenges ahead so you do something about it - whether that is ramp up your sales effort, have a fire sale to raise funds or sell off or rent some premises.

KPI: Cash Ratio

The key performance question that the cash ratio helps to answer is: 'To what extend can we meet our debts from the cash in the business?' This metric is the most conservative liquidity KPI because it only considers cash as an asset.

Cash Ratio = Current Cash/Current Liabilities

Inventory and account receivable are not included in this measure because they are not definite enough. Inventory needs to be sold and the customer needs to pay. It may be harder to make this happen than it looks: Although accounts receivable details orders that have been made, the customers have not yet paid for the orders so it's not absolutely certain that you will receive that cash.

As a result the cash ratio is always lower than the quick or current ratio. It is an assessment of the immediate position, and your ability to meet current liabilities without cashing payment or selling more inventory.

KPI: Days of Working Capital

The key performance question that the days of working capital helps to answer is: 'How long will we survive after paying all current liabilities?' This metric refers to the amount of current assets you would have after paying all your current liabilities.

Days of Working Capital = Working Capital/Sales Revenue per Day

You calculate working capital by deducting current liabilities from your current assets. And you work out sales revenue per day by dividing your total sales by 365 days.

So, for example, if your current assets were $230 million and your current liabilities were $190 million, your working capital would be $40 million. If your total sales were $130 million your sales revenue per day would be $356,164 which means that you have 112 days (40,000,000/356,164 = 112) of working capital.

A healthy business has 30 days or more working capital.

Chapter 10

Reporting to the Masters: Shareholder and Value-Added KPIs

In This Chapter

▶ Understanding value from a shareholders perspective

▶ Appreciating the importance of opportunity cost

▶ Measuring shareholder return

*P*rofit, revenue, cash flow and liquidity KPIs are important to all companies regardless of sector, industry or whether the business is privately or publicly owned.

Once a company becomes publicly listed, however, investors and analysts will use certain KPIs to decide how strong your business is. Their interpretation of these metrics will influence whether shareholders decide to buy, sell or hold your stock.

In a public company, shareholders wear the trousers. Everything a business does, every strategy it embarks on, every decision it makes is focused on delivering shareholder value, and the KPIs detailed in this chapter help the leadership team know how well they are doing against that objective.

The Ultimate Value Metric: EVA

In the past, profit-based KPIs were considered the best and only real way to measure corporate performance and therefore shareholder value.

But looking at profit and revenue can be misleading for two reasons.

✔ Profit calculations ignore the costs of capital and can therefore distort performance.

✔ Profits can easily be manipulated through legal – albeit creative – accounting practices.

In an effort to draw a meaningful distinction between value and profit that would help investors make a more accurate interpretation, New York based consultancy Stern Stewart created the ultimate value metric – Economic Value Added (EVA), also known as *economic profit.*

Basically EVA estimates the profit of a business when the cost of financing the company's capital has been removed, because value is only really created when the return on the capital employed is more than the cost of that capital.

Why profitable companies might not create value

EVA is an important metric for investors and analysts because it allows the investor to pull back the veil of numbers to establish whether value is actually being created in the business or not.

Many businesses view capital, which is any cash that has been deposited in a company over its lifetime, as 'free'. By ignoring costs associated with capital, irrespective of how this was financed, a company can get a better picture of whether it has actually generated value relative to the economy as a whole.

Understanding opportunity cost

The central premise of EVA is that capital is not free. As well as incurring a real financial cost there is also the opportunity cost of capital to consider.

If an investor has $20,000 to invest in your business they could easily invest that money into any other type of investment such as property, gold, government bonds or another company. If he decides to invest in your business, then the investor is effectively charging you a rent to tie up his cash so that you can use that money to support operations. The investor is therefore compensated for choosing to invest in your business as opposed to making an investment elsewhere, and EVA is the only KPI that takes this cost into account.

Say Company A (a start up in mobile phone apps) earned $100,000 on their capital base of $1 million thanks to strong early sales of their mobile apps. *Return on Capital Employed* (ROCE) – which I explore in Chapter 11 – is 10 per cent, a good result, especially as the business has only been operating for a couple of years.

To get off the ground Company A borrowed some money and also sold shares to investors who agreed on a required return in exchange for their investment. Obviously if the investor bought shares in Company A then their money was tied up and they couldn't use it elsewhere. Investing money into start ups of this nature carries some significant risks and investors therefore expect a higher return. If therefore shareholder expectations and obligations to service debt add up to an investment costs of capital of 15 per cent, then it means Company A may be enjoying an 'accounting profit' of 10 per cent but the business actually lost 5 per cent for its shareholders.

Conversely if Company A had $100 million in capital, including debt and equity finance and the cost of that capital (including interest in the debt and cost of underwriting the equity) is $15 million Company A would only add genuine value to its shareholders when profits exceeded $15 million a year. Traditional profit metrics don't factor in the cost of capital and can present an overly flattering picture as a result. If Company A generates an income of $30 million, EVA would only be $15 million.

Measuring opportunity cost in practice

The key performance question EVA helps to answer is: 'How well are we delivering value to our shareholders?' This metric is usually reported on a monthly basis. Use this formula:

Economic Value Added (EVA) = Net Operating Profit After Tax (NOPAT) – (Weighted Average Costs of Capital (WACC) × Economic Capital Employed)

Calculating EVA in practice is a notoriously thorny and complex matter so if it's one you want to use I suggest you get some help from a qualified accountant to do it.

Normally, the equity cost of capital for an organization is calculated through the Capital Asset Pricing Model (CAPM). A firm's nominal equity cost of capital is calculated as a base risk-free rate plus 'beta' – the latter being a general equity risk premium adjusted for a firm-specific risk measure. In short, therefore, the equity rate is the return investors are seeking to achieve when buying a company's common shares. This is expressed as:

the firm's equity investors' expected return (future) = risk-free return (future) + the firm's beta (a relative measure of volatility) × general equity risk premium (history)

The equity risk premium represents the excess return above the risk-free rate that investors demand for holding risky securities. So, with a risk-free rate of 7 per cent, a beta of 1.1 and an assumed equity risk premium of 4 per cent, a company would have the following cost of equity:

Cost of equity = 7 per cent + (1.1 × 4 per cent) = 11.4 per cent.

The cost of debt is the rate of return that debt-holders require in order to hold debt. To determine this rate it stated that the yield had to be calculated. This is typically worked out using discounted cash flow analysis, i.e., the internal rate of return. The cost of tax should be calculated after tax as follows:

Cost of debt after tax = cost of tax before tax × (100 – marginal tax rate)

You can find the data you need to calculate EVA in the profit and loss statement. The component parts needed to calculate EVA require a bit more work to establish than many of the other financial indicators. However you only need to calculate WACC every year. How costly this metric will be to initiate will depend on how readily you can get your hands on the necessary data. If it already exists and just needs to be extracted then it will just require the addition of a new formula in your accounting system. If some of the information is missing it could be a costly measure to establish so you will need to be very sure you need it.

Keeping an Eye on Your Share Price

Investors decide to buy, hold or sell their shares based largely on the movement of your share price. Understanding how attractive your shares are to existing and potential investors is therefore important.

If your share price drops because your business didn't do as well as expected, or because a negative news story affects your business then millions, sometimes billions, can be wiped off the value of the shares almost overnight.

Who can forget the catastrophic collapse of one of the UK's most successful jewellery business following the then CEO's careless remark at an Institute of Directors dinner. Gerard Ratner thought he'd add a few jokes to his speech at the last minute and proceeded to tell the audience about the earrings his store sold adding, they were, 'Cheaper than an M&S [Marks & Spencer] prawn sandwich but probably wouldn't last as long.' Another clanger he felt compelled to share was, 'We also do cut-glass sherry decanters complete with six glasses on a silver-plated tray that your butler can serve drinks on – all for $4.95. People say, 'How can you sell this for such a low price'? I say, 'Because it's total crap".

Unbeknown to Ratner there was a journalist in the room and the story ended up in the press. Even though he'd only been joking, the remarks made it look like he was mocking his own customers, and they stopped buying. His 'jokes' wiped an estimated $500 million of the share value of the business, he was forced to resign and the business under his name did not survive for long.

It's all relative: comparing businesses

Ultimately share price is relative and investors will not make their decisions in isolation – they will compare your share price to other businesses in your sector and beyond.

Not only does this comparison help investors compare different businesses accurately but it also provides managers with insights into how easy or otherwise it's going to be to attract investment capital, and whether or not the business is ripe for a takeover bid. If the share price of a business is trading lower than it should be, then that business can make an attractive takeover target, so keeping a close eye on share price is critical to your on-going strategy.

The KPI most often used to make this comparison is the *Price/Earnings ratio*, usually known as the P/E ratio. This metric looks at the relationships between the share price and the company's earnings.

Looking at historic performance the P/E ratio measures the price an investor is paying for $1 of the company's earnings. Or it can be expressed as the time it will take for the investor to recoup their initial investment assuming it maintains the same earnings as the year before. A higher P/E ratio therefore means that the investor is paying more for each $1 of net income or has to wait longer for their return on investment so the stock is often more expensive compared to one with a lower P/E ratio.

Measuring P/E ratio in practice

The key performance question P/E ratio helps answer is: 'To what extent is the current share price attractive to investors?' The data required to calculate P/E ratio is available from your company accounts and the current share price. This metric is usually measured on a quarterly or annual basis.

P/E Ratio = Current price per share/Earnings per share

For example if Company X is reporting earnings per share of $4 and the share price is $40 per share then:

P/E Ratio = 40/4 = 10

Compare that to Company Y that reported earnings per share of $10 and a share price of $40 per share then:

P/E Ratio = 40/10 = 4

Company X has a P/E ratio of 10 and Company Y has a P/E ratio of 4 which means that Company Y is a much better investment because it will take just 4 years to recoup the investment as opposed to 10 years with Company X.

The biggest problem with P/E ratio is that it uses past earnings to arrive at current value. And yet the mantra of stock investing is that 'past performance does not guarantee future performance' – as evidenced by Ratners Jewellery chain.

Increasingly investors are looking at the forward P/E ratio – share price divided by the expected earnings for the next year. This revised metric can be particularly useful when profits from the previous year have been distorted by a divestment, corporate write-down or one off windfall.

Tracking Total Shareholder Return (TSR)

Ultimately investors want to know how much money is going to be returned to them either through in increase in share value or through dividends. The metric that they use to measure this is called *total shareholder return* (TSR), and it is useful to investors in analysing the best companies to invest in, or the ones they believe will deliver the best return on investment.

TSR is a measure often used for evaluating current performance.

Competition is stiff on the stock market

In any sector in any industry competition is fierce and businesses are not only competing for customers they are competing for investors. TSR is often used as a key measure to determine senior executive compensation because it puts stock performance in direct comparison to other companies in their sector.

This puts additional performance pressure on senior executives because it's not enough to deliver high performance – that performance must be comparable or better than competitors or other organizations with a similar profile, otherwise they risk losing the investor to a competitor.

Investors will use TSR to decide whether to stay invested in the business or to sell the shareholding and invest elsewhere.

Measuring TSR in practice

The key performance question TSR helps to answer is: To what extent are we delivering value to shareholders? This metric is usually reported annually or twice yearly. Assessing TSR across the year is preferable because it allows for seasonal or other market fluctuations and therefore gives a more accurate picture of share performance.

> Total Shareholder Value = (Net Share Price for the period + Dividend)/ Share price at the start of the period × 100

Say for example you wanted to assess the TSR for Company C over a year. To calculate the net share price you need to know the share price at the start of the period in question and the price at the end. So Company C's share price was $30 on the 1st of January 2013 and $35 on the 31st December 2013, making the net share price $5. The company also paid $12 in dividends which is added to the $5 to make $17. The TSR for Company C is 56.66 per cent ($17/$30 x 100).

The TSV is always expressed as a percentage, which makes it very easy to compare across business and allows for benchmarking against industry or market returns.

Obviously TSR is only relevant to publicly listed companies and is not applicable to privately owned enterprises. Although useful it can't be calculated at a divisional or business unit level and as a metric it is 'backward-looking'. TRS only reflects the past overall return to shareholders and offers minimal insight into likely future returns.

Chapter 11

Measuring Your Financial Efficiency

In This Chapter

▶ Understanding how well resources are being used

▶ Knowing what investors want

▶ Measuring how hard the assets are working

*P*rofit and growth are important metrics but measuring how well you use resources is also critical. After all, there is no point fighting tooth and claw to increase front-end sales revenue when inefficient processes, operational waste or poor cost control wipes out all the front-end effort.

Business involves many ways of spending revenue and using resources. Financial efficiency KPIs can help to separate those options and guide decision making, so you make the right decision more of the time.

Assessing the Return on Investment

Return on investment (ROI), also referred to as *rate of return* (ROR) or *rate of profit* (ROP) is a financial KPI used to measure the efficiency of an investment. It can be calculated during or after making an investment or used in the decision-making process prior to a potential investment.

Obviously, if you can assess the costs and projected benefits associated with a particular investment before you part with any hard-earned cash, then you are better able to compare options and build a strong business case around the best investment. As a result, ROI can help management make the 'go' or 'no go' call when faced with investment decisions.

There are two types of ROI – *micro ROI* and *macro ROI*.

Micro ROI looks at particular elements within larger programmes the company is involved in. These programmes usually take anywhere from a few months to a year to come to fruition. Examples of micro ROI include:

✔ A social media sales promotion

✔ Running a staff training programme

✔ A print and TV advertising programme

Effectively, micro ROI can be applied to any project, promotion or investment a business spends money on or is considering spending money on, where a positive return is expected within a year.

Macro ROI is focused on the overall performance of major business initiatives that are ends in themselves rather than elements of a business function. Examples of macro ROI include:

✔ The installation of a new software program

✔ Assembly line upgrade and improvement

✔ Investing in a delivery fleet to manage the supply chain more closely

The return on macro investments takes more than a year to come to fruition, often several years.

ROI calculations can also be used to compare a number of different investment options in order to find the most promising one.

Every investment must yield a return

Every business wants to make sure that investments yield a return, and that the allocation of valuable resources is worthwhile, adds value and makes more money for the business. This is especially true for a publicly listed company that has obligations to deliver value to shareholders.

Resources are usually finite so you and your executive team must decide how best to spend the money it makes – often choosing between a number of investment opportunities. ROI can be a very important and useful KPI to measure in these situations to ensure that as many investments as possible yield a positive benefit for the business.

Of course you need to remember that ROI by itself is not enough to assess an investment because it does not factor in the likelihood of the expected returns coming about. It compares expected cost to expected benefits – both of which could be wrong so the more certainty you can establish around these variables the better the decision making.

Understandably, ROI is a key metric tracked by investors because it measures a business's ability to generate positive returns on their investments on an ongoing basis.

Measuring ROI in practice

The key performance question ROI helps to answer is: 'To what extent are we making efficient investments?' You collect the data for this metric from the accounting data.

You can calculate ROI in a few different ways, although they all seek to compare returns to costs by calculating a ratio or percentage. Simple ROI is:

ROI = (Gains from investment – Cost of investment)/Cost of investment

To calculate the percentage you simply multiply it by 100:

ROI = (Gains from investment – Cost of investment)/Cost of investment × 100

For example, say you want to invest in an integrated marketing campaign with print adds, social media and TV. The cost of the campaign is $350,000 and the expected return is 600,000. Simple ROI is 0.71 or 71 per cent.

($600,000 – $350,000)/$350,000 × 100 = 71.43 per cent

The ROI calculation gives you an insight into how much return you will get from your investment, and obviously you want this to be a positive figure. Negative results would indicate that you are making a loss. In this example, you are making a gain of 71 per cent on your initial investment. An individual ROI calculation gives you an insight into the expected returns, multiple ROI calculations allows you to compare investments.

You can also look at ROI over specific time periods to calculate, for example, an annual rate of return, especially if the investment is made over a number of years. The formula you use for that is:

(Profit/Cost) × (Year/Period) × 100

For example, say you are considering a social media sales promotion that would run for 90 days. It would cost $175,000. Expected sales are $320,000. Profit is expected to be $145,000.

($145,000/$175,000) × (365/90) × 100

0.83 × 4.06 = 3.36 × 100 = 337% annual rate of return

ROI can be very helpful in the decision making process. That said, it's not always easy to match specific returns like anticipated profit to specific costs like marketing campaigns.

You must also make sure you are comparing like with like and not confusing *annual* and *annualised returns*.

An *annual* rate of return is the return on an investment over a one-year period, such as January 1st through to December 31st. An *annualised* rate of return is the return on an investment over a period other than one year (such as 90 days in the example above) multiplied or divided to give a comparable one-year return. For example, a one-month ROI of 2 per cent could be stated as an annualised rate of return of 24 per cent (2 per cent × 12 months = 24 per cent). Or a two-year ROI of 10 per cent could be stated as an annualised rate of return of 5 per cent (10 per cent/2 years = 5 per cent).

This allows you to compare investments of different time frames. For example, if you have three investments, one over 10 years, one over 5 years and another over 2 years, the annual rate of return provides you with a figure to compare them.

There are several ways to calculate ROI which gives the KPI flexibility, but that same flexibility also means if can be manipulated to suit the user's purpose.

Measuring the Return on Capital Employed

Return on capital employed (ROCE) is considered a key profitability KPI for investors seeking to compare investments and find the business that is making the best use of its capital to increase profit, growth and shareholder value. So whether you are an investor or an executive wanting to ensure your business looks enticing to investors ROCE is a very important metric. And that is true even if your business is not a publicly listed company.

ROCE differs from ROI because it considers debt and other liabilities whereas ROI doesn't. As a result it is often a better indication of overall financial performance.

Understanding ROCE

ROCE compares earnings with the capital employed in the company to assess profitability. The main components used in the KPI calculation are operating profit and capital employed.

There are a number of ways to reach the earnings ratio or operating profit, but a common approach is to use *earnings before interest and tax* (EBIT) while capital employed is the capital investment necessary for the company to function and grow. (EBIT is a variation or part of the KPI EBITDA detailed in Chapter eight).

ROCE either uses the reported capital numbers at the end of the period in question or the average of the opening and closing capital over that period – known as *return on average capital employed* (ROACE).

This KPI indicates how well management have utilised owners' and creditors' investment. It is also commonly used as a decision-making metric, helping management decide how best to use capital between projects. Plotting this metric consistently over time illustrates an efficiency and profitability trend and helps executives and investors decide whether the business is improving or otherwise. In essence, ROCE shows you how much your business is gaining from its assets, or how much it is losing from its liabilities.

Measuring ROCE in practice

The key performance question ROCE helps to answer is: 'How well are we generating earnings from our capital investments?' The data for this metric is collected from analysis of the accounting data.

ROCE is usually measured on an annual basis and is an easy KPI to measure as the information needed is readily available in the accounting data. Again, you can calculate ROCE as a simple ratio number or as a percentage. This formula calculates the percentage:

ROCE = EBIT/Total capital employed × 100

It can be particularly useful to compare your ROCE to the ROCE of other companies in your industry or sector as it will give you an idea of how efficient your use of capital is against your competitors.

For example say you would like to know how efficient your business is operating in comparison to your nearest competitor. Your business has EBIT of $10 million on sales of $200 million in 2013. Your competitor has EBIT of $15 million on sales of $200 million. Initially you may be a little concerned because your competitor looks to be performing better with an EBIT margin of 7.5 per cent ($15m divided by $200m multiplied by 100) whereas your EBIT margin is only 5 per cent ($10m divided by $200m multiplied by 100).

But you decide to look more closely to capital employed to measure efficiency rather than just earnings. Your total capital employed is $50 million and your competitors is $100 million.

Your ROCE = $10m/$50m × 100 = 20 per cent

Your competitor's ROCE = $15m/$100m ×100 = 15 per cent

What ROCE demonstrates is that although you're not generating as much revenue as your competitor your business is doing a better job of squeezing value from its capital than your competitor. The higher your ROCE the better the business is at deploying the capital in the business wisely.

One drawback of ROCE is that it measures return against the book value of assets in the business. Obviously assets depreciate, which means that the ROCE will increase even if cash flow remains unchanged. As a result older, more established businesses often have a higher ROCE than newer businesses even though the newer businesses may be more efficient.

Another criticism is that ROCE can be used too stringently. Say your cost of capital is 10 per cent and you have an ROCE target of 30 per cent. You may discount potential investments that do not deliver a return of at least 30 per cent. But if the cost of capital is 10 per cent then any investment that delivers a return of greater than 10 per cent should be considered, as it is still adding value to the business.

Gauging Return on Equity (ROE)

Companies can either finance their operations through *equity* (investments from shareholders) or by *debt* (borrowing money). This metric focuses on equity and measures how much profit your business is creating from the money invested by shareholders.

Many analysts consider ROE as the single most important KPI for investors and the best marker of management performance.

As expected with profitability and efficiency KPIs, the higher the better. Companies with high ROE are better able to grow the business without turning back to shareholders for more capital or incurring debt.

Why should you measure ROE

Shareholder equity is an accounting creation that represents the assets created by the paid-in capital of the shareholders and the retained earnings of the business.

ROE is particularly useful because it looks behind the bluster and sanitised propaganda of annual reports. As legendary investor Warren Buffett pointed out some years ago, achieving higher earnings year on year is not actually that hard. You could stick your cash in a high interest account or sack half your workforce and your figures would look fabulous, but those actions tell the investor nothing about efficiency and how well the business manages their capital and uses it to create value.

A business with a high return on equity is more likely to be one that is capable of generating cash internally. If your company has a high ROE then it is demonstrating a good profitability and efficiency track record.

Measuring ROE in practice

The key performance question ROE helps to answer is: 'How efficiently are we using the investments that shareholders have made to generate profits?' The data needed for ROE comes directly from the income statements of the business.

Shareholder equity is calculated from the balance sheet by taking total assets and subtracting total liabilities. This leaves the amount of equity owned by the shareholders. Again, you can calculate ROE as a simple ratio number or as a percentage. This formula calculates the percentage:

ROE = (Net income for period in question/Average shareholder's equity over same period) × 100

Say for example your net income for 2013 was $11.5 million. Your shareholder equity at the start of 2013 was $48 million and $52 million at the end of 2013. Your average shareholder equity for 2013 was $50 million ($48 million + $52 million / 2).

ROE = 11.5/50 × 100 = 23 per cent

To get a sense of whether your ROE is good or bad you need to compare it to other companies in your industry.

The DuPont formula

The DuPont formula or *strategic profit model* is another, albeit more complex way of measuring ROE that breaks ROE down into three important components:

✔ Net margin

✔ Asset turnover

✔ Financial leverage

The DuPont Formula states that:

ROE = (Net income/Sales) × (Sales/Total assets) × (Total assets/Average shareholder equity)

or

ROE = (Net margin) × (Asset turnover) × (Financial leverage)

Splitting ROE into these three parts makes it easier to understand changes in ROE over time.

For example, if the net margin increased, every sale would make more money for the business which in turn would increase overall ROE.

If the asset turnover increased, the business would create more sales for assets owned, which again would result in a higher ROE.

And finally, if financial leverage increases it means that the business is using more debt than equity to finance operations and growth. Again this will increase ROE because interest payments to creditors are tax deductible while shareholder dividends are not.

Increased debt will only ever make a positive contribution to your ROE if the return on assets or the way the money is used delivers a higher return than the cost of the capital. For example if you borrowed money at 10 per cent interest rate and used the money to upgrade a production line then the return on the production line would need to exceed 10 per cent in order to make it worthwhile.

In years gone by a ROE of 20 per cent plus was considered very good and achievable. Realistically however these figures are probably unsustainable and certainly CEOs have been issuing repeated earnings revisions in an attempt to recalibrate inflated expectations around return.

Understanding Return on Assets (ROA)

All businesses must invest in assets such as property, machinery or equipment in order to generate a return. It's obviously crucial to invest in the right assets – ones that will maximise income and assist growth and profitability.

Return on Assets helps you to work out how profitable your business is in relation to the assets it controls. As such it is another financial metric that is designed to expose corporate efficiency.

If the ROA is low it indicates that the income has been low compared to the amount of assets the business.

Why does ROA matter to companies?

ROA provides investors or would be investors with a good idea of how effective a business is at converting the money it has to invest into net income.

Anyone can make a company look good if they throw enough money at it. If you consider some of the technology start-ups of the late 1990s, just before the dot. com bubble burst, they generated huge investment from expectant shareholders. But even though they were swimming in cash they were not able to convert that investment into income or long-term, consistent shareholder value.

Measuring ROA in practice

The key performance question ROA helps to answer is: 'To what extent are we able to generate profits from the assets we control?' The data needed to calculate ROA comes directly from the income statements of the business and it is usually calculated every year, but reported on a *rolling quarterly basis* (that is, calculated for the past four quarters, each quarter).

> ROA = (Net income for period in question/Total assets at end of period) × 100

The problem with this formula is that it can be too simplistic. For a start, businesses fund their assets through *equity finance* (selling shares to shareholders) or *debt finance* (borrowing money). If a business borrows more money then it will usually result in higher interest rates and the simple ROA formula does not account for capital costs. Plus it can be misleading. Say you owned a fleet of delivery vehicles for 11 months of the year and then decided to sell them all in December. The income for the year in question was earned using those delivery vehicles. Yet come December they are not part of the business or included in total assets even though those assets were integral to earnings, therefore distorting the ROA.

To account for these problems a more accurate formula would therefore be:

> ROA = (Net income for period + Interest expenses in period)/Average assets during period × 100

For example say your company earned $15 million in net income in 2013. The cost of capital during the same period was $1 million. Your assets at the start of 2013 were $20 million and $25 million at the end of 2013. Your average assets would therefore be $22.5 million ($20m + $25m/2).

> ROA = $14 million/$22.5 million × 100 = 62 per cent

There is no benchmark for ROA as it varies significantly between industries. It is therefore most useful to compare ROA with similar businesses.

Part IV

Developing Customer, Sales and Marketing KPIs

```
                          Example Company
                          Income Statement
                For the Year Ended December 31, 2014

Sales Revenue:
Total Sales                           $1,505,500
 - Sales Returns                          - 2,000
 - Sales Discounts                        - 3,500

Net Sales Revenue                                        $1,500,000

Less: Cost of Goods Sold:
  Beginning Stock                      $150,000
   + Purchases                          800,000
   + Freight-In                          10,000
   - Purchase Discounts                 - 15,000
   - Purchase Returns                    - 5,000
   - Ending Stock                      - 140,000
Cost of Goods Sold                                        - 800,000
Gross Profit                                              $700,000

Operating Expenses

Selling Expenses:
   Freight-Out                          $60,000
   Advertising Expense                   55,000
   Sales Commissions Expense             40,000
Administrative Expenses:
   Office Salaries Expense              150,000
   Office Rent Expense                  120,000
   Office Supplies Expense               30,000
Total Operating Expenses                                  - 455,000
Operating Income                                          $245,000

Other Incomes and Expenses:

Gains on Sale Equipment                $20,000
 - Loss on Sales of investments         - 10,000
 - Interest Expense                     - 12,000
Net Other Incomes and Expenses                            - 42,000
Net Profit                                                $203,000
```

For Dummies can help you get started with lots of subjects. Go to www.dummies.com to learn more and do more with *For Dummies*.

In this part . . .

- ✔ Use KPIs to understand what your customers really think of you, and whether they would recommend you to others.

- ✔ Measure how satisfied your customers are with your service, and pinpoint what makes them happy.

- ✔ Track how valuable individual customers are to you, and how likely they are to remain your customers.

- ✔ Measure the size of the market you're in, and what its potential for growth might be.

- ✔ Get a handle on your place in the market: your market share, your potential for further success, and how to drive and enhance the power of your brand.

Chapter 12

The Customer is Always Right: Measuring Your Customer Success

In This Chapter

▶ Establishing if your customers would recommend you

▶ Understanding customer satisfaction and loyalty

▶ Working out how valuable your customers are to you

*Q*uite simply, business success depends on your ability to attract customers and keep them happy over the long term. Of course, not all customers are the same. Chances are they don't all buy the same product or service and they almost certainly experience different levels of service depending on who they happen to deal with on the day, or whether your online purchase system crashed just as they were about to complete their order.

Some customers may love your customer service and attention to detail, some may think it needs work. Some customers may love your prices where others don't really care about the cost because they are fully focused on the quality. This variability means that measuring how your customers feel about your business can often seem an overwhelmingly messy and daunting process.

But it doesn't need to be. The KPIs detailed in this chapter will help you to measure your customer success which will in turn predict your business success.

Asking if Your Customers Would Recommend You (NPS)

Clearly, understanding how satisfied your customers are will have a direct bearing on how loyal they are to your business. If they are satisfied they are more likely to stay and buy from you again. If they are not satisfied they are more likely to buy what they need from your competitors.

Unfortunately most customer surveys that seek to measure satisfaction are complex, time consuming and expensive. Plus they can be notoriously difficult to interpret. So what to do?

Developed and trademarked by Fred Reichheld, Bain & Company and Satmetrix, the Net Promoter Score (NPS) is one option. Introduced by Reichheld in his 2003 *Harvard Business Review* article as the 'one number you need to grow' the metric is based on just one simple question: 'How likely is it that you would recommend [insert company or product name] to a friend or colleague?'

Faced with complex and unwieldy customer surveys or just one question - it is easy to see why NPS became a popular customer assessment KPI.

NPS is based on the fundamental premise that every company's customers can be divided into three groups:

- ✔ **Promoters**: Loyal enthusiastic customers who will continue to buy from you and recommend you to others. Promoters fuel growth.

- ✔ **Passives**: Satisfied but unenthusiastic customers who may or may not buy from you again. Passives are vulnerable to a well-positioned competitor offer and don't necessarily feel any loyalty to you.

- ✔ **Detractors**: Unhappy customers who can actively damage your business through negative word of mouth. Detractors can impede growth.

By asking your customers this one question you can establish how many promoters, passives and detractors your business has and therefore how your customers perceive you.

How NPS drives loyalty and profitability

Loyalty is a strange phenomenon, especially in business. You might assume that loyal customers buy more, more often and therefore make more money for the business. But what constitutes loyalty? What NPS illustrates is that having happy customers is not enough. You need to endeavour to have really happy, enthusiastic customers who will tell anyone who will listen how wonderful you are.

Obviously the more detractors you can turn into passives the faster you will grow. Think of detractors as the brakes on your business – they can really slow you down. To illustrate just how detrimental detractors can be, pause for a moment and consider the last time you were really happy about a product or service you bought.

Okay: How many people did you tell about that? Now think about the last time you were really unhappy about a product or service. How many people did you tell about that? Human nature dictates that your customers will tell significantly more people when they are unhappy with you than they will when they are happy with you. At the very least you need to turn as many detractors into passives as you can so that they don't actively diminish your results.

If, however, you want to accelerate growth and increase your profit then you also need to turn as many passives into promoters, so they start referring you to others and driving growth.

Interestingly, customer loyalty also increases when they puts themselves on the line for your business. So if a customer recommends you to others and shouts from the rooftops about how fabulous you are, then this active participation in your business builds greater loyalty over time. And that type of loyalty does pay.

Even if your customers are happy they won't necessary tell other people about you or be any more likely to buy from you again. You need to surprise and delight them – only then will they start spreading the word.

Understanding the NPS formula

Using a scale of 0 to 10, where 0 indicated 'not at all likely' and 10 indicated 'extremely likely' customers are asked to answer the question: 'How likely is it that you would recommend [insert company or product name] to a friend or colleague?'

- ✔ Promoters are customers that indicated a score of 9–10
- ✔ Passives are customers that indicated a score of 7–8
- ✔ Detractors are customers that indicated a score of 0–6

Empirical research has shown that there is a striking correlation between the NPS customer's grouping (promoters, passives and detractors) and actual behaviour in the form of repeat purchase and referrals over time.

Further research mapped the NPS rating to the growth rates of organisations and demonstrated that this one simple statistic explained much of the variation in relative growth rates. In other words, companies with a high NPS grew more rapidly than those with a low NPS.

NPS is a great metric. Not only does it hold you and your employees accountable for how you treat customers and help strengthen the connection between this treatment and results but when NPS is combined with appropriate diagnostics and follow-up actions, it drives improvements in customer loyalty and enables profitable growth.

Measuring NPS in practice

The key performance question NPS helps to answer is: 'To what extent are our customers willing to recommend us?' NPS is collected using a customer survey usually conducted over the phone or online. The measure can be collected in two ways:

- ✓ **Top down NPS to rate the overall strength of the customer/company relationship**. This is achieved by setting up an anonymous survey and contact existing customers to ask the NPS question.

- ✓ **Transaction NPS where you survey your key customers by transaction type or size.** Obviously, the more promoters in your high-value customers the better.

The formula for calculating NPS is as follows:

NPS = Percentage of Promoters – Percentage of Detractors

For example say you survey 1000 of your customers. Asking them the one NPS question they respond as shown in Table 12-1:

Table 12-1	A typical response to a customer survey
Score	*Number of Customers*
0	3
1	5
2	2
3	0
4	5
5	10
6	20
7	150
8	300
9	350
10	155

Promoters: 350 + 155/1000 × 100 = 50.5 per cent

Detractors: 3 + 5 + 2 + 0 + 5 + 10 + 20/1000 × 100 = 4.5%

NPS = 50.5 per cent – 4.5 per cent = 46 per cent

Ironically, customers who are most unhappy also present the biggest opportunity for turn-around. If possible, find out who gave you a score of 0–3. These people are seriously unhappy, and as long as you fix their issue, apologise sincerely and endeavour to put things right you may be surprised to find they become your most vocal promoters.

Most companies don't collect customer data frequently enough. At the same time asking customers their views too often will just begin to irritate them. So instead of doing one big survey once a year consider asking the NPS question to 8 or 9 per cent of your customers every month. You are still only asking one question to one customer per year but these insights will allow you to gauge sentiment on an ongoing basis and track the NPS trend.

Although very insightful, NPS will not tell you why customers would or wouldn't recommend your business or products. As the NPS question is just one question, you may want to include two additional open questions at the end of the survey that allow for customers to elaborate, should they wish to. You might for example ask:

- ✔ What do you particularly like about this company/product?
- ✔ What would you improve if you had the chance?

The Canada-based online retailer Zappos ask the NPS questions after receiving an order, and also after a customer speaks with a customer loyalty representative. As well as the NPS question Zappos also seek further information that helps them to move their Detractors or Passive to Promoters by asking customers the additional question: 'If you had to name one thing that we could improve upon, what would that be?'

Once the customer has spoken with the customer loyalty representative, the customer is also asked: 'If you had your own company that was focused upon service, how likely would you be to hire this person to work for you?' Further questions ask 'Overall, would you describe the service you received form (insert name of customer loyalty representative) as good, bad, or fantastic?' and 'What exactly stood out as being good or bad about this service?'

Zappos – rather unsurprisingly – consistently score very highly for NPS.

Measuring How Satisfied Your Customers Are (Satisfaction Index)

Measuring customer satisfaction is probably the most common non-financial KPI used in business because it is perceived to predict future performance. The logic is sound – if you have a happy bunch of satisfied customers then they are more likely to buy from you repeatedly and potentially tell others about your product or service.

For obvious reasons satisfied customers are much more likely to be loyal customers, which also keeps costs down because it is significantly more expensive to attract new customers than it is to keep the ones you have.

It makes sense therefore to measure customer satisfaction so you can fully appreciate how your customers are feeling. It also helps clarify whether you are on track or whether you are losing too many customers to your competitors.

Identifying what makes your customers happy

The challenge with measuring customer satisfaction is that it is a very broad term. What makes one customer satisfied will not necessarily be universally appreciated by all your customers.

As a result you will collect more insightful data if you combine quantitative and qualitative techniques. For example, you could survey your customers for overall satisfaction periodically. This is usually achieved by asking customers how satisfied they are with your product/service, where they are asked to indicate satisfaction on a scale of 1–5 (1 being very dissatisfied and 5 being very satisfied). If you gather this same information regularly over time you can gauge the trend of customer satisfaction.

In addition you could also survey your customers immediately after they have received your product or experienced your service. This approach allows for a mix of performance scales, yes/no answers and qualitative questions, so you can uncover the key distinctions that make your customers happy.

Finally, you may choose to conduct focus groups with customers to gain even richer insights into customer satisfaction levels. Measuring customer satisfaction, especially when you seek qualitative or subjective responses, is a great way of finding out exactly what parts of your product or service are most appreciated by your customers. And although this sounds like common sense, many businesses have gone bust because they made assumptions about what their customers really loved about their product or service.

When you do it properly, measuring customer satisfaction can be one of the most insightful management tools because it helps to highlight any gaps that may exist between current delivery and customer expectations. It thus allows a business to close that gap more quickly and improve customer satisfaction in the process.

Creating your unique index

You can measure customer satisfaction in many ways.

One useful approach is the creation of your own unique Customer Satisfaction Index (CSI). A CSI is simply an aggregation of all the attributes that you believe contribute to customer satisfaction. Again don't assume what creates customer satisfaction – find out what actually does and then measure that.

Since different attributes can contribute differently to the overall customer satisfaction, it's best to weight the individual attributes. For example customer satisfaction for an airline may include on-time departure, quick transit through security and on-board snacks. Clearly the quality of on-board snacks is pleasant but it's nowhere near as important as on-time departure – especially for a business traveller. As a result on-time departure would be weighted to account for its importance relative to other factors.

Within an index you can generate a single customer satisfaction score and describe it according to a scale of satisfaction from 'very dissatisfied' to 'very satisfied'.

Measuring CSI in practice

The key performance question Customer Satisfaction Index (CSI) helps to answer is: 'How well are we satisfying our customers?'

You can create your own unique index based on the factors your initial investigation identified as being central to customer satisfaction, or you can use an existing index.

The widely-used American Customer Satisfaction Index (ACSI) generates a single score based on drivers of satisfaction such as customer expectations, perceived quality, perceived value, customer complaints, customer retention, customer loyalty and price tolerance. The ACSI score is calculated as a weighted average of three survey questions that measure different aspects of customer satisfaction with your product or service.

For example, the ACSI uses customer interviewing and econometric modelling to measure and analyse customer satisfaction. An econometric model in this context seeks to specify the statistical relationship that exists between customer satisfaction and, say, perceived value or price tolerance.

Initially, professional telephone interviewers collect survey responses from randomly selected customers. The data is then put into the model which scores the variables and effectively spits out a customer satisfaction index score or ACSI score.

The index runs from 0–100. Although your ACSI score could theoretically be anywhere between 0 and 100, in practice scores tend to be from the low 50s to the high 80s. The beauty of the ACSI and the UK equivalent the The National Customer Satisfaction Index-UK (NCSI-UK) is that they ask the same questions (tailored slightly to each industry), which means that you can compare your business to others in your sector and to your nearest competitors. The downside is that they might ask questions that are not relevant to your specific business needs.

Customer satisfaction is often measured on a rolling basis and reported quarterly along with any specific insight gained from the qualitative information.

The real gold when it comes to customer satisfaction is the qualitative data that explains why someone is satisfied or not. If you want to make real progress in customer satisfaction and use the measurement to improve performance from this perspective you must collect, analyse and interpret the qualitative data so you can act on the information and improve customer satisfaction.

Don't be over zealous about measuring customer satisfaction as a quantitative 'score'. It's helpful to know you are trending in the right direction but if you are not then it's not that helpful at all.

Plus don't confuse loyalty with satisfaction. Just because your customers are satisfied - even very satisfied does not mean they are loyal and will buy from you again. Think about the last time you stayed in a mid range hotel. No doubt the room was spotless, the service impeccable and the food pleasant. If asked you probably said you were very satisfied with your stay but that didn't necessarily make you feel any loyalty to that hotel or chain. The reason for this seeming contradiction is that the hotel simply delivered on your existing expectations. Cleanliness of room, quality of service etc are just the minimum expected from a good hotel. If those aspects were poor then it would have affected your satisfaction and your loyalty as you probably would not visit the hotel again. But if they are good, it may impact satisfaction but not loyalty. The hotel would have to deliver on something unexpected or go above and beyond for you to feel any genuine loyalty to the hotel.

— Tracking How Likely Your Customers are To Leave (Retention/Churn)

Knowing how satisfied your customers are is one thing, but tracking how likely they are to leave is another. It may be obvious that unhappy customers are more susceptible to a competitor, but that may also be true of customers who are satisfied – even very satisfied.

Customer retention/churn is a popular KPI used to track how many customers you are losing, and is therefore a powerful indicator of future financial performance. Obviously, if you are losing more customers than you are gaining then you are going to run into trouble. Customer satisfaction surveys may indicate whether a customer feels satisfied or not but this metric looks at customer behaviour. What are your customers actually doing? Do they stay or do they leave?

Churn and retention matters!

Keeping the customers you have already managed to attract and sell to is much easier and cheaper than trying to find new customers.

Churn and retention matters because once a customer has bought from you once, they are invested in your product or company, albeit in a small way. The hardest decision for any customer is the initial decision to purchase from one company over another. The reason for that choice may vary, but whatever the reason the customer decided to trust you. Making sure they don't regret that choice is what customer KPIs seek, at least in part, to measure.

Once you have a customer and they have taken that first step and bought the first product or service, it is always considerably easier to sell to that customer again, up-sell them to a more expensive product or cross-sell them a different product from your range.

Customer retention therefore offers you not only repeat sales but increased value of sales and new sales in new products or services. If you fail and your customers leave then you don't just lose one sale – you potentially lose many, varied and valuable sales.

Minimising churn or customer turnover should therefore be a key objective of business.

Measuring it in practice

There are two main KPIs to measure retention and churn so you can establish how many customers you are managing to hold on to and how many you are losing over any given period. They are Customer Retention Rate (CRR) and Customer Turnover Rate (CTR)

KPI: Customer Retention Rate (CRR)

The key performance question Customer Retention Rate (CRR) helps to answer is: 'To what extent are we keeping the customers we have acquired?'

> Customer Retention Rate (CRR) = No. of those customers that are still customers at the end of period/No. customers at start of period × 100

For example say you have 145,000 customers on the 1st January 2014 and 142,500 at the end of 2014

> CRR = 144.500/145,000 × 100 = 99.65 per cent for 2013

CRR measures the percentage of customers a company is able to retain over a specified period. The most common formula provided for this metric is number of customers at the start of a period divided by number of customers are the end of the period, expressed as a percentage. But this formula includes new customers and doesn't differentiate between those new customers and the customers who have stayed with your business. CRR is supposed to tell you how many customers you have retained, not how many customers you have. For CRR to be accurate, you need to look only at how many customers you had at the start of the period in question. Save that file. Then at the end of the period cross reference the saved file with current customers to see how many customers from the saved file you have retained.

If you want to be even more accurate, you can divide the number of customers at risk of leaving at the beginning of a period by the number of customers that remained customers at the end.

Say at the start of December 2013 a telecommunication company had 150,000 mobile phone contacts coming to an end. In telecommunications the CRR can be quite low because people are always shopping around for better deals – especially as their contract comes to an end. By the end of December they had been able to renew 132,000 of those contracts. The CRR would be 88 per cent (132,000/150,000 × 100)

How often you collect CRR will depend on the average lifespan of your customer, contract duration or average purchasing cycle although monthly collection in most businesses makes sense. What is considered high or low will depend on your industry so you need to assess your CRR against other businesses in your sector to get a true picture of retention.

Current retention rates are no guarantee of future retention rates.

Pay particular attention to how you count customers and set that as a benchmark for the future. Be really clear about what constitutes a customer. For example, if a customer is a customer of more than one product of yours, are they counted for each product or only once? If there is more than one customer from one household are they counted as individual customers or one household? Whatever you decide make it a rule in the business so that calculations are meaningful and comparable moving forward.

KPI: Customer Turnover Rate (CTR)

The key performance question Customer Turnover Rate (CTR) helps to answer is: 'How many customers are we losing?' Customer Turnover, also known as customer churn, customer defection or customer attrition looks at the other side of the coin – how many customers are you losing, rather than keeping, over a given period? The data you will to calculate CTR should be easily accessible from your customer records.

CTR = Lost customers over a period/Total number of customers at the end of a period × 100

For example say you have 86,000 customers at the start of May 2013. During May you gain 1,200 customers and lose 2,100. The net customer loss at the end of May is 900 (2100 – 1200). Your CTR would therefore be 1.05 per cent. (900/85,100 × 100)

CTR is an important metric to keep on top of and certainly if the CTR is trending up you can use this insight to dig deeper into what is really going on in the business to cause these results. CTR therefore alerts you to a problem that given the right investigation can help you reverse the tide. It is therefore wise to measure CTR on a monthly or quarterly basis.

Pay particular attention to how you define 'lost' and set that as a benchmark for the future. For example is a customer no longer a customer if they have not bought from you for over 6 months? A year? What is the definition of 'lost'? Whatever you decide make it a rule in the business so that calculations are meaningful and comparable over time.

Gauging Whether All Customers are Equal (Profitability)

Measuring customer success and how your customers feel about you is important but not all customers are equal. The assumption is that you should work hard to keep as many customers as possible as happy as possible but that isn't always necessarily true.

The 80/20 rule applies to customers in many ways. Chances are 80 per cent of your revenue comes from 20 per cent of your customers. It is also probably true that 80 per cent of your complaints come from 20 per cent of your customers. And it's not usually the same 20 per cent!

So before you panic about low retention rates or get flustered about turnover rates you really need to know how profitable your customers are and which customers are financially worth worrying about.

Understanding where the profits are made

Often the temptation is to spend more and more money on surprising and delighting customers in the hope that this additional effort will translate into loyalty and profitability.

While that logic is valid, it doesn't always work. Indeed many businesses have gone bust spending unnecessary money trying to fix or improve things that were not perceived as being an important issue in the first place. This is why the subjective, opinion based data around customer satisfaction can be so useful.

You need to know where your profits are made and what types of customers are contributing most to that profit. That way you can make sure you invest in those relationships and actively seek out other people like those customers to increase profit still further.

Tracking customer profitability

Customer profitability is the difference between the revenues earned from customers and the cost of servicing those customers over a specific period. This metric is therefore the net dollar contribution made by your individual customers.

Profitability is directly relevant to a time period so there is no one measure. In reality there are five main ways to measure customer value:

- ✔ **Historical customer profitability:** This perspective looks at the value earned from a customer relationship over a previous historical period such as a fiscal year, quarter or month. It can be measured as an average of previous periods or it can be time weighted which means that the more recent transactions are considered more valuable than older transactions.

- ✔ **Current customer profitability:** This perspective usually looks at a month to coincide with reporting cycles. This shorter time frame makes profitability more volatile as market changes or seasonal peaks and troughs show up in the month(s) in question rather than being averaged out. This perspective can be useful for working out how particular campaigns, new offers or price changes can influence profitability.

- ✔ **Present customer profitability:** This perspective is a future orientated that typically considers future revenue and costs anticipated for the customer. It is useful when looking at the remaining contractual lifetime of a customer and ranking customers according to value. It is also insightful for modelling the impact of pricing changes before they are implemented.

- ✔ **Customer lifetime profitability:** This perspective is also future orientated and looks further than the current contractual period to what revenue the customer might generate after that and what costs are associated with that revenue.

- ✔ **Time-based activity-based profitability:** This perspective measures the present total cost of providing products or services to a customer. In order to calculate this you need the cost per hour of each group of resources doing the work and the unit of time spent by specific activities. For example, say you calculate that your customer service department costs \$80 per hour and handling a complaint well takes 27 minutes the cost of customer complaint handling is \$36 ($27/60 = 0.45 \times \$80$).

Measuring it in practice

The key performance question customer profitability helps to answer is: 'To what extent are we generating profits from our customers?'

The formula for how you would work this out changes depending on the various perspectives above. The most basic formula would be:

Customer Profitability = Revenue earned from the customer – Costs associated with the customer relationships.

Customer profitability can be an incredibly useful KPI because it allows you to compare customers and establish which ones are making you money and which ones are not.

For example, customer profitability in a US based insurance company found that 15–20 per cent of its customers generates 100 per cent or more of its profit. Further investigation found that the most profitable customers generated 130 per cent of annual profits, the middle 55 per cent of customers broke even and the least profitable 5 per cent lost the company money to the tune of 30 per cent of annual profits.

Knowing which customers are which is clearly very important for long term growth and profitability.

The easiest way to calculate customer profitability is to look as historic data, for example 'How much did I earn from that customer and how much did I spend on that customer?' What costs to take into account and how to allocate them to customers can be quite complex, even when you use existing data. The calculations become more difficult and speculative when you start looking into the future. In the next section, I look at the customer lifetime value KPI, which is the most speculative and difficult, but potentially also the most revealing metric for customer profitability.

Calculating Your Customers' Value (Life-Time Value)

Customer KPIs focus largely on how many customers you have, how many you keep and making sure they are happy. While useful and necessary these KPIs don't tell you how much those customers are worth.

For some companies the customer is profitable as soon as they make their first purchase. Others may only become profitable after several purchases. Calculating your *customers' lifetime value* (CLV) allows you to attribute a lifetime value to each customer so you can immediately see which ones are the most valuable and therefore most important to you.

The ultimate customer KPI!

CLV is actually a marketing metric that allows businesses to highlight their most important customers, so they can focus their marketing attention on the ones that are most likely to buy. This metric combines the:

    ✔ Anticipated length of the relationship between you and your customers

    ✔ Anticipated customer financial value.

Calculating CLV helps an organisation understand how much it can invest in acquiring and retaining that customer so as to achieve positive return on investment. This metric is often used by investors as a way of helping to assess the present and future health of an enterprise.

Measuring it in practice

The key performance question Customer Lifetime Value (CLV) helps to answer is: 'How well do we understand the financial value from our customer relationships?' Calculating CLV can be as simple or as complex as you want. But initially, let's start with the simplest version to give you an idea of CLV.

CLV = (Average Value of a Sale) × (Number of Repeat Transactions) × (Average Retention Time in Months or Years for a Typical Customer)

As an example, let's look at the customer lifetime value of a mobile phone contract customer: The customer spends $30 every month on the contracts, the average time for a customer to stay with the provider is 3 years. The calculation would be:

$30 × 12 months × 3 years = $1,080 = CLV (or $360 per year).

What this simple calculation does not take into account are the costs associated with servicing or retaining this customer. A more acrurate calculation would substract the costs:

If in the same example, the service or retention costs were $300 per year, then the CLV over the 3 years would be:

$1,080 − (3 × $300) = $180 (or $60 per year)

CLV has intuitive appeal because it represents exactly how much each customer is worth in monetary terms, and therefore exactly how much you can afford to spend to keep them happy! And how much the marketing department can spend acquiring new customers just like them. But unfortunately the reality of CLV is quite different, and it is a notoriously difficult KPI to calculate effectively. Regardless of the formula you use, either the simple one above or one of the more complicated versions the accurate calculation of CLV consists of four steps:

1. **Forecast the remainder of the customer lifetime.**

   How long is the customer likely to stay a customer?

2. **Forecast future revenues.**

   How much is the customer likely to spend during those remaining months or years?

3. **Forecast delivery costs.**

   How much is it going to cost to deliver those products or services to the customer in the future?

4. **Calculate the net present value of these future amounts.**

Needless to say whilst these four steps appear straightforward there are not and your forecasting accuracy can impact the reliability and usefulness of this metric.

Measuring Whether Your Customers are Truly Engaged

Customer engagement became increasingly important as more and more companies discovered that customer satisfaction was not a predictor of behaviour in the way it was once assumed. Conventional wisdom suggested that satisfied customers = loyal customers = profit. The problem is that research demonstrated that customers who, by their own admission were satisfied still defected to the competition in alarming numbers. In other words satisfied customers did not equal loyal customers or necessarily increased profit.

For example, in the mid 1990s Xerox found that more than a quarter of their customers who stated they were 'satisfied' defected at the end of their contracts. On digging more deeply into this issue, Xerox found that there was a strong correlation between genuine loyalty and customer longevity when customers described themselves as 'very satisfied' and not just 'satisfied'. When those very satisfied customers were pressed further to explain their satisfaction it almost always came down to the nature of their perceived relationship with Xerox – or engagement. When a customer had developed a strong relationship with their Xerox contact, often over many years their satisfaction increased to very satisfied.

In another more recent example, US-based Rent-A-Car deliberately moved away from basic satisfaction KPIs to their own self-designed KPI metric called the Enterprise Service Quality Index (ESQi). The reason for this move was that internal research demonstrated that a basic satisfaction KPI that indicated whether a customer was satisfied or not was not good enough to help them to establish patterns of behaviour and loyalty. The company discovered that customers who stated they were 'completely satisfied' on a 5-point scale from 'completely satisfied' to 'completely dissatisfied' were three times more likely to return as customers and recommend Rent-A-Car to others than even customers who stated they were 'satisfied'. This analysis found that these customers valued the relationship with Enterprise Rent-A-Car, and so could be described as *engaged*. Today all Rent-A-Car offices are measured against how many of their customers are 'completely satisfied' which has improved results – not least because everyone in those offices is now fully focused on delivering better than expected service, so they can achieve the prized (and rewarded) 'completely satisfied'.

Understanding the different levels of engagement

The task of understanding the different levels of engagement has been significantly simplified by the well-known research firm Gallup. Based on the research respondents answers to just eleven questions, Gallup have categorised customer engagement according to four levels.

- ✔ **Fully engaged customers:** Those who are emotionally attached and rationally loyal to your business. These are your most valuable customers

- ✔ **Engaged customers:** Those who are beginning to feel the stirrings of emotional engagement. These customers are ripe for development and could relatively easily be pushed up to fully engaged.

- ✔ **Disengaged customers:** Those who are emotionally and rationally neutral. These customers are also ripe for development because they are neutral so could be swayed upwards (or pushed downwards).

- ✔ **Actively disengaged customers:** Those who are emotionally detached and actively antagonistic. These customers pose a serious threat to your business – especially in the age of the internet and social media.

As a reminder of just how powerful an actively disengaged customer can be, see the sidebar 'United Breaks Guitars' in Chapter 4.

Gallup's data collected from almost three million customers (*business to consumer* (B2C) and *business to business* (B2B)) in 16 major industries across 53 countries over a four year period reveals that fully-engaged customers deliver, on average, 23 per cent more in terms of profitability, share of wallet, revenue, and relationship growth than the average customer. Actively disengaged customers represent a 13 per cent discount in those same measures.

Companies that have high engagement have outperformed their competitors by 26 per cent in gross margin and 85 per cent in sales growth. Their customers buy more, spend more, return more often, and stay longer.

Clearly customer engagement matters!

Measuring engagement in practice

The key performance question customer engagement helps to answer is: 'To what extent are our customers engaged with our organisation?' This metric is usually measured and reported annually and the data needed comes from a customer engagement survey.

> Customer Engagement Ratio (CER) = Number of engaged customers (percentage): Number of disengaged customers (percentage)

The CER is a macro-level KPI indicator designed by Gallup to measure engaged versus disengaged customers. The metric is the ratio of fully engaged customers for every actively disengaged customer.

For example, say you have 600 engaged customers and 100 disengaged ones, your CER would be 6:1, which would mean that you have six actively engaged customers for every 1 actively disengaged customer. Due to the size and scope of their research data Gallup can then place your business into the appropriate engagement category and describe likely financial consequences.

Chapter 13

Measuring the Market and Your Place in It

- -

In This Chapter

▶ Understanding your position relative to your competitors

▶ Calculating how well you are doing at finding new customers

▶ Appreciating the value of your brand

- -

*M*arket KPIs are crucial to your business. Financial KPIs are important because they allow you to measure your financial performance. Customer KPIs are important because they allow you to gauge the strength of your customer relationships and whether you are growing your customer base or whether it's remaining stagnant or contracting.

But your performance is also always relative to your market. The KPIs I detail in this chapter help you to measure your market, so you can appreciate where you really stand relative to that market and your competition.

Painting a Picture of Your Market (Market Growth Rate)

You need to be able to paint a picture of the market you operate in and understand that market, so you can accurately predict and manage the future. A KPI that can help you do that is the *market growth rate*. This metric lets you see whether your market is expanding or contracting, which is obviously critical for assessing future revenue growth potential.

Your business success is not only determined by how efficiently you run the business and how well you satisfy your customers. It's also dependent on two other key factors:

✔ Your ability to stay relevant to your audience

✔ Your ability to identify future growth opportunities in existing and new markets.

Being able to identifying these markets and evaluating their growth rate is therefore a vital piece of performance data.

Understanding the health of your market

Market growth rate is a key indicator of the health of your business because it helps you to understand how robust your market is. In other words, is your market expanding or contracting? Are there still plenty people who want what you sell or are the numbers falling?

If your growth in sales is equal to or greater than the market growth rate then your business is doing well. This effectively means that you are capturing your share of market growth and there are still plenty people who want what you offer.

If your sales growth is less than market growth rate then you are not capturing your share of market growth and could be in trouble. For example your sales growth could be 10 per cent and you may, quite rightly, think that is pretty good. But if the market is growing at 20 per cent then your competitors are cashing in on that growth more than you are. And you need to know why.

Market growth can be as broad as to include a whole market or economy or narrow enough to include a geographic location or product category.

This metric can also indicate where a product is in its life cycle. For example a high growth rate could indicate that your product is in its *growth phase* where many people want the product but not everyone who wants one, has one yet. Conversely a lower more stable growth rate could indicate product maturation, where most of the people who want one, have one. And a low or negative growth rate means that your product is in decline, in which case you need to use that information to alter your strategy.

Market growth rate therefore delivers critical information about your business in relation to what your market is doing and what your customers are buying.

Just because your business is successful today does not automatically mean it will be successful tomorrow. Corporate history is littered with examples of businesses, often extremely successful businesses, that went into liquidation because they under-estimated the longevity of their market or didn't act quickly enough to alter their strategy.

The video rental company Blockbuster is a classic example of how disastrous a disappearing market can be. At their height the company had about 60,000 employees and more than 9,000 stores worldwide. In the 1990s there was a Blockbuster store on just about every high street in every major town or city. Renting movies for the weekend was a common pastime enjoyed by millions. Then in 2000 Netflix arrived on the scene along with increasingly fast broadband connections and with it alternative ways to watch movies.

Blockbuster's market changed dramatically. Instead of going to a physical store and renting movies, people had new options. They could have films posted to them or they could watch them over the internet. But Blockbuster didn't see the writing on the wall. Ironically they turned down the opportunity to buy Netflix for $50 million, when it was still the new kid on the block. This was a decision they probably deeply regretted. Perhaps if they had paid more attention to their declining market growth rate they could have foreseen the demise of their traditional market and changed their strategy accordingly. They didn't, though, and in 2010 they filed for bankruptcy. By 2013 all company-owned stores closed and the giant that was Blockbuster video was finished.

Options for measuring market growth rate

If you want to know your market growth rate you first need to know the size of your market. You measure the size of the market by the total number of goods or services (or the value of those goods or services) sold in that market during a specified time period (usually one year). Although market data is readily available through benchmarking databases or market research companies, unless market data is well-defined, getting a handle on the size of your market can be quite difficult.

There are different options for measuring market size such as:

> ✔ **Interview and analyse your competitors:** The simplest and cheapest way to measure the size of your market is to ask your competitors, other manufacturers or service providers for their sales figures. If they are publicly-listed companies you may not even need to ask them as you will be able to get the information from the annual accounts. The biggest challenge with this approach is you probably won't want to do it and if

you ask someone else they won't want to do it either! The assumption is that these other businesses will not want to share that information but if you explain what you are trying to do up-front, offer to share the information you find, which will help them too then you will probably be surprised at what information you can find out - if you just ask. Ideally cross reference any information you get with another source such as an annual or quarterly report as they may embellish their results to look more successful than they really are.

- ✔ **Collect information from intermediaries:** For example, if you are producing goods that are sold in supermarkets or online portals, then they are often in a good position to provide you with a breakdown of sales of your product relative to those of your competitor products. However, increasingly they are charging for the privilege of sharing this kind of information.

- ✔ **Survey customers and end-users:** This is the most expensive approach because you need a large sample size to make it valid and it's time consuming to collect and analyse.

Measuring market growth rate in practice

The key performance question market growth rate helps to answer is: 'To what extent are we operating in markets with future potential?'

The data for this metric is accessible through existing market research data. This is obviously the most cost effective as you can piggy back on the research someone else has completed in your market. Alternatively you can conduct the research yourself and the best option is to interview and analyse your competitors to help you to assess the size of your market. You need to know this metric every year and if your market is shifting rapidly you would be wise to measure it quarterly.

> Market Growth Rate (%) = Total sales in the market for this year/Total sales in the market for last year

Sales in this context can be measured in monetary terms or in the number of units. For example say you sell speed boats and jet skis so you want to know the growth rate for each market. The size of the speed boat market for 2012 was $600 million and in 2013 it was $750 million. And the size of the jet ski market for 2012 was $250 million and in 2013 it was $150 million. The market growth rates would be:

> Speed Boat Market Growth Rate = $750/$600 = 1.25
>
> Jet Ski Market Growth rate = $150/250 = 0.6

A market growth rate of below 1 indicates a shrinking market while a market growth rate of above 1 indicates a growing market. On that basis you could be confident in your speed boat market, as there are still plenty of people wanting speed boats. The jet ski market, however, is shrinking so you will need to re-visit your strategy and either identify new markets for jet skis that are currently not exploited or consider getting out of jet skis and into something with a buoyant market growth rate.

 You can also anticipate market growth rate for the next year or years by taking into account trend data and market prediction. Looking ahead in this way can help you to pre-empt any changes to the market so you can alter your approach and minimise the impact.

Understanding Your Place in the Market (Market Share)

Knowing the market you compete in is very important but understanding your place in that market is also vital for business success. One KPI that can help assess your place is relative market share. Essentially, this metric indexes your market share against that of your leading competitors. This allows you to gauge your true market strength relative to the other businesses in your sector and can therefore identify areas of weakness or opportunities for improvement.

Market share is always relative to the market you operate in. A high market share in one industry may be considered average in another. As a result there is no global benchmark for market share that crosses industries and sectors.

Why market share matters

Relative market share matters because major players in any market tend to be more profitable than their competitors. As a result it is considered a strong indicator for increased profit and growth, because the higher the share of the market the more cash will be generated. Plus larger, dominant companies enjoy the benefits or economies of scale which means their size and buying power allows them to negotiate better prices all along the supply chain, therefore reducing costs and increasing profit still further.

This metric, however, supplies more information than just looking at profit, growth and cash flow metrics because it shows where your brand is positioned in relation to your main competitors. This comparison gives you greater insight into what's actually happening outside your business, and what you may need to alter or tweak to super-charge your marketing and capture more market share.

Boston Matrix

Although relative market share was developed in the 1960s it was popularized by the Boston Consulting Group through their famous 'Boston Matrix' which positions products according to their relative share and market growth

However, as the market declines there is still money to be made and often that money can then be used to support other products – either stars or to further explore the Problem Child products.

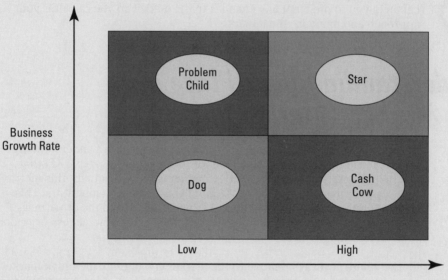

One axis represents relative market share and indicates competitive strength. The other axis represents market growth which indicates market potential. Looking at your product range it is therefore possible to categorise your products or services into one of four quadrants.

- ✔ **Star:** These are products that enjoy high market share within a growing market. Stars make your business lots of money and need to be supported and nurtured with vigorous investment.

- ✔ **Cash Cows:** These products also enjoy high market share, but the market isn't growing anymore and may be stagnant or shrinking.

- ✔ **Problem Child:** Also known as Question Marks these products have a low market share but they compete in a growing market, which means they could potentially exhibit Star quality. But it's a risk – hence the name problem child or question mark.

- ✔ **Dogs:** These products, as the name might suggest, are not good – they have a low market share and serve a small or declining market.

Knowing your relative market share not only for your business as a whole but the products and services you provide can help you to consolidate your operations and focus on what makes you money or could make you money in the future. You need to know which of your products are which so you can make informed decisions about where you want to compete and spend your time and money. It may be that you realise one of your products is a Dog but you may also know that it is a great *loss leader* – in other words you know it doesn't immediately make you money but those that buy this product initially are easily up-sold and cross-sold into different much more profitable products. If however the Dog is just a Dog then you should probably phase that product or service out.

Getting a good picture of your market can be tough

Although market share, relative and otherwise, is an important KPI to measure, it's not that easy to measure and it needs to be viewed in conjunction with other KPIs to help create a complete picture.

There are many ways to measure market share. The easiest is to rank your revenue or measure the absolute volume in units sold or gross sales generated. But even then you need to qualify those measurements. For example even if you have a market share of 70 per cent you may still be losing money and therefore it's not a sustainable strategy. Indeed, the lack of a 'profit' dimension is a major criticism of the Relative Market Share metric.

That said, it is useful to depict market share over time and in comparison to market growth (see Figure 13-1). This provides you with a simple picture to allow you to understand whether your market share growth is in line with the potential and growth of the overall market.

Figure 13-1: Graphic showing market share over time compared to market growth

Volume

Overall Market Growth

Your Market Share (Relative)

Time

Measuring relative market share in practice

The key performance question relative market share helps to answer is: 'How well are we growing market share in comparison to our competitors?' The data you will need to calculate this metric is available from your accounts information and your competitor's annual reports or market research.

The easiest way to measure relative market share is to simply break down the overall market size into the chunks that your company has and then to the same for all the other major players in that market. You can do this by simply applying this formula to yourself and your competitors:

Relative Market Share A (%) = Your Market Size/Overall Market Size × 100

A more formal way of measuring relative market share, often done on an annual basis, is to look at your market share relative to the market share of your biggest competitor:

Relative Market Share B (%) = Your Market Share/Your largest competitor's market share

You can calculate relative market share using units sold, revenue or percentage market share. For example, say Company A sold 7,500 units, creating revenue of \$187,500, and enjoyed a market share of 20 per cent. If the management of Company A wanted to compare their company's performance to Company B, the market leader, which sold 25,000 units generating revenue of \$375,000 and enjoyed a market share of 40 per cent, then they could calculate the relative market share in three ways:

7,500/25,000 = 0.30 relative market share in unit sold terms

187,500/375,000 = 0.5 relative market share in revenue terms

20/40 = 0.5 relative market share in percentage market share terms

These figures then have to be compared with the same figures for other players in the market.

Gauging Your Market Success (Customer Acquisition KPIs)

Knowing how you compare to your competitors and how much market share you have can help you to understand your relative strength in your industry and illuminate opportunities for improvement. But it's also important to gauge your market success through the eyes of your customers.

How successful are your sales and marketing departments at attracting new customers? How successful are they are converting initial interest or *leads* into a paying customer? And how much does it cost to generate those leads in the first place? Customer acquisition KPIs can help you to answer these questions and ensure your sales and marketing initiatives are cost effective and productive.

Knowing the cost of finding new customers

A key function of sales and marketing is to let people know about your business and attract as many of them as possible to buy your product or service. There are, of course, many ways to achieve this. Some, such as TV advertising or brand awareness campaigns can cost a great deal of money. Everything from traditional direct mailing campaigns to social media campaigns cost something to create and execute, so you need to make sure that the costs are justified.

One of the most popular ways of finding out is through the KPI called *cost per lead*. As the name would suggest, cost per lead works out how much it costs to attract each potential customer to your product offering, and it is a powerful leading indicator of likely future revenue. The theory assumes that if you can attract potential customers cost effectively, then sales in the future will be strong.

That said, not all leads are equal, so to make this metric more accurate and indicative of future performance, calculate cost per qualified lead. A *qualified lead* is someone who is definitely in the market for what you are selling and is therefore *sales ready*.

Of course leads do not always convert into sales so it's also important to track conversion rates.

Options for gauging customer conversion

There is no point having thousands of leads if your business can't convert them to paying customers. The customer conversion rate works out how successful your business is at turning opportunities or potential customers into actual customers.

The definition of conversion will differ depending on the medium in which you operate. For example, if you have a chain of physical stores your conversion rate would look at how many people entered yours shops compared to how many actually bought something while they were there. Online conversion may look at product ordering or whether the visitor signed up for membership, subscribed to the monthly sales promotion newsletter, downloaded software, or actively opted-in in some form or another.

Understanding your conversion rate will give you more insight into how well your sales and marketing strategies are working. For example, if you manage to attract 1000 people to your website every month but none of them convert into a sale or even an enquiry, then there is clearly something wrong with your marketing message or the way you are positioning your products or services. You need to go back and work out what your customer really wants.

There are a number of different types of conversion rates that you may want to measure to gain more specific insights such as:

- Visitor to sales conversion rate
- Lead to conversion rate
- Online click-through rates
- Tender or quote to sale conversion rate

Measuring cost per lead in practice

The market success KPIs that are most useful are *cost per lead* and *conversion rate*.

KPI: Cost per lead

The key performance question cost per lead helps to answer is: 'To what extent are the costs for generating new customers justified?' The data needed to calculate this metric should be located in your marketing department.

Cost per lead = Total money spent on marketing campaign/Total leads generated

For example say you spent $90,000 on online banner advertising and you generated 15,400 leads.

Cost per lead = $90,000/15,400 = $5.84

This is a particularly useful metric to track after a campaign or marketing event and can easily be taken a step further to calculate the cost per qualified lead. By regularly calculating your cost per lead, you will be able to use the data to inform your decision making and on-going marketing strategy. For instance, if you exhibit at an industry event and the cost per lead is $2.50 but you run an online social media campaign that yields a cost per lead of $0.20

then so long as the conversion rate is comparable you would be wise to stop doing the events and test your online initiatives against some other type of campaign to see if you can improve on $0.20.

Make sure you calculate cost per lead and cost per qualified lead separately for each marketing initiative or campaign you execute. This will help you make better decisions and give you a much clearer picture of what is working and what is not. If you try to calculate cost per lead or cost per qualified lead across multiple initiatives then there are too many variables that could skew the result and you won't get very meaningful data.

KPI: Customer conversion rate

The key performance question customer conversion rate helps to answer is: To what extent are we able to convert potential customers into actual customers?

Conversion Rate = Number of desired outcomes achieved/Number of Visitors × 100

You can use this basic formula to measure conversion rate for anything you are interested in measuring. For example you could measure the conversion rate for web page views compared to the number of people who then clicked on an advert on that page – also called *click-through rate* (CTR). Or you could measure the number of people who filled a shopping basket online to the number who actually completed the purchasing process and bought what they put in the shopping basket.

For example, say you are a clothes retailer with a chain of shops on the high street. You may be interested in your conversion rate from a number of different perspectives.

First you may want to find out how many people that visit your shops, actually buy something during that visit. If you calculate that across the chain 12,000 people visited your shops over a certain period and 3750 sales were made then your conversion rate would be:

3750/12,000 × 100 = 31.25 per cent

If you were running a promotion during this time so that everyone that bought something in your stores was given a $5 off online shopping voucher, you would then be interested in knowing the conversion rate for that. You know that you distributed 3750 $5 vouchers over the given period and you can tell from your online sales records that 1200 people used the voucher so your conversion rate in this context is:

1200/3750 × 100 = 32 per cent

As you can see from these simple examples the data collection method you need to use to calculate conversion rate depends on what you are measuring. And often it can be simpler to measure on line with the use of free to use web analytics tools to help you track conversion rates along the so-called *conversion funnel* – the path visitors take from the initial prompt to the targeted desired action (for example, a purchase).

In the physical world retailers often use simple counting methods where they have the manager or sales assistant actually count the number of people who enter the shop over a given period of time, and then compare that number to sales made. There are, however, more sophisticated tools that allow you to track customers using camera technology and software that will automatically track and report conversion rates. For example, one of my clients has installed a device that tracks mobile phone signals and therefore any customer who carries one (which is almost everyone nowadays). This allows them to count the number of customers who pass the shop, and the ones that enter the shop. Comparing these numbers with sales transactions gives them a good proxy for conversion rates.

Charting the Power of Your Brand

A strong corporate or product brand is enormously valuable. It represents a promise or value assumption that is capable of influencing consumer behaviour into the future.

Companies with a strong brand like Coca-Cola don't have to work as hard to win customers because they trust the brand and are therefore happy to continue to buy it – even paying a little extra for the peace of mind. This trust translates into future revenue security for the business so charting the power and potency of your brand may be important.

The value of the brand is often referred to as brand equity.

What brand equity means for your business

Brand equity is the positive or negative value that a brand adds to your products and services. In other words if you have a strong positive brand customers will often view your product as being of a higher quality even when there is no measurable difference in quality. As a result they are often happy to pay more than your competitor's products to secure the branded product. Conversely, if your product receives bad press this can negatively impact your brand and sales.

There are three main benefits of positive brand equity:

- ✓ **Price premium:** The ability to charge more for your product or service
- ✓ **Long-term loyalty:** The ability to keep customers coming back and buying again and again.
- ✓ **Increased market share:** If people love your brand and keep coming back you will be able to secure a much higher market share.

Brand equity has become a very important measure in the eyes of investors because it is seen as a proxy or pre-cursor for profit. Often the largest part of a company's market value is in non-tangible assets such as brand, reputation, trademarks and expertise rather than the more traditional tangible assets such as factories, plant and machinery.

If you have a brand then you need to measure and protect it, because if the brand is diminished in the eyes of the customer then there will be a knock-on fall in the overall value of your business. Brand equity is not simply nice to know, but has significant financial implications. This metric allows you to maintain, build and leverage that equity so as to increase return on assets.

Finding your unique formula

In order to measure brand equity accurately you will need to decide what specifically you want to measure. Qualitative measures can help you to identify associations to a brand, its strength, desirability and uniqueness. Consider using face-to-face interviews or focus groups to gather this initial qualitative data.

However you will also need to formulate some quantitative measures to provide a more solid grounding for strategic and tactical recommendations. Quantitative brand tracking studies are often used to measure brand awareness, usage, attitudes, and perceptions. Different aspects of awareness such as recall and recognition may also tell you how strong a brand is and inform your marketing decision making and campaign design to further enhance brand equity.

Measuring brand equity in practice

The key performance question brand equity helps to answer is: 'How much value is driven by our brand?'

The formula for measuring brand equity depends on what you are actually measuring. Some measurements look at brand equity from the company level, some at the product level and others are at the consumer level.

✔ **Company level**: Measures the brand as a financial asset. To calculate brand equity as an intangible asset, work out the value of the company using your market capitalization. Then subtract tangible assets and 'measurable' intangible assets. What is left is your brand equity.

✔ **Product level**: Compares a no-name or private label product to an 'equivalent' branded product. This is the easiest brand equity to calculate because it only requires you to compare selling price. Assuming all else is equal the difference between a branded product and non-branded product is the brand equity. For example a can of Coca-Cola and a can of supermarket cola are the same size, contain the same amount and probably have fairly similar ingredients so you can safely assume that the difference between the selling prices is due to the value of the brand.

✔ **Consumer level:** This measurement seeks to find out what associations the consumer has with the brand. This approach is interested in measuring the awareness, including recall, recognition and overall brand image. You can use free association tests and projective techniques to uncover the tangible and intangible attributes, attitudes, and intentions a customer has regarding your brand. Brands with high levels of awareness and strong, positive attributes enjoy high equity brand.

None of these measures is absolute and definitive but they will give you a sense of your brand equity. Use multiple measures of brand value to create a more complete understanding of your brand.

Part V
Developing Operational and Internal Process KPIs

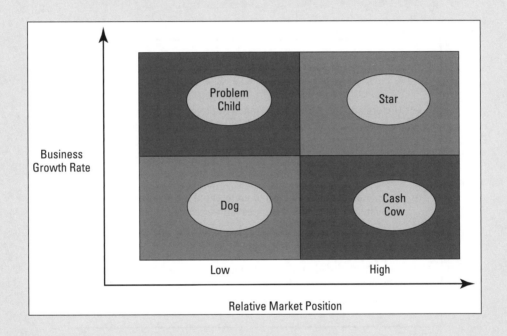

In this part . . .

✔ Understand the crucial importance of project performance, and its three key components: schedule, budget and deliverables.

✔ Assess the quality and efficiency of your business's internal processes and procedures, using Lean and Six Sigma to reduce waste.

✔ Calculate your profitability and understand the importance of innovation to keep your business future-proofed.

✔ Measure the quality of your IT service delivery, and why it's of vital importance to your business.

✔ Get a handle on IT project performance, using the classic three project performance KPIs: project schedule variance, project cost variance and project earned value.

Chapter 14

Measuring Project Performance

. . . .

In This Chapter

▶ Understanding how performance will be measured for each project.

▶ Working out whether you're delivering your project on time and on budget

▶ Establishing whether you are on track for future successful project delivery or not

. . . .

*K*PIs are incredibly useful strategic and operational navigation tools. They allow you to know where you are against expected targets and make real time adjustments to ensure you end up where you want to end up. Often, at an operational level, the execution of strategy is facilitated by the implementation of a number of projects.

It is therefore essential to measure project performance so you know you are going to hit your targets and are fully across the operational implementation of the strategic objectives.

The KPIs detailed in this chapter offer up practical insights into project efficiency and effectiveness.

Why Project Performance Matters

Projects matter because most strategic and change initiatives are delivered via projects. Project performance matters because it's essential to monitor these projects carefully to make sure they deliver the objectives they were initiated to deliver.

Keeping an eye on project performance allows you to assess current performance levels, provide input into future goal setting and decision making, and help anticipate any potential problems. If you don't monitor project performance then you are likely to run into difficulties. There are many ways to screw up a project and there are plenty famous examples to focus your mind on the importance of measuring project performance. For example:

✔ **The new Wembley stadium:** The Football Association's centrepiece was originally scheduled to open in 2003 but it didn't open until 2007.

✔ **Sydney Opera House:** Australia's architectural icon was scheduled to open in 1963 at a cost of $7 million but actually opened in 1973 at a cost of $102 million.

✔ **Concorde:** The supersonic airliner cost 12 times more than scheduled.

✔ **The Channel Tunnel:** The link between the UK and France cost 80 per cent more than budget

✔ **Boston's 'Big Dig' tunnel:** This huge construction project went 275 per cent – or $11 billion – over budget.

Clearly the bigger the project the more you need to pay attention. Project failures and over runs whether time or budget often carry severe consequences – and not just financial. For example, the software giant Oracle has been sued for an alleged $20 million budget overrun of one of their software implementation projects.

If a project is important enough to be initiated it's important enough to measure.

Introducing the Three Components of Project Performance

Projects usually have a defined beginning and end as well as a defined budget. There purpose is to bring about a change or deliver an outcome that is outside 'business as usual' or normal business operations.

There are always three key components of project performance and delivery against all three will determine success. The three components are:

✔ **Schedule:** Is the project on schedule?

✔ **Budget:** Is the project on budget?

✔ **Deliverables:** Is the project delivering the specified outcomes?

If you want to measure the success of your projects and ensure they deliver what you intend them to deliver then you must monitor and measure performance against schedule, budget and quality of output.

Tracking whether your projects are on time (Project Schedule Variance)

The project timeline is usually a critical component to any project. The purpose of the project is to bring about a result, improve an output or deliver an outcome by a specified day. That day may be determined by a myriad of different and sometimes competing factors. It may be that you are hosting an event and you need a venue built by a certain date. There is no movement on that completion date because the event is already locked in. It may be that you need to complete a software development project which is just part of a bigger project and the hand-over must happen on an exact day, or the software will not be completed for the client on time. In other instances the timing is not as critical and the project may have a delivery window of several days. Generally speaking the quicker you want a project completed, the more expensive it will be.

Project Schedule Variance is a simple comparison that allows you to measure the planned or scheduled project time and the actual time taken to complete the project.

If Project Schedule Variance is zero then the project was completed on time. If the variance is negative it shows an overrun. And if the variance is positive it indicates that the project was completed ahead of schedule.

For larger, longer projects it's always wise to monitor progress as you go along rather than just waiting until the completion date to see what 'falls out'. Measuring progress and milestones throughout the project allows you to compare where you thought you'd be at a certain point against where you actually are. That way you can adapt and fine tune to get back on track as soon as possible.

Measuring whether your projects are on budget (Project Cost Variance)

All projects have a budget – or should have – to provide strict financial parameters. It is possible to achieve just about anything in just about any time frame if you have deep enough pockets, but few commercial organisations have the luxury of a limitless budget.

The decision to execute the project in the first place is usually based on detailed expectations around what the project will deliver. Ideally, you should have analysed the project to ensure there is sufficient return on investment to warrant going ahead. If, however, the budget that analysis was based on is subsequently blown, then the return on investment disappears. Measuring whether your projects are on budget is therefore incredibly important throughout the life of the project, to ensure that it delivers what it promises without spending more than you have allocated.

Project Cost Variance is a simple comparison of the planned or scheduled project costs and the actual costs to complete the project.

If Project Cost Variance is zero then the project was finished on budget. If the variance is negative then you sent more on the project than you budgeted for. And if the variance is positive you finished the project with money left in the kitty.

For larger, longer projects it's always wise to monitor budget as you go along rather than just waiting until the end. Measure progress and anticipated spend as you progress so that you can compare what you thought you'd have spent at a certain point against what you actually spent. That way you can adapt and fine tune to get back on budget as soon as possible.

Checking whether your projects are delivering the right value (Earned Value)

Earned Value (EV) is a particularly useful metric for helping you to monitor progress throughout the project, so you can assess whether your projects are delivering the intended value.

EV is a project tracking measure that looks at the cost of work in progress and allows you to understand how much work has been completed compared to how much was expected to be completed at any given point.

In addition to assessing progress to date, the EV metric allows you to project what the likely costs of the complete project will be; assuming performance levels remain as they have been to date. This can be very useful in anticipating over spend before it happens so evasive measures can be taken to minimise the overspend where necessary.

Measuring the KPIs in practice

The most useful project performance KPIs to measure are Project Schedule Variance (PSV), Project Cost Variance (PCV) and Earned Value (EV).

KPI: Project Schedule Variance

The key performance question project schedule variance helps to answer is: 'To what extent are our projects delivered on schedule?' The data for this KPI usually comes from a project management software application or via manual records. PSV is usually measured monthly but can be monitored more often for important short-term projects.

> Project Schedule Variance (PSV) = Scheduled Completion Time (SCT) – Actual Completion Time (ACT)

ACT and SCT are measured in time intervals such as days or weeks.

For example say you are running three separate projects:

- ✔ **Project A:** SCT = 67 ACT = 90
- ✔ **Project B:** SCT = 23 ACT = 19
- ✔ **Project C:** SCT = 56 ACT = 57

The PSV for each is as follows:

> PSV Project A = 67 – 90 = –23
>
> PSV Project B = 23 – 19 = 4
>
> PSV Project C = 56 – 57 = –1

This KPI can also be adapted to measure performance across a business or department. For example if you want to calculate the departmental Project Schedule Variance you simply add the individual project variances for each separate project together for an actual number or calculate a straight or weighted average variance score.

> PSV Department = (–23) + (4) + (–1) = –20

Your target is zero. Ideally you should be aiming to deliver your projects on time every time. Overruns usually come with negative cost and implications for your reputation.

For the most part zero is also better than a positive PSV. If one of your managers consistently delivers ahead of schedule then it is actually likely to indicate weak planning, with too much room and contingency built into the plan. Aim for just-in-time delivery.

KPI: Project Cost Variance

The key performance question project cost variance helps to answer is: 'To what extent are our projects delivered on budget?' The data for this KPI will also usually come from a project management software application, financial planning applications or manual records. PCV is usually measured monthly but should be measured more frequently for important projects.

Project Cost Variance (PCV) = Scheduled Project Cost (SPC) – Actual Project Cost (APC)

For example going back to the three separate projects:

- **Project A:** SPC = $400,000 APC = $500,000
- **Project B:** SPC = $350,000 APC = $325,000
- **Project C:** SPC = $200,000 APC = $300,000

PCV Project A = $400,000 – $500,000 = –$100,000

PCV Project B = $350,000 – $325,000 = $25,000

PCV Project C = $200,000 – $300,000 = –$100,000

To calculate the overall Project Cost Variance simple add the individual project variances for every separate project together for an actual number or calculate a straight or weighted average variance score.

PCV Department = (–100,000) + (25,000) + (–$100,000) = –$175,000

Like the PSV, your target is zero. Ideally, you should be aiming to deliver your projects on budget every time. Overruns can cause financial problems. A positive PCV is, of course, usually a good thing. It means you didn't spend as much as you thought you would. But it could indicate poor planning, and the 'extra' money set aside for that project could have been better used elsewhere.

For longer, larger projects break the costs down into milestones throughout the project to help you see how you are tracking as the project moves forward. That way you can avoid any nasty surprises at the very end.

KPI: Earned Value (EV)

The key performance question earned value helps to answer is: 'To what extent are our projects delivering the intended value?' Again the data you need to calculate EV will usually come from a project management software application or any manual project records. How often you measure EV will depend on the project type but weekly or monthly are common. EV is always specific to an explicit point in time (or *status day*) you select.

In order to calculate EV you require three values:

✔ **The overall budgeted costs for the project:** This is usually referred to as the 'Budgeted Costs of Work Scheduled' or BCWS for short and includes any costs (resource costs and fixed costs) associated with the delivery of the project. You can calculate BCWS for any point in time (status day) along the project delivery timeframe simply by multiplying it by the percentage completion of a project at that given time. For example, if a project is scheduled for 4 months with an overall price tag (BCWS) of $100,000, then the BCWS is $25,000 after month one, $50,000 after month two, and so on. After the first month 25 per cent of the project have been completed, leading to the following calculation: $100,000 × 0.25 = $25,000. For month two it would be $100,000 × 0.5 = $50,000.

✔ **The actual costs used up to run the project up to the status day:** This is usually referred to as 'Actual Costs of Work Performed', or ACWP for short.

✔ **The value of work delivered at the given project status day:** This is the value that has been earned by the project work and is often referred to as 'Budgeted Cost of Work Performed', or BCWP for short. For example, if after 2 months of the project 75 per cent of the work on the project has been completed, then you might expect that also 75 per cent of the total project budget have been spent ($75,000 for our example here).

You can now use these figures to assess project performance. Let's go back to our example of a $100,000 project scheduled over 4 months.

Earned Value (EV) =
Budgeted Cost of Work Scheduled (BCWS) × % complete

The chosen status date could be after 3 months of running the project, at which point 60 per cent of the value of work has been delivered. Or in other words, the project is 60 per cent complete. The earned value, or (BCWP) is $60,000. However, the scheduled value (BCWS) is 75 per cent at this 3 months milestone. This tells us that the project is not on schedule because less value has been earned compared to what was planned.

Now let's look at the actual costs up to that 3 month status date. If we find that $90,000 (because for example a more expensive contractor had to be hired in) it tells us that the project is not only delivering less value than expected but is also over budget.

You can also calculate the factor of overspend or underspend, called Performance Level:

Performance Level = Actual Cost of Work Performed (ACWP)/EV

So for our 3 month status date, we have:

Performance Level = $90,000/$75,000 = 1.2

If we take the assumption that the same level of overspend (or underspend) continues for the rest of the project, then we can use these figure to calculate a predicted forecast:

Predicted Forecast = (Remaining cost × Performance Level) + ACWP

So in this case it would be:

Predicted Forecast = ($25,000 × 1.2) + $90,000 = $120,000

This means that, based on current progress and spending the project will overrun by $20,000.

EV is easily misinterpreted. Although the rhetoric surrounding EV states that it can deliver an objective quantitative measure of project performance in reality its validity hinges on how project progress is reported.

Like all KPIs it's important not to get too hung up on the final number. Instead use EV as a tool to identify and rectify potential problems in the project delivery. EV relies on good reporting and evaluation, so it's important to be aware of the potential for cheating!

There are several ways to manipulate EV. For example:

- ✔ Deliberately scheduling projects for longer than necessary so the driver of the project can complete more quickly and look good.
- ✔ Deliberately inflating the budget so the driver of the project can look good.
- ✔ Deliberately load all the easy tasks at the start of the project so good progress is made initially, keeping a project EV score looking good for a long time.
- ✔ Deliberately exaggerate the task completion percentages.

These types of unwanted behaviours can easily and quickly skew the data and render EV meaningless.

Chapter 15

Measuring Internal Efficiency and Quality

In This Chapter

▶ Tracking efficiency and quality

▶ Establishing how productive your internal operations really are

▶ Making sure you've future proofed your business

*R*evenue, profit and growth are essential outcomes for business success. This particular trio is the Holy Grail of business objectives and yet they are very difficult to achieve consistently if you don't focus on delivering product or service of sufficiently high quality in the most efficient manner possible.

Measuring internal efficiency and quality is therefore essential so you can effectively manage operations to make your resources go as far as possible while maintaining a tight control on quality.

Thankfully there are many KPIs that can help you to monitor progress and output from an operational perspective.

Assessing Quality, Lean and Six Sigma KPIs

Your business exists to provide certain products and services to your customers. This means you can make money. In order to do that effectively you first need to know what it is about your product or service that your customers really values so that you can satisfy their need at an affordable price that will drive growth.

Quality and efficiency are therefore very important – especially in manufacturing. Over the years many process have emerged to manage and monitor quality and efficiency but Lean and Six Sigma are perhaps the best known.

Why Lean matters

The principles of a 'lean business', often simply referred to as *Lean* look at operational efficiency from the perspective of the customer. Lean assumes that any expenditure of resources for any reason other than the creation of value for the customer, that is, something the customer is willing to pay for, is wasteful and should be minimised or eliminated.

Lean matters because profit is not just a function of how much money you make. The other side of the profit coin is how little you spend making your products or services or how efficiently you are able to utilise your resources. Effective and lean operational processes therefore allow you to minimise or eliminates as much waste as possible which means you make more profit.

There are seven types of waste to be considered for improvement:

- **Transportation:** Waste caused by the unnecessary transportation or handling of goods. For example, this may occur due to poor operational layout or excessive materials handling.

- **Motion:** Waste caused by the unnecessary motion of people or equipment. This may come about if people or equipment is moved too often between processes losing valuable time.

- **Inventory:** Waste caused by any work-in-progress (WIP), or finished goods that are in excess of requirements or don't have value a value-adding function. For example, if you use perishable materials and employees don't adhere to the FIFO (first in first out) principle where the goods with the shortest shelf life are used first.

- **Waiting:** Waste caused when people, parts, systems or facilities lie idle, waiting for a work cycle to be completed. For example, an employee may stop work or work slowly while they wait for an upstream process to deliver or for a machine to finish processing.

- **Over-production:** Waste caused by producing products in greater quantities or faster than the customer is demanding. For example if production is making larger batch sizes than is ordered.

- **Over-processing:** Waste caused by unnecessary work that goes beyond what is required to satisfy customer requirements. For example painting or polishing unseen areas that the customer will never see.

✔ **Defects:** Waste caused by anything that the customer would deem unacceptable. For example defects may be caused by operator error, insufficient training or poor supplier materials.

Getting data on the level of waste in your internal processes will allow you to become more efficient and profitable. There is more detail on how to do that later in this chapter.

What does Six Sigma really mean?

Six Sigma is a collection of tools and techniques to improve operational processes. Although pioneered by Motorola in 1986 it was made popular when General Electric adopted Six Sigma very successfully. Today it is widely used by businesses of all sizes in many sectors although it is still seen as a manufacturing focused process.

The term *six sigma* comes from the field of statistics and evaluates process capability. Technically speaking six sigma means that your defect level is below 3.4 per million opportunities. In other words for every million actions or steps in a production process an error is made less than 3.4 times!

As an analogy, consider a goalkeeper of a football team who plays 50 games in a season and who in each game faces 50 shots from the opposing team. If a defect is when the team scores, then a Six Sigma goalkeeper would concede one goal every 147 years! Clearly that is a very low error rate and Six Sigma in practice may not be quite so stringent. Essentially, Six Sigma's purpose is to improve all processes, but not necessarily to the 3.4 defect per million level.

Ultimately you need to determine an appropriate sigma level for each of your most important processes and strive to achieve these, and where possible improve them.

Three assertions are central to Six Sigma:

✔ Stable and predictable process results, including the reduction of process variations and inconsistency, are central to business success.

✔ Business processes have specific characteristics that can be measured. And if they can be measured they can be analyzed, controlled and improved.

✔ Sustained quality improvement can only be achieved when the whole business is committed to that outcome – especially senior management.

What makes Six Sigma so useful is that it is a measurement tool focused on verifiable data and statistical methods, *and* a performance improvement methodology.

The Six Sigma tools are based on the DMAIC principles.

- ✔ **Define** your internal and external customer requirements or expectation of the process

- ✔ **Measure** the current performance; what is the current frequency of defects?

- ✔ **Analyse** the data you collect to determine cause and effect and opportunities for improvement; why, when and where the defects occur.

- ✔ **Improve** the target process by designing solutions to improve, fix or prevent problems.

- ✔ **Control** the improvements to keep the process on the new course; ask 'How can we ensure that the process stays fixed?'

The implementation of this DMAIC process is done through an in-house team of Six Sigma-certified employees, known as Master Black Belts, Black Belts or Green Belts depending on their experience and level of involvement.

The promise of reaching Six Sigma performance levels is that you will significantly decrease customer dissatisfaction and achieve superior and sustainable financial rewards.

Finding your ways to track quality

Whilst the obsession with quality is universal thanks to quality pioneers such as W Edwards Deming, Josef Juran and Philip Crosby, the definition of quality is not unique.

Each business will perceive quality in a different way. For example, a bakery may consider they have produced a quality product when their cakes look fabulous. A restaurant may regard quality as the serving of locally sourced ingredients, where as a telecommunication company may believe they deliver quality because of the expertise of their customer service staff.

Even within the same sector, quality can mean radically different things. In car manufacturing for example one company may consider safety to be central to a quality product. Another company may consider design aesthetics to be central to their quality while another may be focused on the environmental pedigree of their cars or the performance.

The dimensions of quality for your business ultimately come down to whether or not your product or service fully meets (and ideally surpasses) your customers expectations and whether it is fit for purpose. As such it is your customers, not you, who decide whether you are delivering on quality.

It makes sense therefore that if you want to measure quality effectively you need to understand what your customers' value. Your quality index will be unique to you as there is no quality index template. It should be a bespoke group of between 5 and 10 KPIs that measure the various dimensions of quality as identified by your customers.

Measuring the KPIs in practice

The quality, lean and Six Sigma KPIs that are most useful are *Six Sigma Level* and *Quality Index*.

KPI: Six Sigma Level

The key performance question Six Sigma level helps to answer is: 'How capable are our processes in delivering error-free work?'

In order to answer this KPQ you need to know what a defect is and count the opportunities which exist for those defects to occur. In the context of Six Sigma a defect is anything outside of customer specifications, while a Six Sigma opportunity is the total number of times a defect could occur with a process.

First you need to calculate the *Defects Per Million Opportunities* (DPMO).

DPMO = (Number of defects × 1,000,000)/(Number of units × Number of opportunities)

The number for defects is the total number of defects found, the number of units is the number of units produced and the number of opportunities means the number of ways to generate defects.

For example say a online retailer wanted to examine their order and delivery process. To collect the data they examined 50 orders and found:

- ✔ 11 deliveries were not made on time
- ✔ 3 occasions where the order was wrong
- ✔ 4 instances where the product was damaged

DPMO = (11 + 3 + 4) × 1,000,000/(50 × 3) = 120,000

By comparing the result to the Sigma Conversion Table (see Table 15-1) the manager of the online retailer can establish that 120,000 defects per million opportunities is equivalent to a sigma performance level of between 2 and 3 (the number of defects is higher than 66,800 but lower than 308,500).

Table 15-1	Sample Sigma Conversion table	
Sigma Level	*DPMO*	*% Error*
1	691,500	69.15%
2	308,500	30.85
3	66,800	6.68
4	6,200	0.62
5	230	0.00023
6	3.4	0.00034

If you implement Six Sigma then be sure to choose strategically relevant projects as well as those that are likely to deliver some financial gain. If you don't, you run the risk of focusing too heavily on cost cutting without aligning your action to genuine performance improvement. A combination of the two is the best way to reap the considerable benefits Six Sigma can deliver.

KPI: Quality Index

The key performance question your Quality Index helps to answer is: 'How is the organisation ensuring that it is delivering products/services that are fit for purpose?'

In order to create your quality index you need to find out what your customers value most about your product or service. And that means asking them properly not guessing! Once you know what they value you must then identify KPIs that will allow you to monitor the various aspects of quality they have identified so you can ensure ongoing delivery against their expectations.

The KPIs you choose may be equally weighted or you may choose to attach higher value to certain KPIs. For example if your customers buy from you because they believe your product is safe and durable they may also like the colour range that you provide. But the safety is likely to be much more important to the customer than the colour it comes in and should be weighted accordingly.

Be careful not to turn the creation and maintenance of a quality index into a 'tick box' exercise. The purpose of the quality index is to highlight areas for continuous improvement.

Calculating Your Internal Productivity

When growth and profitability are at stake you must be able to measure internal productivity. You should be squeezing all the intended benefit from your resources – whether that means people, processes, plant or products.

Knowing the *capacity* of your business – what your business is capable of producing at any given time – is important, so that you can measure actual performance against that yardstick.

One of the key metrics for calculating internal productivity is the *Capacity Utilization Rate* (CUR). This metric provides insights into the extent to which a company actually uses its installed productive capacity. It therefore explores the relationship between actual output (what *is* being produced with the installed equipment) and the potential output that could be produced if everything was operating at maximum efficiency.

Looking at waste levels

Low capacity utilisation means there are potential inefficiencies in the internal processes of an organisation. It indicates waste, and waste costs money.

It also indicates opportunities to increase revenue without necessarily incurring additional costs. For example if you identify that you have an 80 per cent capacity utilization rate there is 20 per cent un-used but available capacity. This means that you can produce more products to sell without spending any more money on equipment, plant and machinery or people. As such capacity offers a significant opportunity to increase revenue, growth and profit.

Different ways to measure waste

In the effort to run a profitable and efficient company, waste obviously matters, yet most businesses have very little appreciation of how much waste is already built into their operational processes. Plus they don't really appreciate the considerable number of ways waste can manifest itself inside a business.

There are many different ways to measure waste, because there are many different types of waste. For example, there is the waste related to inefficient use of resources, but there is also the waste related to the actual production process and the environmental impact that waste can and does have. Some of the waste KPIs you can choose from – and what they measure – are:

✔ **Time to Market:** This metric measures the time it takes from the initial idea for a new product to the point where that new product is ready for distribution. As an indicator it reflects how well your research, design, manufacturing and managing processes are integrated, and how quickly you can translate a great idea into a winning product. Wasted time in this process may cost your business money through the loss of your first mover advantage (benefit for being the first significant player in any market) and can allow competitors to pull ahead.

✔ **First Past Yield (FPY):** This metric measures the waste in the system caused by defects. Defects decrease operational effectiveness, increase costs through rework costs and reduce profit. It is essential that you know what defects are costing you and where they are happening. FPY helps you measure the yields of every step along the process, detect defects and rework requirements early so they can be fixed instead of remaining hidden until the customer complains!

✔ **Overall Equipment Effectiveness (OEE):** This metric is a composite KPI that measures wasted capacity which takes process availability, efficiency and quality into account. It rolls up a number of output wastes into a single index which reduces complex production problems into a useful and intuitive information source for overall production effectiveness.

✔ **Process or Machine Downtime Level:** This metric looks at the waste caused by non-productive time. If machines or people are not able to do their job because of hold-ups, breakdowns or poor management or organisation skills then your business is losing money. You will never reach 100% capacity for all machinery, plant or people but you should know where it's happening so you can minimise it as much as possible.

✔ **Energy Consumption:** This metric looks at your energy consumption and will help you identify where you can reduce consumption and minimise waste. Energy is a huge issue for business. Energy costs are escalating at an alarming rate so identifying ways to conserve energy and reduce waste is going to be increasingly important.

✔ **Waste Reduction Rate:** This metric looks at the efficiency and effectiveness of your operations as well as the environmental and social impact of your operations. As well as being important to manage costs it's also a growing area of competitive advantage as consumers become more demanding and discerning about how the products they buy are made. How are you dealing with waste products in the production process, for example? Cost-effective waste minimisation is a valuable investment that will always pay dividends for your business.

✔ **Waste Recycling Rate:** This metric looks at how effective you are at recycling waste products you create in the business process. While it may not be possible to eliminate all waste products you absolutely must minimise the impact that waste has on the environment. If you send waste to landfill sites or incinerators for example then there is commercial as well as environmental implications. A better solution would be to reuse or recycle the waste as much as possible and this metric helps you gauge how well you are achieving that objective.

Measuring waste in practice

The KPIs most often used for measuring waste are Capacity Utilisation Rate (CUR) and Process Level Waste.

KPI: Capacity Utilisation Rate

The key performance question Capacity Utilisation Rate helps to answer is: To what extent are we leveraging our full production/work potential? This metric is often measured daily or weekly, depending on what is being assessed. For example, you could calculate the CUR for a single machine hourly while for an entire factory or company you could calculate the CUR weekly or monthly.

> CUR = Actual Capacity over specified time period × 100/Possible Capacity over specified time period

For example say your production plant could potentially produces 20,000 units per day but only produces 15,000 units per day. The CUR is:

> 15,000/20,000 × 100 = 75 per cent

Your CUR is particularly useful for working out when you unit costs will change because additional investments have to be made to increase capacity such as buying a new machine, recruiting more staff or finding a bigger business location. If you are currently producing 15,000 units at a cost of $0.75 per unit and your CUR is 75% then you can produce up to 20,000 units without raising the costs per unit.

KPI: Process Level Waste:

The key performance question Process Level Waste helps to answer is: To what extent are our processes lean and effective?

All businesses should aim to have effective and lean operational processes that seek to minimise or eliminate waste. Under the principles of Lean waste is considered any activity that does not add value to the end customer.

Formula: This metric doesn't have one formula because it looks at many different types of waste. As a result you will need to collect this data manually by following and observing the various processes. Individual measures will have to be designed for each waste type.

An example of how productive process level waste assessment can be how-ever can be seen in Portakabin. Portakabin is an international company that produces portable buildings. You will no doubt have seen a Portakabins on building sites or outdoor events.

The modular buildings are made in a factory and then put up wherever the customers need them. As part of their commitment to lean production methods Portakabin regularly conducts exercises to measure process waste levels. This has allowed the company to identify and cut out waste from the manufacturing system including improved module design, re-use or changes to materials used, pre-cut steel beams, boards and floors to remove the need for trimming.

Measuring process waste levels takes a lot of time and effort because of the manual data collection processes that are required. But it can make a signifi-cant difference to profitability and customer satisfaction.

Focus on the areas where you can reduce waste easily. For example you would be better to re-design a process that can be done fairly quickly and without great expense than you would be moving plant and heavy machinery or re-designing the distribution area.

Monitoring rework levels

After WWII businesses and manufacturers could pretty much create anything and people would buy. Quality wasn't an issue because even a bad product was better than no product at all. But as the world economies got back on their feet quality began to matter and competition gave consumers choice.

Japan and China started to really prosper and on investigation US and European companies realised that they were able to produce better goods at lower prices because they were paying attention to quality and employing the principles of Total Quality Management (TQM).

One of the key principles of TQM is that quality needs to be built into the manufacturing process rather than just inspected for quality at the end. If a product is defective or found to be of poor quality – it's too late by then. However building quality into the process dramatically reduced costs because it minimised the instances where a product would have to be re-worked.

For US and European manufacturers seeking to emulate their Eastern compet-itors monitoring rework levels became a key quality KPI. Rework is defined as a product that fails to meet the specifications but, with some alterations can be brought up to scratch.

Why rework levels matter

Clearly rework matters because getting your product or service right first time is much more efficient than having to go back and do something again. It wastes resources, time and manpower.

You should always be aiming for no rework or zero defeats. As well as providing your business with cost benefits it establishes how effective your business is at delivering what your customers want without further fine-tuning, correction or revision.

Plus if you focus on quality all the way through the production process you ensure that problems are flagged quick enough to rectify "in-situ" so that the quality of the product is not compromised moving forward. It also avoids the waste that can occur after a failure or defeat is already built into the product. If a product is only inspected at the end but a defeat was built early on in the production process then the product is defective and will need to be re-done. So all the other additional processes that occurred after that initial defeat were wasted and simple added to the cost as often they will also need to be redone once the initial defeat is fixed.

Monitoring rework level also matters because it sends a very clear message to employees to focus on getting the products right first time. This metric can also illuminate where additional training is required to improve performance.

Measuring rework levels in practice

The key performance question Rework Level helps to answer is: How effectively are we driving waste out of our processes? How often you measure rework will depend on your industry or sector. Manufacturers would be wise to measure rework levels weekly whereas service companies may only need to measure rework on a monthly basis. The formula is

Number of defective products requiring rework over a specific period/ Total number of products produced over a specific period × 100

So for example if your company produces 1,500 widgets a month and 112 of them need to be reworked.

112/1500 × 100 = 7.46 per cent rework level

The information you need access to in order to calculate rework level will be available from the processes that create your product or service.

Be careful to avoid a "blame culture" when it comes to rework levels. If this metric is perceived as an invitation for a witch hunt or to track down and shame poor workmanship then problems are more likely to be covered up and hidden. Instead foster a culture of openness and use rework level as a companywide invitation to move closer to zero defects and elevated performance.

Scrutinizing order fulfilment

Whether your customers are happy with you or unhappy with you largely comes down to how well you meet their expectations. We've covered the quality expectations they may have but customers also have delivery expectations.

When your customers buy from you they expect to receive their goods or services reasonably quickly. Technology has made most customers impatient so you need to scrutinize your order fulfilment process to make sure it is meeting and preferably exceeding expectation.

One of the key metrics to help you monitor order fulfilment is order fulfilment cycle time (OFCT).

OFCT is a continuous measurement defined as the time from order confirmation to receipt of the goods or services. And as a KPI it applies equally well to goods or services.

OFCT, also known as customer order cycle time considers performance from end-to-end rather than looking at one individual part of the operational process. This is important because it helps to identify opportunities that may be missed in conventional efficiency programs.

For example you may decide to focus your efforts on reducing machine down time but if machine down time only account for 5% of the total OFCT then any gains in that area will be minimal. If on the other hand you identify rework level at 25% then clearly gains in that area are going to make a significant different to order fulfilment.

Understanding what your customer sees

The only part of the supply chain your customer sees is the ordering process and the delivery process. As such you are effectively being judged by those two processes. How easy is it to order and how quickly do I get my products or services once I order.

For some customers how you create your product or service is important and they will always care about the quality and price but responsiveness is increasingly important. Understanding what your customer sees and managing those processes closely is therefore critically important. And it's only going to become more so.

Customers are becoming more and more discerning and less and less accommodating or forgiving of error. Flawless and efficient deliver will often mean the difference between repeat sale and a defection to your competition.

Measuring OFCT helps to improve efficiency because the re-engineering that is usually required to reduce cycle time often leads to significant improvements as the process becomes more and more responsive to internal and external customer needs

Measuring it in practice

The key performance question Order Fulfilment Cycle Time (OFCT) helps to answer is: 'How efficient are our processes?' The formula for OFCT is:

OFCT = Average actual cycle time consistency achieved to fulfil customer orders.

This is calculated through an analysis of the end-to-end order fulfilment process over a specific period of time. In order to calculate the cycle time for each order you need to pay attention to each step of each sub-step within the overall process. In each case the cycle time starts from the day the order is placed to the day the customer receives all the goods or services they ordered.

Measuring end-to-end processes can be tricky because it requires data from various different functions and departments – each with their own power-bases and potentially agendas.

To manage these challenges it may be wise to appoint an end-to-end process manager who is skilled in change management and has the authority to make any necessary improvements.

Dissecting delivery

Whereas OCFT looks at the end-to-end process of fulfilment it can also be worthwhile to focus in on and dissect delivery. In a world of instant gratification if ordered products or services are not in the customers hands in a matter of days then questions are asked and often the rating of the overall service will drop off.

Delivery matters.

And delivery is especially important if you supply products or services to other companies that operate a just-in-time supply chain to minimise inventory and expense.

Did you provide what the customer expected?

On time delivery metric therefore provide vital insight into your ability to deliver what the customer expects when the customer expects it.

In addition delivery metrics give you valuable information about the effectiveness of your internal processes and highlight inefficiencies in your supply chain.

The key metric used to monitor whether your deliveries arrive at the customer – either internal or external on time and in full is delivery in full, on time rate (DIFOT). This metric ensures you are aware of when the customer takes receipt of the complete order. In the end your customers don't really care when you shipped the goods, or whether they have part of the order they will judge you based on when they receive what they ordered in full.

Measuring it in practice

The key performance question Delivery in full, on time (DIFOT) rate helps to answer is: To what extent are our customers getting what they want at the time they want? The data you will need to calculate the DIFOT rate is contained in your order tracking system. If you use a third party in your supply chain then you will need to gain information from them too in order to calculate this metric.

DIFOT = Units or orders delivered in full, on time/Total units or orders shipped × 100

For example say you run an online electrical retailer. The days of telling a customer their washing machine will be delivered sometime on Tuesday between 8am and 6pm are going. Customers expect a delivery window of an hour or two at the most – and rightly so. Who has the time to hang around all day waiting for a washing machine to be delivered?

The delivery drivers have a handheld mobile device that records delivery and the customer must sign acceptance. The device also tracks if the order is rejected or incomplete.

In the first week of March 2013 you received 487 orders for various large white goods. Of those 398 were delivered in the designated delivery window meaning that 89 were not delivered on time or within the designated window. 480 were delivered in full meaning that 7 orders which contained multiple orders did not deliver all the products orders. And 2 order were rejected as being the wrong product, but those order were also late so must be removed from the calculation as they are already accounted for in the on-time delivery calculation.

On-time delivery = 398/487 × 100 = 81.72%

In-full delivery = 480/487 × 100 = 98.56%

DIFOT = (487 − (89 + 7 − 2))/487 × 100 = 80.69%

Your DIFOT rate will depend on your industry but in today's competitive environment no company should let their DIFOT rate slip below 95%.

This metric can be difficult and costly to measure if you don't already have an internal or automated order and delivery tracking system.

Investigating inventory

Part of measuring internal productivity is investigating inventory and how inventory changes over time. For example are you losing inventory becayse of damage or expiration?

The metric that can help you keep a handle on inventory is the Inventory Shrinkage rate (ISR). Inventory shrinkage looks at the loss of products between production and purchase. Obviously, loosing inventory for any reason will push up your costs and reduce your profit margin. If these escalating costs can't be stemmed then they may eventually be passed on to your customers, which could in turn impact repeat purchase and customer loyalty.

Managing inventory properly is therefore critical to your on-going efficiency and profitability.

The key reasons for shrinking inventory

There are many different reasons for inventory shrinkage such as breakages, damages caused by poor handling or storage, administrative mistakes, misplaced goods and perishable goods not sold in time. If for example a company has sell by dates or best before dates and the inventory is not managed in an ordered fashion according to these dates than inventory can be wasted.

Sloppy dispatching and poor handling may be the cause of some inventory shrinkage but unfortunately the biggest culprit is often theft. It is estimated that about 44% of inventory shrinkage is down to employee sticky fingers and another 35% due to shoplifting!

Investigating inventory and specifically inventory shrinkage may be a distressing business but it is absolutely essential if you are to pinpoint areas of loss and stem the loss occurs.

Plus when everyone in the business knows that inventory is scrutinized and measured regularly the thieves or would be opportunist thieves will probably think twice about foolishly risking their job.

Measuring it in practice

The key performance question Inventory Shrinkage Rate (ISR) helps to answer is: To what extent are we losing inventory along our internal processes?

The data needed to calculate ISR is collected from the inventory management system, manufacturing data, purchasing data, stock taking information as well as sales and shipping data. Ideally this metric should be measured every 6 months or more frequently is it is considered high.

Inventory can either be measured in actual stock-keeping unit (SKU) or in financial terms using average selling prices.

$$ISR = (\text{Inventory you should have} - \text{Inventory you do have})/\text{Inventory you should have} \times 100$$

For example a knitwear accessories manufacturer may create 5000 scarves, 5000 pairs of gloves and 5000 hats ever month. Unfortunately there is flood damage in the warehouse and a box of 200 scarves is ruined. In addition a stock take at the end of the month shows that a further 150 hats and 100 pairs of gloves are missing.

$$15,000 - 14550/15,000 \times 100 = 3\% \text{ ISR}$$

 It is common only to look at Inventory Shrinkage Rate inside a business but it can be really illuminating to look at IRS all along the supply chain to assess where most of the shrinkage is occurring. That way you and your suppliers can seek to minimise shrinkage for the benefit of all parties.

Asking Yourself Whether You're Future Proof

Just because business is good today doesn't mean it will automatically be good tomorrow. Every business needs to be plan for the future and ensure revenue, profit and growth are secure moving into the future.

Do you know where tomorrow's sales are coming from? Do you know about your market and whether it's growing or contracting? Have you thought about future customer needs and product innovation in order to future proof your business?

Your innovation pipeline

Innovation is a critical component for most businesses. What customers want today may not be what they want tomorrow and you need to be ahead of the curve so you can pre-empt any changes in demand and adapt accordingly.

The innovation pipeline is the name of the new ideas, products of services that have potential and it is increasingly important for all businesses to foster a strong innovation pipeline so they can rise to the challenges of shifting markets and customer demands.

Innovation is key but hard to measure

Clearly paying attention to the demand for existing products and seeking to introduce new product and service offerings that go on to replace failing product lines or diversify the business into new areas is important for on- going growth and profitability. Yet according to a study conducted by McKinsey a large percentage of companies, even those that rely heavily on innovation don't measure their innovation performance or potential.

When there is an attempt to quantify and measure innovation it is usually pretty crude such as identifying the proportion of revenue spent on research and development (R&D). However the amount spent on R&D does not necessarily tell us anything meaningful about how innovative a business is. A higher spend on R&D may indicate that new products or services are more likely to be developed but it is by no means guaranteed.

The KPI called Innovation Pipeline Strength (IPS) can help you to estimate revenue potential of the new products or services in development as well as the potential of completing the innovation and taking it to market. After all innovation for innovations sake it pointless – you need to know that there is a market and eager customers willing to buy the product or service in development otherwise why bother.

By measuring Innovation pipeline strength you will gain an understanding about the future potential and insight into the potential return on your R&D investments.

Measuring innovation in practice

The best KPIs to help you future proof your business are Innovation Pipeline Strength (IPS) and Return on Innovation Investment (ROI^2)

KPI: Innovation Pipeline Strength (IPS)

The key performance question Innovation Pipeline Strength (IPS) helps to answer is: To what extent have we got a strong innovation pipeline? In order to calculate this metric you will need to look at the key innovation projects and estimate the potential future revenue they will generate. IPS is usually measured on a quarterly basis.

Formula: IPS = Sum (Innovation project x Future revenue potential)

For example, a company might have 3 new products in the pipeline:

- ✔ Product A, with a future revenue potential of $100,000
- ✔ Product B, with a future revenue potential of $200,000
- ✔ Product C, with a future revenue potential of $300,000

In this case, IPS would be:

> IBS = $100,000 + $200,000 + $300,000 = $600,000

IPS is an estimation of future revenue generated by the innovation currently in development which means there are by definition uncertainties around the risks and opportunities involved in taking it to market.

KPI: Return on Innovation Investment (ROI²)

The key performance question Return on Innovation Investment (ROI²) helps to answer is: To what extent are our investments in innovation generating a return? Innovation is important but it's also important to measure the effectiveness of that innovation to ensure that it's justified and delivers a return. The data needed to calculate this metric is available through the accounting data and project data and ROI² is usually measured at the end of an innovation project or as a percentage return over a specific periods of time.

> ROI² = Net Profit from new product or service/ Innovation costs for the products and services

For example as a simple ROI² calculation, an innovation project costs $150,000 to implement, and you derive $200,000 in net profits.

> ROI² = $200,000/$150,000 = 1.33

This means that for every dollar you spend on the innovation project, you get $1,33 back in return. Obviously, if you have a ROI² of below 1 your return is negative and you are making a loss. Any ROI² above 1 is making a profit.

ROI² is most commonly used as a retrospective KPI taking into account actual costs versus actual profits. However, by using estimations about future revenues and projected costs, it is possible to estimate future ROI². This is especially useful to manage investment between competing products. If a product looks great but will cost a fortune to implement then it would be wise to shelve that product until such time as implementation costs are reduced and focus on other developments that look set to deliver a higher return on investment.

According to a 2010 Boston Consulting Group report half of all mangers are unhappy with their return on innovation investment Measuring ROI^2 helps to ensure that the business is future proofed and the innovation is worthwhile. This metric also allows you to compare investment between initiatives so you can compare results from innovation to marketing initiatives or other types of investment to see what delivers more reward.

The problem with any ROI metric is that the definition can be modified to massage the results. ROI is therefore very susceptible to manipulation. To make sure it's a meaningful metric that drives performance improvements be clear on the definition and stick to it.

Chapter 16

Measuring IT Performance

In This Chapter

▶ Appreciating the growing importance of IT and the need to measure it

▶ Metric for measuring IT service delivery

▶ Monitoring IT projects effectively

*T*here are few businesses today that are not dependent on IT in some form or another. Whether from the simple desk top computer that allows employees to do their job through to complex networks and bespoke technology that are paramount to business success.

If your business depends heavily on IT or you need IT systems to deliver your product or service to your customer effectively and efficiently then you would be wise to measure IT performance through the adoption of some of the IT-focused KPIs detailed in this chapter.

Why IT Matters More Than Ever

Technology has significantly assisted business success. Now you can

- ✔ Easily and cheaply communicate with suppliers and customers.
- ✔ Sell online without a physical presence on the high street.
- ✔ Venture into new markets unhindered by geographical location.
- ✔ Reduce costs and become much more efficient.

But these advantages do come at a price.

For example most businesses today handle and store personal data. In days gone by, that data would be held in physical ledgers or in some paper filing system. Now everything is stored electronically, and as such it is vulnerable to attack and misappropriation.

There have been many examples of valuable personal data going missing or being carelessly lost by employees. In November 2007 news broke in the UK that two computer discs holding personal information on 25 million British citizens had been lost in the mail. The data included names, addresses, National Insurance numbers and in some cases bank information. These types of IT failures and breaches of security are fairly common and can end up costing the business a lot of money not to mention the reputational damage and loss in customer confidence.

In addition there has also been a marked rise in cyber crime, including remote hackers shutting your system down and demanding a ransom. Hackers often target valuable personal data, including credit card details or bank details which are then sold on to undesirables seeking to exploit the data in some way. Add to that the constant threat of viruses, worms or malware that can cause havoc to an IT system, and you begin to see that the misuse of IT poses a serious threat even while IT itself provides significant opportunities.

One survey by PricewaterhouseCoopers (PwC) found that 92 per cent of firms with more than 250 employees, and 83 per cent of smaller firms, with up to 25 employees, stated they had experienced a security incident in the last year – more than double in just 24 months. According to PwC a security breech in a large firm can cost anywhere between £280,000 and £690,000.

Clearly IT matters more than ever.

Measuring IT service delivery

Obviously, it's important for customer satisfaction and repeat purchase that you provide good service across your business including IT service.

For example, most IT functions have a *help desk* that provides both internal employees and external customers with technical support in some form or another. When users call the help desk or send an email they would like their query resolved quickly, so they can get back to whatever it was they were doing before the IT started to go wrong.

The benefits of measuring IT service delivery are clear. If you resolve a customer IT problem at first contact, you are improving operational efficiency, reducing costs, and improving user satisfaction all at the same time. If you don't resolve the problem, it can impact productivity and cause on-going frustration. These unresolved issues usually lead to repeat calls, which in turn add direct and indirect cost to your help desk operations.

Research has indicated that 34 per cent of customers who don't get their query or problem resolved quickly are likely to go to your competitor. In addition, 30 per cent of call centre operational costs can be attributed to *not* being able to resolve the query in the first contact, so it really is important to measure service delivery and get it right.

While it may be easier for you to assess product quality – because it's often easier to define and measure it – you must also measure the quality of IT service delivery.

Defining and measuring service delivery

Understanding the quality of service you deliver to your customers is important when considering your operational efficiency.

The best way to define and measure service delivery is through the KPI known as SERVQUAL which was developed in the mid-1980s. The methodology is designed to measure quality of service by comparing the service expectations a customer has with the actual service experience.

SERVQUAL breaks service quality into the following dimensions, also often referred to as the acronym RATER:

- ✔ **Reliability:** Are your people able to perform the promised service dependably and accurately?

- ✔ **Assurance:** Do your people convey confidence and trust through their knowledge and courtesy?

- ✔ **Tangibles:** Do the appearance of physical facilities, equipment, personnel, communication materials and so on reassure your customers?

- ✔ **Empathy:** Do your people provide caring, individualised attention to customers?

- ✔ **Responsiveness:** Are your people willing to help and respond to your customers' needs?

When it comes to measuring the quality of the service you provide SERVQUAL is particularly useful because it is both a measurement and management model.

The authors of the methodology also identified five gaps that can result in a perceived drop in service by customers. Often simply being aware of these gaps can provide valuable insights into service improvement.

The five gaps are:

- ✔ **Gap between management perception and consumer expectation:** This gap arises when people inside the business don't fully appreciate or understand what the customer actually wants. For example, you may believe that your customers want cheaper product but what they really want is access to a real person when they call you business with an issue or query. This is why measuring your customer KPIs in part 4 are so important so you can be sure you cater to what your customers want and not what you *assume* they want.

- ✔ **Gap between management perception and quality of service specification:** This gap arises when management has not set an appropriate performance standard. Even if you know what your customers really want, you have to then lay out a benchmark for what constitutes quality service. For example, your customers may tell you that they want to get through to that real person quickly. You need to define what *quickly* means so that the people delivering the service know what they are aiming at. The performance standard may therefore be to answer the call within five rings and resolve at least 90 per cent of all calls in the first call.

- ✔ **Gap between service quality specification and service delivery:** This gap arises when a shortfall exists between the performance standard and actual performance. For example a gap would arise if your people were consistently answering calls later than five rings and were only able to resolve 10 per cent of the calls in the first conversation. This shortfall in performance may be caused by poor communication or training. If your people are not informed about why the performance standard is in place they may feel that it's just some unnecessary arbitrary rule to make their life more complicated. If however they understand that it is what the customers have asked for they may be more inclined to get on board and meet those standards.

- ✔ **Gap between service delivery and external communication:** Marketing, advertising and what your people say to customers all have a profound effect on what they expect from your business. This gap arises when the promised level of service doesn't materialize when it's expected. For example if an insurance company advertises that in the case of a claim their customers are assigned a personal claim handler who will be their sole point of content and that doesn't happen then the customer has every right to be frustrated by that gap in service.

- ✔ **Gap between expected service and experienced service:** This gap arises when there is a difference between the expected service and the service experience. Often this gap is caused by a combination of gap 1 and gap 4 and often represents a breakdown in communication.

Understanding the gaps between service expectation and actual service perception will provide companies with an insight into the customer service areas where they are not delivering the service levels customer were expecting.

Measuring service delivery in practice

The IT service delivery KPIs that are most useful are *Service Quality* (SERVQUAL) and *Help Desk First Call Resolution* (HD FCR).

KPI: Service Quality (SERVQUAL)

The key performance question SERVQUAL helps to answer is: 'To what extent are we delivering service quality to our customers?'

SERVQUAL is established using two questionnaires of 22 questions which measure expectation and perception of the service on a scale of 1 to 7 (1 being strongly disagree and 7 being strongly agree). In addition, respondents rank the five dimensions of the RATER scale (Reliability, Assurance, Tangibles, Empathy, and Responsiveness) to identify relative importance. This is achieved by allocating 100 points across the five dimensions.

Finally you calculate the *gap score* for each dimension by subtracting the Expectation score from the Perception score. A negative gap score indicates that the actual service was less than what was expected. Obviously you are aiming for a neutral or positive gap score!

For example, say ABC Bank is keen to see how their customers perceive their quality of service. First they have to establish what customers expect from a bank. This is achieved through 22 expectation statements which ask customers to rank their expectations around what an excellent bank would look like. Customers are therefore asked to rate each of the statement from 1–7 for statement such as:

1. Excellent banking companies will have modern-looking equipment.
2. The physical facilities at excellent banks will be visually appealing.
3. Employees at excellent banks will be neat in their appearance.
4. Materials associated with the service (brochures or statements) will be visually appealing at an excellent bank.
5. When excellent banks promise to do something by a certain time, they do.
6. When a customer has a problem, excellent banks will show a sincere interest in solving it.
7. Excellent banks will perform the service right the first time.

The customers are then asked to complete a perception statement which relates to their perceptions of ABC bank in particular. Again they are asked to rate the statement from 1–7 for statements such as:

1. The bank has modern looking equipment.
2. The bank's physical features are visually appealing.
3. The bank's reception desk employees are neatly dressed.

4. Materials associated with the service (such as pamphlets or statements) are visually appealing at the bank.

5. When the bank promises to do something by a certain time, it does so.

6. When you have a problem, the bank shows a sincere interest in solving it.

7. The bank performs the service right the first time.

Feel free to adapt the SERVQUAL methodology and amend the dimensions and questions slightly to make it a better fit for your business

Domino's Pizza modified the classic dimensions into the following six outcome items:

1. Domino's has delicious home-delivery pizza.

2. Domino's has nutritious home-delivery pizza.

3. Domino's home-delivery pizza has flavourful sauce.

4. Domino's provides a generous amount of toppings for its home-delivery pizza.

5. Domino's home-delivery pizza is made with superior ingredients.

6. Domino's prepared its home-delivery pizza crust exactly the way I like it.

KPI: First Call Resolution (FCR)

The key performance question FCR helps to answer is: 'How effectively are we resolving our customer queries at first contact?' Understanding help desk first call resolution will provide an insight into the effectiveness and efficiency of the IT help-desk operations as well as insights into the costs and user satisfaction levels with the IT support.

There are different ways to collect the necessary data in order to measure FCR. The easiest option is by comparing the number of IT calls (or emails) with the number of cases resolved at first contact. This data can normally be collected from the agent logs – where IT operators detail whether calls have resolved or escalated.

FCR call statistics are calculated as follows:

Total number of calls/Total number of resolved at first call × 100

For example say your IT help desk logged the following statistics over two months:

Month 1: 4500 calls   3890 resolved at first call
Month 2: 5400 calls   5000 resolved at first call

Based on Call Statistics the FCR for month 1 would be

$(3890/4500) \times 100 = 86.44$ per cent

and for month 2

$(5000/5400) \times 100 = 92.59$ per cent

Over-emphasis on FCR can sometimes distract from the fact that not all contacts add value. For example, if your user manual or technical information that accompanies your product is not clear enough you may get more calls than you should. The easiest way to solve this and avoid the unnecessary cost is to improve the clarity of the supporting documentation.

Measuring IT project performance

It is very common for IT related objectives to be delivered via projects such as new software design projects, hard ware or software implementation projects, or website development projects.

Unfortunately, IT projects have an especially poor track record for successful implementation. In fact, research indicates that up to 70 per cent of IT projects fail to deliver their objectives. According to the British Computer Society (BCS), only 16 per cent of IT projects – at best – can be considered truly successful.

Failure in the context of IT projects is the same as failure in any project. Either the project wasn't delivered on schedule, wasn't delivered on budget or didn't deliver what it was supposed to deliver.

If you want to ensure that your IT projects are successful then you need to measure IT project performance using the classic project KPIs.

Using the classic three project KPIs

There are three classic project KPIs that are particularly useful for keeping your IT projects on track. They are:

- *IT Project Schedule Variance* (IT PSV)
- *IT Project Cost Variance* (IT PCV)
- *IT Project Earned Value* (IT EV)

IT project schedule variance measures actual progress against the agreed schedule to help ensure the IT project is delivered on time.

IT spending can be notoriously high as companies seek to invest in increasingly more sophisticated systems to automate processes as well as collect, store and analyse data. In fact one burgeoning area of IT expense is systems that promise a plethora of KPIs . . . all at the touch of a button.

Unfortunately the financial track record of IT projects is not much better than schedule with an estimated 1/3 of all IT projects in the private sector running between 10–20 per cent over budget. And it's not better in the public sector – the implementation of Universal Credit, a single welfare payment to replace the multitude that currently exist in the UK is still on-going but it is already significantly over budget. It is also estimated that website projects typically end up costing 25 per cent more than the agreed budget. IT Project Cost variance allows you to measure whether an IT project has gone over budget and if so by how much.

For larger, longer-running IT projects however you really want to measure progress as it's happening rather than retrospectively which is what ITPSV and IT PCV do.

IT EV is particularly useful because it looks at the cost of work in progress and allows you to understand how much work has been completed compared to how much was expected to a particular date.

In addition to assessing progress to date, the IT EV metric allows you to project what the likely costs of the complete project will be; assuming performance levels remain unchanged moving forward.

Measuring IT project performance KPIs in practice

The IT project performance KPIs that are most useful are IT Project Schedule Variance, IT Project Cost Variance and IT Project Earned Value.

KPI: IT Project Schedule Variance

The key performance question IT project schedule variance helps to answer is: To what extent are our IT projects delivered on schedule?

> IT Project Schedule Variance (IT PSV) = Scheduled Completion Time (SCT) – Actual Completion Time (ACT)

ACT and SCT are measured in time intervals such as days or weeks.

For example say you are running three separate IT projects:

- **IT Project A:** SCT = 105; ACT = 129
- **IT Project B:** SCT = 25; ACT = 25
- **IT Project C:** SCT = 40; ACT = 35

IT PSV for each is as follows:

IT PSV Project A = 105 – 129 = –24

IT PSV Project B = 25 – 25 = 0

IT PSV Project C = 40 – 35 = 5

If you want to calculate the total IT Project Schedule Variance (i.e. the schedule variance of all projects combined) you simply add the individual IT project variances for each separate IT project together for an actual number, or calculate a straight or weighted average variance score.

Total IT PSV = (–24) + (0) + (5) = –19

If IT Project Schedule Variance is zero then the project was completed on time, as promised. If the variance is negative it shows an overrun and if the variance is positive it highlights competition ahead of the planned completion date. Positive numbers may indicate poor planning or the IT project's owner deliberate attempt to add too many contingency days into the project so they can look good when it's finished ahead of time.

KPI: IT Project Cost Variance

The key performance question IT project cost variance helps to answer is: 'To what extent are our IT projects delivered on budget?'

IT Project Cost Variance (IT PCV) = Scheduled Project Cost (SPC) – Actual Project Cost (APC)

For example, going back to the three separate projects:

- ✔ IT Project A: SPC = $800,000 APC = $950,000
- ✔ IT Project B: SPC = $150,000 APC = $152,000
- ✔ IT Project C: SPC = $350,000 APC = $300,000

The IT PCV for each project is

Project A = $800,000 – $950,000 = -$150,000

Project B = $150,000 – $152,000 = -$2,000

Project C = $350,000 – $300,000 = $50,000

To calculate the overall IT Project Cost Variance simple add the individual project variances for every separate IT project together for an actual number or calculate a straight or weighted average variance score.

Total IT PCV = (–$150,000) + (–$2,000) + ($50,000) = –$102,000

If IT Project Cost Variance is zero then the project was completed on budget, as promised. If the variance is negative it shows an over spend and if the variance is positive it shows the project was delivered under budget. Like the IT PSV a positive numbers may indicate poor planning or the IT project's owner deliberate attempt to add inflate the estimated budget so they can look good when it's finished under budget.

KPI: IT Project Earned Value

The key performance question IT EV helps to answer is: 'To what extent are our IT projects making the desired progress?'

IT Earned Value (IT EV) = Budgeted Cost of Work Performed (BCWP) × per cent complete

BCWP is the total budgeted costs for labour and resources for the project.

Performance Level = Actual Cost of Work Scheduled (ACWS)/EV

Actual Cost of Work Scheduled is the total amount in labour and resources that has been spent on the project to date.

For example, say you have initiated an IT Project and the BCWP is $200,000. So far the ACWP or what's actually been spent so far is $145,000 but the project is only 30 per cent complete.

The IT Earned Value (IT EV) = $200,000 × 30 per cent = $60,000

Part VI
Measuring Your Most Important Assets: Developing HR and People KPIs

⭐ **Company X**   Commercial Strategy Map Example

Financial Objectives	**1.0 Deliver Shareholder Value** Ensure we create long-term value for our shareholders		
	1.1 **Grow Sales**	1.2 **Maximise Profits**	1.3 **Manage our Investments**
Customer Objectives	2.1 **Improve Brand Awareness in Europe**	2.2 **Enter Midmarket Segment in Europe**	2.3 **Build Strong Relationships with Top Customers**
Internal Processes Objectives	3.1 **Gather Market Intelligence**	3.2 **Optimise our Processes in Plant X**	3.3 **Innovate and Integrate our Products**
Internal Processes Objectives	4.1 **Implement IT Suite**	4.2 **Roll out Lean Training**	4.3 **Improve our Internal Communication**

For Dummies can help you get started with lots of subjects. Go to
www.dummies.com to learn more and do more with *For Dummies*.

In this part . . .

✔ Discover how satisfied and engaged your staff are, and whether they'd recommend you to anyone else.

✔ Understand the importance of 360-degree feedback in building up a picture of how your people see your company.

✔ Find out just how much value the people your business employs are generating.

✔ Measure how good your business is at attracting and keeping talent by charting recruitment effectiveness and retention rate.

✔ Dealing with the pitfalls and challenges of measuring training success.

Chapter 17

Measuring People Performance

In This Chapter

▶ Measuring how satisfied and engaged your employees are . . . and understanding the difference between the two

▶ Working out whether your employees would recommend you . . . and understanding why they should

▶ Making performance appraisals meaningful and useful

*P*eople are your most important assets. They are also probably your biggest cost, so it's really vital that you know what they are doing and whether they are happy, productive and engaged. It is clearly important that your people are doing what they are supposed to be doing, working hard and adding value to the business; generally speaking, they are only likely to be doing that if they are happy and engaged – at least most of the time.

Considering the importance of people, I am constantly surprised at how few businesses really measure their people in any meaningful way. In fact most companies do this really badly and it's almost always the least well measured section of a performance framework.

Many businesses conduct basic staff surveys – often copied from some other company's staff survey or one that managers have found online. Alternatively, businesses will use over-simplified metrics: examples include the number of training days staff have completed or simple measures of absenteeism. These may provide a number –great for slotting into a performance dashboard – but none of these methods give meaningful insights and they certainly don't help improve people performance.

The KPIs I detail in this chapter offer up a solution to this challenge and provide worthwhile ways to measure people performance so you can ensure that your people are happy, productive and engaged. That way they really will be your biggest asset and not your biggest liability.

How Satisfied and Engaged are Your People?

Employee satisfaction is one of the most established of all the non-financial KPIs. This is largely because of the recognised correlation between happy employees and happy customers – and happy customers mean happy shareholders.

Employee satisfaction is a powerful leading indicator of customer satisfaction, which is in itself a leading indicator of profit. A leading indicator is one that is focused on the future and allows us to make predictions about what will happen in the future.

As a result most businesses at least try to measure employee satisfaction in some form or another. But there is a growing recognition in business that satisfaction is not a good enough measure.

In the same way that customer satisfaction doesn't tell the whole story about customer loyalty, employee satisfaction doesn't tell the whole story about staff productivity. For example, an employee might be 'satisfied' because he has an easy job or likes the people he works with or is paid well, but this 'satisfaction' doesn't necessarily mean he is productive or committed to delivering the corporate vision. Ironically it may be the most dissatisfied employees that are the most performance-oriented and really want to do all that they can to deliver to the organizational vision and mission. In such cases their dissatisfaction may be a reflection of their inability to do that well enough and not a reflection of their commitment.

As a result, employee engagement surveys emerged as a mechanism for assessing employee *contribution*, rather than just satisfaction, which could be misleading.

Whatever metric you use, it's clear that if you want to hunt down performance improvements and increase revenue and growth you must measure how satisfied and engaged your people are.

Satisfaction and engagement matters

In 2007 Gallup estimated that 73 per cent of US employees were actively disengaged, costing the US economy up to $350 billion per year in lost productivity. In other words, the disengaged employees either just turned up to work and went through the motions or they actively sought to do as little as possible.

If your employees are disengaged your business will almost certainly be haemorrhaging money, as well as losing key talent.

Conversely, high engagement can provide significant commercial advantages. Leading global HR consultancy Towers Watson found that companies with highly engaged employees generate more marketplace power than their competitors. Their data collected over 36 months for 40 global companies showed that companies with a highly-engaged workforce turned in significantly better financial performance than those businesses with a disengaged workforce.

In a separate analysis, Tower Watson found that organisations that consistently show higher engagement levels than average produced shareholder returns 9.3 per cent higher than the returns for the S&P 500 Index.

Measuring satisfaction and engagement in practice

Employee satisfaction index and employee engagement level are the two main KPIs for measuring how happy, productive and committed your people are to your business objectives.

KPI: Employee Satisfaction Index

The key performance question Employee Satisfaction Index helps to answer is: 'To what extent are our employees happy in their job?'

Employee Satisfaction, often referred to as *climate* is usually measured through a survey. In order to get really meaningful data the survey must be anonymous, so people feel free to express their opinions without the possibility of reprisal or career limitation. However, what that survey measures will depend on what aspects of your business you want to find out about. For example, you may be specifically interested in how satisfied your employees are with one or more of the following:

- Leadership and direction
- Internal Communications
- Staff development opportunities
- Culture
- Facilities
- Work, pay and conditions

Your Employee Satisfaction Index may be completely different to your competitors'. You need to work out what you want to measure and create a survey that measures and weighs those things.

The formula therefore relates to how you value the different elements or questions of your survey. You can either give them all the same ranking or weigh different parts higher or lower.

For example, say you sent an engagement survey about departmental leadership to everyone in the marketing department – 50 people. In the survey they were asked to rank their agreement or disagreement with 3 statements from strongly disagree (1) to strongly agree (5).

> Statement 1: I trust our leaders? – with an average score of 3
>
> Statement 2: Our leaders are strong communicators? – with an average score of 4
>
> Statement 3: I feel supported by our leaders? – with an average score of 2.

If the department feels they are all equally important, it could simply create the index by adding the scores up and dividing them by 3 (the number of questions):

$$(3+4+2)/3 = 3$$

This metric is particularly useful because it allows you to examine the data across different classifications or parameters such as age, level of responsibility, department, location, and so on.

You can also conduct additional statistical analysis, such as correlation or regression to identify issues which are driving satisfaction and the relative impact of these issues on satisfaction. Correlation analysis measures the strength in the relationships between variables and regression analysis measures how much one variable affects another.

This metric is usually measured through an annual survey. However a better way to measure the trend and get an on-going read of employee satisfaction is to survey 10 per cent of the workforce every month for 10 months. That way everyone still only completes the survey once a year but you have 10 data points not one and that insight can allow you to make in-time corrections to ensure on-going high satisfaction scores.

Make sure you use the insights you gain from the employee survey and fix as many of the things that are causing dissatisfaction as possible. If you uncover low satisfaction and do nothing about it, it will only make matters worse!

When your people feel you are listening to them, that what they say matters and that you are genuinely trying to address the issues they raise, then not only will they continue to complete the surveys – giving you additional on-going insights – but they are also much more likely to bring you good ideas and process improvements too.

KPI: Employee Engagement Level

The key performance question Employee Engagement Level helps to answer is: 'To what extent are our employees committed to playing their part in the delivery of our vision and mission?'

Like the satisfaction index, employee engagement is measured via a survey. The most common survey is probably the one devised and deployed by the Gallup Organisation.

Gallup's survey consists of just 12 questions and is focused on uncovering the specific behaviours or characteristics that will make a quantifiable difference to performance in the workplace. Employees answer the 12 questions through straight yes/no responses, and the results are then turned into a score. You can find the full list of questions at: `https://q12.gallup.com/Public/en-us/Features`

Based on your employees' responses you can see the percentage of employees that are actively engaged, engaged, disengaged or actively disengaged and the likely financial consequences of engagement.

There are other ways to measure engagement and you can certainly create your own survey around key things that you want to establish. The benefit of the Gallup survey is that you can compare your results to other businesses and your competitors.

Engagement surveys should be short and focused, and it's probably best to secure an external provider to conduct the research and deliver the results. The external provider should, however, be able to demonstrate a link between high engagement scores and superior financial performance. They should also be able to drill down into the data to explain what parts of the business have disengaged employees so you can find appropriate solutions.

Like satisfaction surveys, engagement surveys must trigger behavioural change. If they don't they can do more harm than good, as employees become even more de-motivated and disengaged.

Would your Employees Recommend Your Business?

In many ways, your employees are your internal customers. It matters what they think of your business. When your employees believe in what the business is seeking to do, align themselves with the corporate values and admire the ethical, environmental or financial performance of your company, then that pride shines through in the way they treat and interact with customers and suppliers.

In years gone by it didn't really matter whether employees liked the business they worked for, as they did their jobs. In fact the cliché of 'them and us', indicating the divide between management and other employees, showed that there really wasn't much love lost. But in an age where every thought, slight and observation can be shared with the online universe, having employees on your side is increasingly important.

Employees are often seen as presenting the unfiltered truth about businesses, untouched by propaganda or marketing spin. So when a business has employees that love the business and shout about that passion from the rooftops, people listen.

Furthermore, if you consider the power of sites like LinkedIn at finding new employees and sourcing talent, what other employees say about a future employer matters. A cursory search for a business name online will often uncover blog posts or discussion threads from unhappy employees, which can quickly alert people to whether the business is a good business to work for or not.

Perhaps the best measure for whether your employees would recommend you is the *staff advocacy score*. Similar to the Net promoter Score (see Chapter 12) that asks customers whether they would recommend the product, business or service the staff advocacy score asks employees if they would recommend your business to a friend.

The extent to which your employees would advocate your business to others is an important KPI to measure, because it is closely linked to staff satisfaction and loyalty. These in turn have implications for customer loyalty, your brand and profitability, not to mention your ability to attract new talent and keep the talent you already have.

Measuring the trends

You typically measure the staff advocacy score annually but I believe this is a mistake because it just provides one *datapoint* – a single snapshot of how employees view the business at any one given time.

Clearly this score will fluctuate throughout the year, and will depend on the individual experiences of the people you ask but also on the collective performance of the business and what opportunities and threats the business faces throughout the year. For example employees of a large clothing manufacturer may be rocked by news that the company uses factories in the developing world that employ children to produce some garments. If they are asked whether they would recommend the business after such a story they are likely to say 'No'. If several months later, however, the story turns out to be false then they may bounce back to 'Yes'.

It is therefore much more useful and insightful to measure the trend of whether your people would recommend you to others – either as a place to buy products or a place to work. This can easily be done simply by surveying a percentage of your workforce every month until everyone has completed the survey over the course of one year.

That way you still only survey each employee once a year but the resulting data is much more useful. Ongoing data can also alert you to problems long before they escalate into an online public relations nightmare.

Measuring staff advocacy in practice

The main KPI for measuring whether your employees would recommend your business is the Staff Advocacy Score.

The key performance question Staff Advocacy Score helps to answer is: 'To what extent are our employee's advocates of our business?' You derive the data you need to calculate this metric from a staff survey that asks just one question: 'How likely is it that you would recommend this company as an employer to a friend?'

The respondent is then asked to rank their response on a scale from 0 – 10 (0 being not likely to 10 being very likely). Based on the response to this single question you can then group your employees into three categories:

- ✔ **Advocates (9-10):** Advocates are loyal, enthusiastic employees who will promote you as a potential employer.

- ✔ **Passives (7-8):** Passives are satisfied but unenthusiastic employees. Not only are they unlikely to positively influence someone to join the business but they are more likely to leave the business.

- ✔ **Detractors (0-6):** Detractors are unhappy employees who could potentially damage your brand and put people off working for you through negative word of mouth.

The formula for calculating the Staff advocacy score is:

Staff advocacy score = percentage of advocates – percentage of detractors

For example say you survey 1000 of your employees and ask them the staff advocacy question. 982 employees respond as shown in Table 17-1:

Table 17-1	Typical staff advocacy score data
Score	*Number of Employees*
0	4
1	3
2	2
3	0
4	8
5	150
6	60
7	130
8	100
9	350
10	175

$$\text{Percentage of Advocates} = \frac{(350+175)}{982} \times 100 = 53.46 \text{ per cent}$$

$$\text{Percentage of Detractors} = \frac{(4+3+2+0+8+150+60)}{982} \times 100 = 23.11 \text{ per cent}$$

$$\text{Staff advocacy score} = 53.46 \text{ per cent} - 23.11 \text{ per cent} = 30.35 \text{ per cent}$$

Although the staff advocacy score will give you a neat, simple number to slot into performance dashboards, it won't tell you why employees are advocates or detractors. Seeing as the score is based on one question it is always wise to include a couple of additional open qualitative questions to gather more detail. Consider asking what employee particularly like or dislike about the company and/or how they would improve things if they could.

This additional detail will identify areas for improvement which could effectively move detractors to passives or advocates, and passives up into advocates. Ironically if you address what is making someone really unhappy they can often before your most vocal advocates.

Looking All Around – 360 Degree Feedback

Great companies are built by great employees. Conversely, poor companies are often the result of poor employees. You need to measure people performance so you know which your business is! In order to drive growth and profitability, you need to develop and motivate your employees. That ensures that you maintain the skill level required in the business, and that you keep your talented employees. Performance reviews or appraisals play an important role in that development process as they allow line managers to have a constructive review of an employee's performance. If done well, performance appraisals provide a positive experience that contributes to the overall employment and career development experience of an employee and helps to strengthen the relationship between line managers and their reports.

Unfortunately performance appraisals are rarely done well. Most performance reviews are woefully inadequate, demoralising and almost entirely focused on the negative. As a result, the mere mention of, 'performance review' or 'performance appraisal' creates universal eye-rolling.

Performance review training for managers may encourage them to deliver a few cursory compliments before focusing on what the individual didn't do well but the employees know what's coming.

Performance reviews by their nature are always looking backwards – not forwards – and almost always reflect the opinion of just one person. If an employee doesn't get on with his or her manager, then this strained dynamic can influence the performance review even when it shouldn't.

Understanding the need for a full picture

In an effort to improve this dreaded annual dance and bring about genuine improvement it was clear to most managers and HR professionals that a broader, fuller picture of performance was required. 360-degree feedback is the result.

360-degree feedback provides an individual with a broad assessment of their performance based on the views of those who have a stake in their performance. Those stakeholders may be their supervisor, manager, co-workers, customers (internal and external), suppliers and so on. The person being assessed also has the opportunity to assess their own performance and it is often the comparison between this self-assessment and the perception of other stakeholders that allows each individual to understand his or her effectiveness. Often these insights, which can illuminate training and development needs, actually help the individual to improve.

Because 360-degree feedback is scored, this approach offers a more objective basis for pay rises and promotions than the old type of performance review, which was very subjective.

Measuring 360-degree feedback in practice

The key performance question 360-degree feedback helps to answer is: 'How well are our people performing in the eyes of those who have a stake in their performance?' Data for the 360-degree feedback is collected through an annual survey – usually web-based.

There is no one formula for the creation of 360-degree feedback, because what is asked and measured will depend on what is considered important within your business. There are, however, certain areas that are almost always included. These are:

- ✔ **Question number:** Always number the questions in a 360-degree feedback to make reference and analysis easier.

- ✔ **Key skills or capabilities:** This should always be tailored to the key skills required for the person to do his or her job. For example a marketing manager may be assessed for key skills of communications, planning, reporting, creativity and problem solving. A warehouse supervisor may be assessed for key skills of organisation, planning, communications, people management, problem solving.

- ✔ **Skill component or element:** This will seek to dig deeper into the essential component parts of the key skills. For example the marketing manager may be assessed on active listening skills (within communications) or generates ideas (within creativity) or finds innovative solutions (within problem solving). The number of components per key skill will vary with every position and should only focus on things that really matter to performance.

- ✔ **Specific feedback questions:** These questions should relate to skill component for example the feedback question for the active listening component may ask, 'Does the person take care to listen and understand properly when you/others are speaking to him/her?'

- ✔ **Tick-box or grade box:** Usually the grading is presented as a Likert scale which asks the assessor to rate the person being assessed on a score from 1–5 or 1–10, where 1 is very poor and the higher number is very good. Be sure to clarify the rating system and make sure everyone is clear on the definitions of each score, so that accurate comparisons can be made between results.

For the 360-degree feedback to be as useful as possible it is often completed anonymously. In other words, the people doing the assessing and scoring the individual are not known to the individual.

Confidentiality is important to both parties in the feedback process. Those doing the assessing are likely to be more honest about the individual's performance when they can remain anonymous. After all, it would be a brave employee indeed who highlighted his boss's performance failings when it was that exact person who determined whether or not the employee is promoted or gets a pay rise. The person being assessed may also feel very anxious about the process if he or she is not assured that the results will remain confidential.

To help ensure confidentiality:

✔ **Select a neutral administrator.** You can either recruit a representative from HR or hire an external consultant to administer the 360-degree feedback so than anonymity is assured.

✔ **Create user-names and passwords for access to the online survey.**

✔ **Make sure the online systems encrypt the response data and the data is stored on secure servers.**

A good 360-degree feedback survey should only ask relevant questions that can impact performance and direct improvement. Focus on important observable behaviour, question one behaviour at a time and use clear language.

In an effort to raise management performance internet giant Google set out to answer two questions:

✔ 'What is it that makes a great manager?'

✔ 'What are the behaviours that make managers struggle?'

Based on some extensive research that involved interviews with their managers, 360-degree feedback surveys of their employees, and regression analysis of things such as job performance and employee satisfaction, Google was able to identify eight behaviours that make a great manager in Google:

✔ Is a good coach

✔ Empowers the team and does not micromanage

✔ Expresses interest/concern for team members' success and personal wellbeing

✔ Is productive and results-orientated

✔ Is a good communicator – listens and shares information

✔ Helps with career development

✔ Has a clear vision/strategy for the team

✔ Has important technical skills that help him/her advice the team

In addition the research alerted them to the top three reasons why managers were struggling in their role:

✔ Has a tough transition (for example, suddenly promoted, hired from outside with little training)

✔ Lacks a consistent philosophy/approach to performance management and career development

✔ Spends too little time on managing and communicating.

Google then acted on these insights and now gear the 360-degree feedback surveys for managers around these aspects. Conducted twice a year the surveys have allowed Google to instigate an early warning system to detect both great and struggling managers. Google has also revised its management training in light of these findings.

How Much Value Are Employees Generating?

Knowing whether your people are delivering on their objectives and performing well is one thing. Quantifying the value your employees generate is another.

As your biggest cost base it's important that you understand how much value your employees add to the financial performance of the organisation. Most businesses will employ a range of HR KPIs, and yet research suggests that less than half actively track the impact of employees on financial business performance.

Because of the cost implications of hiring more and more people, most businesses aim to deliver as much revenue as possible with the fewest number of employees. Putting revenues in relation to the number of employees that were needed to create that revenue is an important productivity measure.

Measuring the value your employees generate in practice

There are two main KPIS for measuring how much value employees generate – Human Capital Value Added (HCVA) and Return per Employee (RPE).

KPI: Human Capital Value Added (HCVA)

The key performance question Human Capital Value Added (HCVA) helps to answer is: 'To what extent are our employees adding value to the bottom line?' You can collect the data needed to calculate this metric from the financial accounting system or financial statements, and you usually calculate it quarterly.

> HCVA = Revenue – Total Costs – Employment cost/Average full-time Employees

Total costs are the difference between the Revenue and Profit Before Taxes and employee costs are pay and benefits. Here *full-time employees* means *full-time equivalent*, so if you have 5 full-time employees and 2 that work half days, then Average Full Time Employees here would be 6 (5 + 0.5 + 0.5).

For example, say Company A employs 800 employees and enjoys revenue of $50 million. Total costs are $22 million and employment costs are $15 million.

> HCVA = 50,000,000 – 22,000,000 – 15,000,000/800 = $53,750

Looking at costs of full time employees alone can sometimes distort the picture because most businesses incur further employee related expenses such as the cost for contingents, absence, and turnover. These can be added to the formula.

An alternative formula for calculating HCVA is:

> HCVA = Operating Profit + Employment Cost/Average Full Time Employee

KPI: Revenue per Employee (RPE)

The key performance question Revenue per Employee (RPE) helps to answer is: 'How productive are our employees?' You can easily collect the data needed to calculate this metric from the financial statements, and you usually calculate it quarterly.

> RPE = Revenue/Number of equivalent full-time employees

If a company generates a revenue of $1,000,000 and has 29 employees, then the RPE would be $34,482 per employee ($1,000,000/29).

Although there are no general rules or benchmarks for RPE, it is a commonly used KPI, so data around this metric exists. The higher the RPE the better as it is an indication of productivity and efficiency. The metric is especially useful when comparing it to other companies in your sector. Below is a sample of RPE results for some large companies.

Chapter 18

Measuring Human Resources Performance

In This Chapter

▶ Putting Human Resources under the spotlight

▶ Measuring how good your business is at attracting and keeping talent

▶ Analysing the effectiveness of training.

*T*o provide an accurate business-wide picture of performance it follows that all areas of a business should be measured in some form or other. The finance department is usually the department that is most used to measurements, but increasingly sales, marketing, customer services and operations are measured to help a business know where it is against its objectives.

Human Resources (HR) is not exempt from inspection. Often HR is only really challenged when there is an economic downturn or the business is seeking to squeeze costs. But HR measurement is important all the time, especially around two of their main functions – recruiting and training.

The KPIs detailed in this chapter allow you to measure HR performance so you can establish just how effective your recruitment is, whether you are consistently hiring the right people and whether your training is delivering a measurable return or not.

Charting How Well You're Recruiting

Recruitment is an expensive business and that's true at any level, not just senior executives. You need to advertise the vacancy, sift through the applications and whittle them down to a short list. You need to interview those people, often more than once, and when you have chosen someone they need to be inducted into the business and trained. Then and only then do you find out whether the choice was a good one or not.

It's important for any business to fill vacancies quickly, but getting it wrong can be very costly.

On the one hand, failure to fill open jobs quickly has a number of negative consequences. If there aren't enough people to complete the work, existing workers can become frustrated and overworked (risking further loss). Lost revenue becomes a real possibility as the business can't keep up with demand. If there aren't enough staff, the business won't be able to run to capacity, missing out on potential growth. In addition, cost implications develop as you scramble to fill the gaps with costly temporary or agency staff.

On the other hand, filling vacancies too quickly at the expense of a thorough vetting process can lead to even greater problems down the track – especially at a senior level. Most senior positions are arranged through a recruitment agency, which can take a large fee for the process. In addition, if the person is not a good fit for the business they can set you back even further.

Getting recruitment right is clearly important.

Finding and keeping talent

One of the traditional metrics used to measure how good you are at finding talent is Time to Hire. This metric is calculated as the time between the initial approval or posting of a vacant position and the final acceptance of a job offer from a qualified and approved candidate.

As a strategic KPI this metric is primarily interested in measuring the elapsed time between recognising a need and filling that need when the chosen candidate starts work. Obviously, getting the right people into the right jobs as quickly as possible is going to benefit your productivity and financial performance, so time to hire is an important metric to track.

In addition, once you have the right people you need to keep them. Metrics that can help to shed light on your ability to retain talent are *churn rates*, *absenteeism* and *average tenure*. If people are joining your business and leaving quickly, or they are taking too many unauthorised days off, or always using up their allocation of sick leave then something is wrong – either in the recruitment process or the business. And you need to know which so you can solve the problem and keep the people you want.

No business will always get recruitment right. People change their minds or receive better offers. They may get into a business and find they just don't fit, or that their priorities change.

In addition, not everyone who leaves your business will be a loss! Measuring employee churn rate against regretted churn can help you make sure you are keeping the people you want to keep and helping the rest to move on.

Moving beyond the trivial

Competition for the best talent is fierce and that is not going to change. The very best people will have options and you need to know what those other options look like. You need to be offering an attractive salary package, and it needs to remain attractive when the individual you are looking to attract then looks at what your competitor is offering.

Understanding how the salary your company pays compares to the salary your competitors are paying, or the industry standard, not only helps you to position your offer properly but also gives you insight into how tempted your existing talent may be to leave and work for someone else.

Pay is never the only reason someone joins or stays with a particular firm but it is naive to assume that other factors will be enough if the pay difference is too wide. Comparing your salary rates with others will help you ensure you remain competitive without paying too much or too little. Knowing this information is also good for pay review meetings, especially if you are already paying a competitive salary.

Measuring recruitment effectiveness in practice

A number of KPIs exist that can help you measure your recruitment effectiveness and your ability to find and keep good people. The most popular ones are *Time to Hire*, *Salary Competitiveness Ratio*, *Absenteeism Bradford Factor*, *Average Employee Tenure* and *employee churn rate*.

KPI: Time to Hire

The key performance question Time to Hire helps to answer is: 'How well are we able to fill vacant positions in our business?' The data you will need to calculate this metric may be in your HR system or you may need to find it out manually. Ideally you should measure Time to Hire quarterly.

> Time to Hire = Elapsed time between Time of posting and Time to Start (in working days)

For example if you advertise for a Warehouse supervisor on the 18th of August 2014 and the chosen candidate starts on the 8th of September 2014 then the Time to Hire is 22 days.

Once established, Time to Hire can be averaged for specific job roles or calculated across the entire company. As a metric it's most useful to compare between job roles because time to hire will vary between industry and job roles – usually increasing with the seniority of the position.

Benchmarks for commercial companies range from 20 to 80 days. Public service organisations are however notoriously poor around time to hire. In 2010 the US time to hire in the public sector was 110 days – dropping from a staggering 180 days!

KPI: Salary Competitiveness Ratio (SCR)

The key performance question Salary Competitiveness Ratio (SCR) helps to answer is: To what extent are we offering a competitive salary to our employees?

> SCR (Competitor) = Salary offered by your company/Salary offered by your competitor

or

> SCR (Industry) = Salary offered by your company/Average salary offered in the industry or sector

For example if you were paying $167,000 and your competitor was paying $189,000 for the same role then your competitor SCR would be 0.88.

If you operate in a competitive market the general rule of thumb is that you will need to offer equal or slightly higher pay than your competitors, so a ratio of 1 or over. If your company is already very attractive – perhaps you have a strong brand or excellent non-financial benefits – then you may secure the talent you need with an SCR of 0.9 or 1.

That said, measuring this metric can be easier said than done. Some industries are fairly open about how much they pay their staff where others are not.

One way to cheaply research salary is to look at competitor recruitment adverts in national newspapers or industry magazines, or use online recruitment websites to get an idea of what certain jobs in certain industries are paying.

KPI: Absenteeism Bradford Factor

The key performance question Absenteeism Bradford Factor helps to answer is: 'To what extent is unauthorised employee absenteeism a problem in our business?' People take time off work for many reasons, health, family emergencies or because they 'feel entitled to a day off'. Unfortunately short, unplanned absenteeism has been found to be much more disruptive that long term absenteeism. Obviously neither is great but this KPI was developed to identify the people who are taking too many unauthorised days off so the reasons can be reviewed.

Absenteeism Bradford Factor = Total number of days of unplanned absence × (Total number of individual episodes of absence)^2

For example if one of your employees was absent for one day, 10 times in a quarter, his total number of days off is 10 and the total number of episodes is 100 because it's the number of episodes squared (10×10). His Absenteeism Bradford Factor would be:

$10 \times 100\ (10 \times 10) = 1000$

Say another employee took 10 days unauthorised time off in one go. There are still 10 days of unplanned absenteeism but the number of episodes is only 1 (1×1). So that employee's Absenteeism Bradford Factor would be:

$(10 \times 1)/(1 \times 1) = 10$

Consider stepping in to review performance and seek to solve any issues at the following benchmarks:

- ✔ **Annually:** 80 or higher
- ✔ **Quarterly:** 27 or higher
- ✔ **Monthly:** 12 or higher

This metric can be particularly useful to link to reviews and intervention. For example you may institute a system whereby you issue a verbal warning to anyone who exceeds 51 points in any six month people. If improvements are not made then this will be followed by a written warning at 201 points and a final warning at 401 points prior to termination.

KPI: Average Employee Tenure

The key performance question Average Employee Tenure helps to answer is: 'To what extent do our employees stay loyal to our company? The data you need to calculate this metric will be available in the HR records and is usually calculated annually or six monthly.

Average Employee Tenure = Sum of all tenures/Number of full-time employees

For example say Company B employs 100 people:

- ✔ 5 people have been there for 1 year or less.
- ✔ 16 people have been there for 2 years
- ✔ 22 people have been there for 3 years
- ✔ 30 people have been there for 4 years
- ✔ 10 people have been there for 5 years
- ✔ 3 people have been there for 6 years
- ✔ 6 people have been there for 8 years
- ✔ 8 people have been there for 10 years

$$(5 \times 1) + (16 \times 2) + (22 \times 3) + (30 \times 4) + (10 \times 5) + (3 \times 6) + (6 \times 8) + (8 \times 10)/100 = 4.19$$

When you consider the cost, time and disruption associated with staff turnover keeping talent is every bit as important as attracting it in the first place. Longer tenure usually indicates stability however it can mean that employees are complacent.

Review this metric alongside employee churn rate to get a fuller picture of what is going on with your workforce.

KPI: Employee Churn Rate

The key performance question employee churn rate helps to answer is: 'How well are we retaining our staff?' The data you need to calculate this metric will be available in the HR records. Some industries have a higher churn rate than others so may wish to measure this metric monthly, for others quarterly may be sufficient.

Total number of leavers over a specific period/Average total number employed over same period × 100

The total number of leavers should include everyone who left the business regardless of reason – even if they were dismissed. For example in the first quarter of 2013 Company A dismissed three people, two more left because of illness, an additional eighteen left to take other positions and two retired. Company A employed 540 people on average in that quarter.

25/540 × 100 = 4.63 per cent

Even in industries such as call centres, hospitality and retailing where churn is common there is a growing appreciation that churn is expensive and should wherever possible be reduced.

Analysing How Well You're Training

Training and personal development is not just about increasing skills and making people more productive: It's also a key factor in attracting the right talent. Broadly speaking, talented individuals want to know that they are going to be developed once they are with a company, so they can increase their knowledge base and therefore value.

Analysing how well you're training your staff is therefore an important consideration.

That said, CEOs and business leaders want assurances that the training they are investing in is working and that the skills they are training people for are showing up back in the work place. When they can't get those assurances then training can often be one of the first areas to be pruned back on during a downturn. It is therefore essential that HR professionals can demonstrate validity.

The pitfalls and challenges of measuring training

The trouble with corporate training is that it is notoriously ineffective. Estimates suggest that up to 80 per cent of training never delivers the benefits it was initiated to deliver. In addition, a lot of corporate training focuses on soft skills such as leadership or communication. The term *soft skills* relates to how someone interacts with others. Such skills are considered harder to measure. It is, for example, much harder to measure how much a person inspires a group or how much emotional maturity they demonstrate in a difficult situation than it is to measure how many training days they attended last year.

Just because something is hard to measure doesn't mean it shouldn't be measured, and training is increasingly coming under the microscope. A growing library of best practice is emerging to trace how training expenditure affects financial performance. In other words, businesses are looking to trace the return on investment for every training dollar spent.

Although the need to measure training effectiveness was first brought to the attention of businesses by Donald Kirkpatrick in the 1950s, most businesses have struggled to achieve a useful measure in practice. The Kirkpatrick model, which is still used by companies around the world, has since been developed further by Dr Jack and Patti Phillips of the ROI Institute. Their *training ROI* methodology has since become the gold standard.

Measuring it in practice

The key performance question training ROI helps to answer is: 'How effective is our training in driving business results?' To use the Phillips methodology you must be accredited in their approach. You collect data in several ways, including surveys. Participants are questioned to ascertain their satisfaction with the training programme immediately after the event and follow-up questionnaires and surveys are delivered to participants and their managers several weeks after the training event to assess behavioural or performance changes.

Later still, data is collected to measure the training programme impact on areas such as output, quality, cost and customer satisfaction and the ROI is calculated.

The Phillips ROI model assesses five levels of training evaluation:

- ✔ **Level 1: Reaction and planned action.** At this level, participants' reaction to and satisfaction with the training programme is measured. Also captured are the planned actions that the delegates intend to implement back in the workplace.

- ✔ **Level 2: Learning.** This level is where an assessment is made on what participants believe they have learned in the programme (often through an end-of-class evaluation).

- ✔ **Level 3: Application.** At Level 3, data is collected to determine whether participants have implemented the HR programme successfully. This measures changes in on-the-job behaviour or actions as the programme is applied, implemented or utilised. Typically, questionnaire and survey instruments will be used to access this information.

- ✔ **Level 4: Business impact.** At this level, the actual business results of the programme are identified and a monetary value applied to the behavioral/skills changes. Typical Level 4 measures include output, quality, cost, time and customer satisfaction. However, even though the HR programme may produce a measurable business impact, the costs for the HR programme may still be too high.

- ✔ **Level 5: Return on investment.** This is where the actual ROI is calculated. Essentially, the ROI calculation is identical to the ROI ratio for any other business investment where the ROI is traditionally reported as earnings divided by investment.

  ROI = Benefits/Costs

If a company has run a training course that cost $50,000 and the benefits have been $75,000 then the return would be:

$75,000/$50,000 = 1.5

This means for every 1 dollar of investment the company is getting 1.5 dollars back.

Although most HR departments conduct evaluations to measure training satisfaction, whether someone is satisfied with the training, enjoyed the training or can remember a few salient points from the training doesn't mean that the training has been effective.

Getting to grips with Training ROI presents a real opportunity for HR departments to demonstrate the effectiveness of training and gain credibility. Too often HR is seen as a second-tier department that needs to prove its validity as a value adding organisation rather than a cost centre. Providing genuinely impactful training that positively influences the bottom line can do a great deal to reposition HR as an *investment* rather than a *cost*.

Part VII
The Part of Tens

For Dummies can help you get started with lots of subjects. Go to www.dummies.com to learn more and do more with *For Dummies*.

In this part . . .

- Develop effective KPIs by understanding the importance of strategy, ensuring that the right people have ownership of them and communicating them with maximum impact.

- Avoid the pitfalls involved in trying to measure everything, linking KPIs to incentives and failing to act on KPIs.

- Use the most important KPIs to work out how profitable your business is, what your customers think of you and how good you are at retaining key people.

Chapter 19

Ten Tips for Developing Effective KPIs

. . . .

In This Chapter

▶ Starting with strategy

▶ Ensuring the right people own the KPIs

▶ Communicating your KPIs for maximum impact and understanding

. . . .

*T*o ensure that you collect *only* commercially relevant data – the sort that drives results and supports fact-based decision making – stick to the following ten tips for developing effective KPIs.

Map Your Strategy

Always start with strategy. Without a firm stake in the ground about what your business is seeking to achieve, it is incredibly easy to end up with a dauntingly long list of possible indicators that you feel you could or should measure.

Your strategy therefore acts as a starting point from which you can then design appropriate KPIs. But it'll only work if it's clear! All too often companies create a 30- or 40-page strategy document that no one ever reads or understands. A really great way around this is to put the key strategic objectives on a single page to create a strategy map.

Identify the Questions You Need to Answer

Linking your KPIs to your strategy will immediately narrow your focus and make the relevant ones more obvious. Identifying the questions you need to answer will further narrow your focus, because questions give the indicators context.

Once you are clear on the questions the data needs to answer you can make sure that every indicator you subsequently choose or design is not only relevant to your strategy, but also provides the answers to very specific questions – the ones that will guide your strategy and inform your decision making.

Define Your Data Needs

Once you know what questions you are trying to answer, you need to define your data needs to establish what KPIs, metrics or data you need in order to answer those questions.

Forget about reality for a moment and consider what information and knowledge you want to have in an ideal world.

Everything can be measured!

Evaluate All Existing Data

Most companies are full of data. Often, KPIs are already being collected for all sorts of different reasons by different divisions and different managers. So it makes sense to evaluate all existing data to work out whether what you need is already being collected by someone, somewhere in the business, or perhaps it's almost being collected and a few tweaks to the collection process would deliver exactly what you need.

Perform a gap analysis by comparing what data you would ideally like to have with what you already have to see what's missing. Ask yourself what you need to change, tweak or implement to ensure the data collection is completely aligned with the strategy and will fully answer the questions you need answered. And then come up with the right indicators to deliver those objectives.

Find the Right Measurement Methodology

Once you know what information you need to collect, you need to find the right measurement methodology. Especially if you have to develop new KPIs or tweak existing ones.

For example, if you have a survey or an existing database in place, you have to evaluate whether you can you extract what you need from that. Sometimes finding the right methodology will mean pulling the data from different sources or aggregating it up. Knowing what you need is one thing, working out how to access and measure that information is another. Finding the right measurement methodology is critical.

Assign Ownership

Effective KPIs require two types of ownership. The first is the ownership of how the meaning and interpretation of the KPI is used. Someone must always be in charge of looking at the KPI, interpreting its meaning, monitoring how it's changing and what that means for the business. Obviously, it's important that those people were involved in the selection and creation of the KPI so they buy-in to its relevance otherwise they just won't use it!

The other type of ownership is of the data collection. Sometimes you can automate the process, but more often than not data collection will require some human interaction. Perhaps certain personnel are involved in transferring data from one database to another, or they have to collect it manually. Again those people need to understand why they are doing that and why it's so important.

Identify the Right Measurement Frequency

Measurement frequency has to be in line with the reporting frequency otherwise the data may lose impact and/or relevance.

For example, if you collect customer satisfaction data through a survey in the summer and report on the findings in the winter, then the findings are already six months out of date. It's always preferable to align measurement frequency with how and when the data is used in the organisation, because all data has a 'shelf-life'.

Ensure Costs and Efforts are Justified

Too often organisations spend a huge amount of time, money and effort collecting, analysing and reporting on data that is never actually used in the business.

It's vital that you ensure the cost and effort is justified. If you are not going to use the information, or the data does not answer the questions you need answered, don't waste time collecting it. If you consider staff surveys, for example, the cost can often run into six figures, and that doesn't even include downtime needed for staff to complete them, or the work involved in collating them. So, unless you have a *very* good reason for conducting the survey that is directly linked to your strategy, why do it? It's always worth stepping back for a moment to work out whether you really need the information you are about to collect and whether it will drive strategy and improve performance sufficiently to justify the time and cost involved.

Find the Right Supporting Data

KPIs are incredibly powerful in the right hands, but we need to acknowledge that we also have access to vast quantities of supporting data which is every bit as insightful and useful as traditional KPIs.

By finding the right supporting data, you can triangulate and verify your findings. So instead of having one data point you have several data points which can help to validate your findings.

Think of this like walking into a pitch black room – your KPI is your torch and you can shine the light into a corner and figure out what's in the room. But if you could also switch on a lamp and turn the light on in your smart phone you would get a much richer picture of the room, much more quickly. The datafication of our world, by which a vast amount of information is being created and stored every minute, means we now have billions of datapoints of supporting data that can potentially transform the pitch black into a magnificent starry night. By finding the right supporting data you can make much better sense of the world, much more quickly, which in turn can help decision making in real time.

Finding the Right Picture to Communicate your KPI

Finally, it's always wise to think about how best to communicate your KPIs so that their insights are obvious, engaging and apparent to all.

Many KPIs are communicated in long reports full of numbers or tables, perhaps with traffic light graphics to indicate urgency. This is not good enough. Really effective KPIs will illustrate trends and variations in data, and engage the reader. In addition, there is no point hiding the insights in excessive reports that no one ever reads.

Seek to find the right picture so that the nuggets of wisdom extracted from the data are clear, unambiguous, accessible and therefore actionable to and by everyone who needs them.

Chapter 20

The Ten Biggest KPI Mistakes to Avoid

- -

In This Chapter

▶ Measuring everything

▶ Linking KPIs to incentives

▶ Failing to act on KPIs

- -

*T*he use of KPIs is one of the business topics that has been so widely written about and discussed in management and leadership circles that most people think 'They have it covered'. And yet like most familiar things this familiarity can breed contempt. Below are the ten biggest mistakes people make when instituting a KPI methodology or framework. Avoid them at all costs!

Measure Everything That is Easy to Measure

This is by far the biggest mistake that people make with KPIs – they work out what is easy to measure and measure *everything* that is easy to measure regardless of its relevance to the business.

Senior executive teams will often brainstorm KPIs and what they could measure. Usually the indicators they end up with will be the ones they have heard of, read about in a management journal or indicators they are *already* measuring. Obviously this is not the best way to develop KPIs because the resulting list is very often overwhelmingly long, the indicators are not relevant to the strategy of the business and do not answer the most critical questions.

Measure Everything Everyone Else is Measuring

A trap that many businesses fall into is looking to other companies and competitors to see what they are measuring, and then just doing the same.

For example a business leader may notice that many businesses are conducting staff surveys or customer experience surveys and think that they'd better do one too. Rather than taking a step back and working out what questions they need to ask they look elsewhere at the questions other businesses are asking and follow suit. As a result what they measure is often just regurgitated existing KPIs, or metrics prompted by external sources or the most recent leadership book. The ones they *should* be measuring are the ones that are directly relevant to that business.

Not Linking KPIs to Strategy

KPIs are only really useful if they are aligned to your strategy and inform strategic decision making. Anything else is just window dressing. When KPIs are not linked to strategy or determined by strategy then the company is always wasting huge amounts of time and money collecting information that is never then used by the business.

Not Separating Strategic KPIs from Other Data

There is no shortage of data and information inside most businesses, including financial,sales, customer, legislative and compliance data.

The problem, however, is that often all the KPIs are lumped together in one long KPI report or on an indecipherable dashboard. Business leaders and decision makers are time-poor; they don't want to have to wade through pages and pages of KPIs to ferret out the really critical ones. As a result the ones that could really direct strategy and inform decision making are lost in a sea of irrelevant information.

Hardwiring KPIs to Incentives

Hardwiring KPIs to incentives is really dangerous in business, and so easily creates unintended consequences.

The true purpose of a KPI is to help people inside the business know where they are in relation to where they want to be. KPIs act like a compass on a sea voyage. But once those KPIs are linked to incentives, they stop being a navigation tool and become a target an individual has to hit to secure an incentive such as bonus or pay rise. And as soon as that happens the individuals involved can become very creative in how they manipulate the information – or their behaviour – to ensure they receive the incentive.

When the number of people on waiting lists became an incentive-linked KPI within the National Health Service (NHS) a few years ago, managers, administrators and doctors just got creative and delayed putting patients on a waiting list in the first place. This had the effect of massaging the data, giving the impression of diminishing waiting lists.

Not Involving Executives in the KPI Selection

What I see in my work with senior executives is that they get excited about strategy and the big picture. Those who are interested in numbers might want to design specific KPIs (finance directors, for example), but most executives are not. As a result, senior executives who work on the strategy know that they need KPIs and dashboards to monitor and understand what's happening, but they then delegate the process of identifying or designing the right KPIs to someone else.

This is a mistake. The senior executives must be involved in the decision making process, otherwise they will not feel ownership of what is created. If they don't feel ownership of the KPIs, they won't use them. It's very important that the senior team think about the KPIs, engage with the questions they are seeking answers to and sign off the chosen KPIs, so that there is a clear, strong, understood connection between the strategy, the KPIs and the questions those KPIs will answer.

Not Analysing Your KPIs to Extract Insights

Another common mistake with KPIs is that no one inside the business is really analysing the data to extract business relevant insights. No one is working out how the data relates to corporate or industry benchmarks or how the metric has changed over time and what that might mean for the business.

This is often down to a disconnection between the decision makers and those who are doing the reporting. Often, the analysis is done at lower levels of the organisation and reported to the top. Those lower down don't understand the relevance of the data, so are just presenting it. Those at the top delegated the KPI design to others, so are not connected to the way the information is presented. It's vital that someone at the right level looks at the data and deciphers what it all actually means for the business.

Not Challenging Your KPIs

Once a business has identified or designed the right KPIs, it often never questions or challenges them as to whether they remain relevant, linked to strategy or useful in helping the business answer critical questions. It is important to make sure that you are always collecting the right data, collecting it often enough and are using what you collect so don't be afraid to challenge your KPIs.

If you don't KPIs can easily become a 'tick box' exercise that allow managers to say they have them and they look at them rather than being a real time navigation tool for better outcomes and performance.

Not Updating Your KPIs

The business strategy and information needs of companies are rarely static. They change, yet too often the KPIs do not.

Too often companies go through the process of designing their KPIs and then they run with exactly the same KPIs for five or ten years, even though their strategy has changed several times during the same period. Whenever there is a change in strategy, corporate priorities or the questions you need to answer, you need to review and update your KPIs to make sure you only measure what you need to measure, and that the KPIs remain relevant and aligned to the new strategy.

Not Acting on Your KPIs

KPIs can shape strategy and inform fact-based decision making inside business, but only if those inside the business act on them. In the end it doesn't matter how great your reporting system is or how brilliantly you've aligned the KPIs to strategy, how cleverly you've sought answers to business critical questions or even how well you've captured and presented the relevant KPIs: If they are not used as they were intended to be used, then it's all been a waste of time and effort.

Chapter 21

The Top Ten KPIs to Use

In This Chapter

▶ Working out how profitable the business is

▶ Establishing whether your customers would recommend you

▶ Working out what your employees think of your business

There are 1000s of KPIs that are commonly used in business. That's a lot of information, a lot of data collection and a lot of report reading! But don't panic . . . here are the top ten KPIs you absolutely must know about for your business.

Revenue Growth Rate

The purpose of business is to make money or revenue. Revenue, also known as turnover, is the income that the business generates through sales of goods and services.

Revenue growth rate helps you to answer the question: How well are we growing the business. This KPI is simply this quarter's (or any other time frame such as month or year) revenue compared to the previous quarter (or any other time frame). This data can be extracted from the general ledger and captured in the income statement.

Always compare like with like for a meaningful comparison.

Net Profit Margin

Net profit margin helps you to answer the question: 'How much profit are we generating for each dollar in sales?' This metric is also known as return on sales or net income margin and it is a key metric in explaining how well a business is run. A low net profit margin could indicate that the operating costs are too high or there is something wrong with your pricing strategy. This information you need to calculate net profit margin is available on your income statement and is calculated as follows:

Net profit margin = Net profit/Revenues × 100

Cash Conversion Cycle (CCC)

The most common cause of business difficulties is liquidity. The business simply runs out of cash. This KPI helps to avoid this by helping you to answer the question: How well are we doing at maintaining a healthy cash position?

This metric takes three things into account:

- ✔ The amount of time required to sell inventory (*days inventory outstanding* or DIO)

- ✔ The amount of time required to collect receivables (*days sales outstanding* or DSO)

- ✔ The amount of time you have to pay your bills without incurring penalty (*days payable outstanding* or DPO)

You can get the data you need to calculate CCC by analysing the sales records to establish the information in the preceding list. Calculate it using the following formula:

CCC = DIO + DSO – DPO

Net Promoter Score

This KPI seeks to answer the question: To what extent are our customers satisfied and loyal? Instead of seeking the answer through customer surveys, which are notoriously expensive and subjective, NPS was developed as 'the one number you need to know'. On a scale of 0 to 10 (where 0 is very unlikely and 10 is very likely) your customers are asked one simple question: How likely is it that you would recommend (your company or your product or service) to a friend or colleague?

'Promoters' are those that score 9 to 10 and are loyal advocates of your product or service, likely to keep buying and recommend you to others. 'Passives' and those that score 7 to 8 who may be satisfied but unenthusiastic about your product or service which means they are potentially vulnerable to your competitors offering. 'Detractors' are those customers who score 0 to

6 in response to the above question. These customers are unhappy and can potentially damage through negative word of mouth. Calculate NPS using the following formula:

NPS = Percentage of Promotors – Percentage of Detractors

Customer Engagement

This is a particularly useful metric for those businesses whose strategy involves building a loyal customer base. This KPI seeks to answer the question: 'To what extent are our customers engaged with our organisation?' Loyalty and engagement go beyond satisfaction. Indeed many companies have found that satisfied customers still leave the business. Satisfaction is often not enough.

There are many ways to measure customer engagement but one of the most popular is Gallup's customer engagement ratio know as the CE[11] because it seeks answers to 11 engagement questions – eight emotional attachment questions and three rational loyalty questions – to quantify customer engagement.

Customer Profitability

Customer profitability is the difference between the revenue earned or sales made over a period of time and the costs associated with the customer relationship during the same period. This KPI seeks to answer the question: 'To what extent are we generating profits from our customers?'

Customer profitability is not a static score and covers several different timeframes.

- **Historical value:** looking at value earned over an extended period of time such as previous financial year.

- **Current value:** Looking at value earned over a shorter time span such as a month.

- **Present value:** Looking at expected value earned and cost streams in the future

- **Life-time value:** Looking at projected revenue and costs streams from the existing relationship and new business expected to be conducted with that customer.

Relative Market Share

This KPI allows you to index your business or brand's market share against that of your leading competitors. It therefore helps you to answer the question: 'How well are we developing our market share in comparison to our competitors?' You can find the information you need to calculate this KPI from analysis of annual reports or market research, often available in the public domain. Use the following formula:

> Relative market share (per cent) = Organisation's market share/Largest competitor's market share

Capacity Utilisation Rate (CUR)

CUR helps business leaders to answer the question: 'To what extent are we leveraging our full production/work potential?' This KPI allows business leaders to measure if the business is working to capacity. You may have to calculate the data required to measure this KPI manually at the start but you can then automate collection based on output. Use the following formula:

> (Actual capacity in time period t)/(Possible capacity in time period t) × 100

Staff Advocacy Score

Happy employees are more productive; they provide better customer service and deliver consistently better performance. The staff advocacy score is the KPI that will help you to measure staff moral and whether your people are on your side. This KPI seeks to answer the question: To what extent are my employees advocates of our business?

Usually collected via a survey the staff advocacy score is similar to NPS but for staff not customers. On a scale of 0 to 10 employees are ranked as Advocates (score 9–10), passives (7–8) and Detractors (score 0–6). Staff advocacy score is therefore percentage of advocates – percentage of detractors.

Sustainability Index

The Sustainability Index is a KPI companies can create based on a number of other indicators including carbon footprint, water footprint, energy consumption, waste recycling, supply chain miles, and others. Every organisation can create their own unique composite formula based on the sustainability issues most relevant to their business or industry.

Consumers are increasingly interested in sustainability as well as where and how company's products are produced. Those businesses that can demonstrate a favourable sustainability index will increasingly gain a competitive advantage from their effort.

Index

• A •

absenteeism, 254
Absenteeism Bradford Factor, 257
absolute target, 24
actively disengaged customers, 181
Advanced Performance Institute, 4,
    102, 105
advocates, employees as, 245
Analyse Six Sigma tool, 210
analysing
  competitors, 185–186
  Key Performance Indicators (KPIs) to
    extract insights, 272
  training, 259–261
analytics, 100–103
annual rate of return, 156
applying
  KPI design template, 81–90
  quantitative methods, 76–77
ASCI score, 172
assessing
  about, 21–22
  brand equity, 195–196
  brand power, 194–196
  cash, 135–140
  cash conversion cycle (CCC), 137–138
  cash flow, 137–140
  churn, 174–175
  cost per lead, 192–194
  customer conversion, 191–192, 193–194
  customer engagement, 180–182
  customer Key Performance Indicators
    (KPIs), 16
  customers' lifetime value (CLV), 179–180
  delivery in full, on time rate (DIFOT),
    220–221
  Earned Value, 204–206
  eliminating fear of, 35–36

employee Key Performance Indicators
    (KPIs), 18
engagement of customers, 182
engagement of employees, 241–243
financial efficiency, 153–161
financial Key Performance Indicators
    (KPIs), 14–15
identifying frequency of, 267
impact of Internet and social media, 51
Innovation Pipeline Strength (IPS),
    222–224
internal efficiency, 207–225
internal productivity, 213–222
Inventory Shrinkage rate (ISR), 222
IT performance, 227–236
IT project performance, 233–236
IT service delivery, 228–233
Key Performance Indicators (KPIs),
    202–206
liquidity, 141–143
market growth rate, 185–186, 186–187
market share, 190
mistakes with, 269–270
Net Promoter Score (NPS), 168–169
operational Key Performance Indicators
    (KPIs), 16–17
opportunity cost, 147–148
order fulfilment cycle time (OFCT), 219
people performance, 239–252
Price/Earnings (P/E) ratio, 149–150
profit margins, 129–132
profitability, 123–129, 176–178
Project Cost Variance, 204
Project Schedule Variance, 203
quality, 207–225, 210–211
recruiting, 253–258
recruitment effectiveness, 255–258
retention, 174–175
return on assets (ROA), 161

assessing *(continued)*
 return on capital employed (ROCE),
  156–158
 return on equity (ROE), 158–160
 return on investment (ROI), 153–156,
  155–156
 revenue growth, 132–134
 rework levels, 216
 Satisfaction Index, 171–172
 satisfaction of employees, 241–243
 service delivery, 229–230
 Six Sigma Key Performance Indicators
  (KPIs), 211–212
 staff advocacy, 245–246
 360-degree feedback, 248–250
 total shareholder return (TSR), 150–151
 training, 259–261
 trends, 244–245
 usefulness to answering questions, 72
 usefulness to decision-making, 72
 waste, 213–215
 whether projects are on budget, 201–202
 whether projects are on time, 201
assessment criteria, in KPI design
  template, 84
assigning ownership, 267
assumptions
 managing, 93
 testing, 94–96
assurance, as dimension of SERVQUAL, 229
Audience and Access Rights, in KPI design
  template, 82
Average Employee Tenure, 257–258
average tenure, 254

B2B (business to business), 181
B2C (business to consumer), 181
balance sheet, 140
Balanced Scorecard (BSC)
 about, 13, 44, 46–47
 customer perspective, 50–51
 customising, 59–60
 financial perspective, 48–49
 future value, 54–55

 internal process perspective, 51–53
 mapping, 55–60
 perspectives of, 47–48
Baldridge Award, 60–61
bar graph, 111–112
Beane, Billy (general manager), 96
best practice performance reports, 108
bias, removing through experiments,
  97–100
"blame culture," 216
Blockbuster, 185
'boss-watching,' 30
Boston Matrix, 188–189
bottom line, 124
Bradford, Rob (managing director), 52
brand equity
 about, 194–195
 measuring, 195–196
brand power, charting, 194–196
BSC (Balanced Scorecard)
 about, 13, 44, 46–47
 customer perspective, 50–51
 customising, 59–60
 financial perspective, 48–49
 future value, 54–55
 internal process perspective, 51–53
 mapping, 55–60
 perspectives of, 47–48
budget, as component of project
  performance, 200
bullet graph, 114
bulletin boards, 79
business experiments, learning from, 96–97
business intelligence, 100–103
business risks, 62
business to business (B2B), 181
business to consumer (B2C), 181
businesses, comparing, 149

• *C* •

calculating
 about, 21–22
 brand equity, 195–196
 brand power, 194–196
 cash, 135–140

cash conversion cycle (CCC), 137–138
cash flow, 137–140
churn, 174–175
cost per lead, 192–194
customer conversion, 191–192, 193–194
customer engagement, 180–182
customer Key Performance Indicators (KPIs), 16
customers' lifetime value (CLV), 179–180
delivery in full, on time rate (DIFOT), 220–221
Earned Value, 204–206
eliminating fear of, 35–36
employee Key Performance Indicators (KPIs), 18
engagement of customers, 182
engagement of employees, 241–243
financial efficiency, 153–161
financial Key Performance Indicators (KPIs), 14–15
identifying frequency of, 267
impact of Internet and social media, 51
Innovation Pipeline Strength (IPS), 222–224
internal efficiency, 207–225
internal productivity, 213–222
Inventory Shrinkage rate (ISR), 222
IT performance, 227–236
IT project performance, 233–236
IT service delivery, 228–233
Key Performance Indicators (KPIs), 202–206
liquidity, 141–143
market growth rate, 185–186, 186–187
market share, 190
mistakes with, 269–270
Net Promoter Score (NPS), 168–169
operational Key Performance Indicators (KPIs), 16–17
opportunity cost, 147–148
order fulfilment cycle time (OFCT), 219
people performance, 239–252
Price/Earnings (P/E) ratio, 149–150
profit margins, 129–132
profitability, 123–129, 176–178
Project Cost Variance, 204

Project Schedule Variance, 203
quality, 207–225, 210–211
recruiting, 253–258
recruitment effectiveness, 255–258
retention, 174–175
return on assets (ROA), 161
return on capital employed (ROCE), 156–158
return on equity (ROE), 158–160
return on investment (ROI), 153–156, 155–156
revenue growth, 132–134
rework levels, 216
Satisfaction Index, 171–172
satisfaction of employees, 241–243
service delivery, 229–230
Six Sigma Key Performance Indicators (KPIs), 211–212
staff advocacy, 245–246
360-degree feedback, 248–250
total shareholder return (TSR), 150–151
training, 259–261
trends, 244–245
usefulness to answering questions, 72
usefulness to decision-making, 72
waste, 213–215
whether projects are on budget, 201–202
whether projects are on time, 201
Capacity Utilization Rate (CUR)
about, 213, 215
as one of top ten Key Performance Indicators (KPIs), 278
Carroll, David (musician), 52
cash, tracking, 135–140
Cash Conversion Cycle (CCC)
about, 137–138
as one of top ten Key Performance Indicators (KPIs), 276
cash cow products/services, 188
cash flow
about, 15
measuring, 137–140
cash flow Key Performance Indicators (KPIs)
about, 135
tracking cash, 135–140

cash flow solvency ratio, 140
cash ratio, 142–143
cause and effect maps, 56–59
cause and effect relationships, testing, 92–96
CCC (Cash Conversion Cycle)
  about, 137–138
  as one of top ten Key Performance Indicators (KPIs), 276
challenging Key Performance Indicators (KPIs), 272
charting
  about, 21–22
  brand equity, 195–196
  brand power, 194–196
  cash, 135–140
  cash conversion cycle (CCC), 137–138
  cash flow, 137–140
  churn, 174–175
  cost per lead, 192–194
  customer conversion, 191–192, 193–194
  customer engagement, 180–182
  customer Key Performance Indicators (KPIs), 16
  customers' lifetime value (CLV), 179–180
  delivery in full, on time rate (DIFOT), 220–221
  Earned Value, 204–206
  eliminating fear of, 35–36
  employee Key Performance Indicators (KPIs), 18
  engagement of customers, 182
  engagement of employees, 241–243
  financial efficiency, 153–161
  financial Key Performance Indicators (KPIs), 14–15
  identifying frequency of, 267
  impact of Internet and social media, 51
  Innovation Pipeline Strength (IPS), 222–224
  internal efficiency, 207–225
  internal productivity, 213–222
  Inventory Shrinkage rate (ISR), 222
  IT performance, 227–236
  IT project performance, 233–236
  IT service delivery, 228–233

Key Performance Indicators (KPIs), 202–206
liquidity, 141–143
market growth rate, 185–186, 186–187
market share, 190
mistakes with, 269–270
Net Promoter Score (NPS), 168–169
operational Key Performance Indicators (KPIs), 16–17
opportunity cost, 147–148
order fulfilment cycle time (OFCT), 219
people performance, 239–252
Price/Earnings (P/E) ratio, 149–150
profit margins, 129–132
profitability, 123–129, 176–178
Project Cost Variance, 204
Project Schedule Variance, 203
quality, 207–225, 210–211
recruiting, 253–258
recruitment effectiveness, 255–258
retention, 174–175
return on assets (ROA), 161
return on capital employed (ROCE), 156–158
return on equity (ROE), 158–160
return on investment (ROI), 153–156, 155–156
revenue growth, 132–134
rework levels, 216
Satisfaction Index, 171–172
satisfaction of employees, 241–243
service delivery, 229–230
Six Sigma Key Performance Indicators (KPIs), 211–212
staff advocacy, 245–246
360-degree feedback, 248–250
total shareholder return (TSR), 150–151
training, 259–261
trends, 244–245
usefulness to answering questions, 72
usefulness to decision-making, 72
waste, 213–215
whether projects are on budget, 201–202
whether projects are on time, 201

charts and graphs
  about, 110–111, 115–116
  bar graph, 111–112
  bullet graph, 114
  line graph, 112–113
  pie chart, 113
  scatter chart, 113–114
  speedometer dials/gauges, 115
Cheat Sheet (website), 3
cheating, creating awareness of, 73
Chocolate Cake analogy, 92
choosing
  frameworks, 44–45
  Key Performance Indicators
    (KPIs), 271
churn
  about, 173
  importance of, 173
  measuring, 174–175
churn rate, 254
click-through rate (CTR), 193
CLV (customers' lifetime value)
  about, 178–179
  measuring, 179–180
Coca-Cola, 99
collecting
  data. *See* data collection
  meaningful data, 71–72
colour, in graphs and charts, 116
combining data, 80–81
communicating
  about, 105–106, 268
  decision makers, 106–110
  developing management dashboards,
    116–119
  graphs and charts, 110–116
  importance of, 106
companies
  level of measuring brand equity, 196
  why they need Key Performance
    Indicators (KPIs), 8–11
comparing businesses, 149
competitors
  analysing, 185–186
  interviewing, 185–186
completeness, of indicators, 87

conducting
  peer-to-peer assessments, 78–79
  qualitative surveys, 78
confidentiality, in 360-degree feedback, 249
consumer level, of measuring brand
    equity, 196
contribution, 240
Control Six Sigma tool, 210
conversion funnel, 194
cost per lead, measuring, 192–194
costs
  about, 86–87
  of finding new customers, 191
  justification of, 73, 267–268
  opportunity, 146–147
creating
  awareness of cheating, 73
  improvement and performance preview
    meetings, 37–41
  Satisfaction Index, 171
  surveys, 76–77
CRR (Customer Retention Rate),
    174–175
CSI (Customer Satisfaction Index). *See*
    Satisfaction Index
CTR (click-through rate), 193
CTR (Customer Turnover Rate), 175
culture
  about, 12
  establishing, 33–36
CUR (Capacity Utilization Rate)
  about, 213, 215
  as one of top ten Key Performance
    Indicators (KPIs), 278
current customer profitability, 177
current position. *See* working capital ratio
current ratio, 141–142
current value, 277
customer acquisition Key Performance
    Indicators (KPIs)
  about, 190–191
  cost of finding new customers, 191
  gauging customer conversion, 191–192
  measuring cost per lead, 192–194
customer conversion rate, measuring,
    193–194

Customer Engagement
  levels of, 181–182
  measuring for customers, 180–182
  as one of top ten Key Performance
    Indicators (KPIs), 277
customer Key Performance Indicators
  (KPIs), assessing, 16
customer lifetime profitability, 177
customer order cycle. *See* order fulfilment
  cycle time (OFCT)
customer perspective, as perspective of
  Balanced Scorecard (BSC), 47, 50–51
Customer Profitability
  about, 14, 176
  advantages of, 125
  gauging, 123–129
  importance of, 127
  measuring, 128–129, 177–178
  measuring in practice, 128–129
  Net Promoter Score (NPS) and,
    166–167
  as one of top ten Key Performance
    Indicators (KPIs), 277
  perspectives on, 125–127
  sources of profit, 176
  top line compared with bottom line, 124
  tracking, 176–177
  types of, 126
Customer Retention Rate (CRR), 174–175
customer satisfaction, 16
Customer Satisfaction Index (CSI). *See*
  Satisfaction Index
Customer Turnover Rate (CTR), 175
customers
  about, 165
  actively disengaged, 181
  churn, 173–175
  cost of finding new, 191
  customers' lifetime value (CLV), 178–180
  disengaged, 181
  engaged, 181
  fully engaged, 181
  measuring engagement of, 180–182
  Net Promoter Score (NPS), 165–169
  profitability, 176–178
  retention, 173–175
  Satisfaction Index, 169–172
  surveying, 186

customers' lifetime value (CLV)
  about, 178–179
  measuring, 179–180
customising
  Balanced Scorecard (BSC), 59–60
  Strategy Map, 59–60

• *D* •

dashboards, management, 116–119
data
  challenges with, 81
  checking for existing methods and, 71
  combining, 80–81
  defining needs, 266
  evaluating, 266
  identifying types of, 76
  measurement, in KPI design
    template, 86
  reporting, frequency, 85–86
  supporting, 268
data collection
  about, 71–73
  frequency of, 85
  from intermediaries, 186
  meaningful, 71–72
  methods, 75–81, 83
data source, in KPI design template,
  84–85
data usage, in KPI design template, 82
datafication, 9–10, 100–101
days of working capital, 143
dead wood, 36
debt, 158
debt finance, 161
decision support tools, Key Performance
  Indicators (KPIs) as, 10–11
decision-making
  assessing usefulness to, 72
  getting attention of decision-makers,
    106–110
decision-making, fact-based
  about, 29–30
  creating improvement and performance
    preview meetings, 37–41
  implementing key components of fact-
    based management, 30–36

decisions
  isolating, 71
  on Key Performance Indicators (KPIs),
    70–75
Defects Per Million Opportunities (DPMO),
    211–212
defects waste, 209
Define Six Sigma tool, 210
defining data needs, 266
deliverables, as component of project
    performance, 200
delivery, 219–221
delivery in full, on time rate (DIFOT), 220
detractors
  about, 166
  employees as, 245
developing
  Key Performance Indicators (KPIs),
    65–90, 265–268
  Key Performance Questions (KPQs),
    66–69
  management dashboards, 116–119
DIFOT (delivery in full, on time rate), 220
disengaged customers, 181
dog products/services, 188
double-blind tests, 98
DPMO (Defects Per Million Opportunities),
    211–212
DuPont formula, 160

• **E** •

Earned Value
  about, 202
  measuring, 204–206
earnings before interest and tax (EBIT), 157
earnings before interest tax, depreciation
    and amortisation (EBITDA), 128–129
Economic Value Added (EVA), 145–148
efficiency, 17
efficiency, financial
  about, 15
  assessing return on investment (ROI),
    153–156
  measuring, 153–161

measuring return on capital employed
    (ROCE), 156–158
  measuring return on equity (ROE),
    158–160
  return on assets (ROA), 160–161
efficiency, internal
  calculating internal productivity,
    213–222
  future planning, 222–225
  measuring, 207–225
effort, justification of, 73, 267–268
EFQM (European Foundation for Quality
    management), 60–61
eliminating fear of measurement, 35–36
empathy, as dimension of
    SERVQUAL, 229
Employee Churn Rate, 258
employee engagement, 18
Employee Engagement Level, 243
employee Key Performance Indicators
    (KPIs), assessing, 18
Employee Satisfaction Index, 241–243
employees
  as advocates, 245
  recommendations from, 244–246
  value generated by, 250–252
end-users, surveying, 186
Energy Consumption, 214
engagement, customer
  levels of, 181–182
  measuring for customers, 180–182
  as one of top ten Key Performance
    Indicators (KPIs), 277
engagement, of employees
  about, 240
  importance of, 240–241
  measuring, 241–243
Enterprise Service Quality Index (ESQi),
    180–181
equity
  brand, 194–195
  defined, 158
equity finance, 161
ESQi (Enterprise Service Quality Index),
    180–181

establishing
  culture, 33–36
  operational performance improvement
    meetings, 39
  personal performance discussions, 39
  processes, 33–36
  senior management buy-in, 30–31
European Foundation for Quality
    management (EFQM), 60–61
EVA (Economic Value Added), 145–148
evaluating data, 266
executives, involved in KPI
    selection, 271
experiments, removing bias through,
    97–100
expiry date, in KPI design template, 86

• *F* •

fact-based decision-making
  about, 29–30
  creating improvement and performance
    preview meetings, 37–41
  implementing key components of fact-
    based management, 30–36
FCR (First Call Resolution), 232–233
financial efficiency
  about, 15
  assessing return on investment (ROI),
    153–156
  measuring, 153–161
  measuring return on capital employed
    (ROCE), 156–158
  measuring return on equity (ROE),
    158–160
  return on assets (ROA), 160–161
financial Key Performance Indicators
    (KPIs)
  about, 123
  assessing, 14–15
  gauging profit, 123–129
  measuring profit margins, 129–132
  measuring revenue growth, 132–134
financial perspective, as perspective of
    Balanced Scorecard (BSC), 47, 48–49
financing activity, 137

First Call Resolution (FCR), 232–233
First Past Yield (FPY), 214
Fishing analogy, 8–9
focus groups, 78
formulas
  in KPI design template, 84
  Net Promoter Score (NPS), 167
FPY (First Past Yield), 214
frameworks
  about, 12–13, 43
  alternative, 60–62
  options for, 43–44
  project management, 62
  selecting, 44–45
frequency
  of data collection, 85
  of data reporting, 85–86
  measurement, 267
fully engaged customers, 181
future planning, 222–225
future value, improving and
    driving, 54–55

• *G* •

GAAP (Generally Accepted Accounting
    Principles), 129
General Electric, 209
Generally Accepted Accounting Principles
    (GAAP), 129
Google, Inc.
  about, 67
  testing business assumptions at, 95
grade box, in 360-degree feedback, 248
graphs and charts
  about, 110–111, 115–116
  bar graph, 111–112
  bullet graph, 114
  line graph, 112–113
  pie chart, 113
  scatter chart, 113–114
  speedometer dials/gauges, 115
gross profit, 125–126
gross profit margin
  about, 130, 131–132
  compared with product mark up, 132

• H •

hardwiring Key Performance Indicators (KPIs) to incentives, 271
Harvard Business Review (HBR), 46
HCVA (Human Capital Value Added), 251
headlines, in reports, 109–110
health, of market, 184–185
historical customer profitability, 177
historical value, 277
human capital, as component of Learning and Growth perspective, 54
Human Capital Value Added (HCVA), 251
human resource performance
  about, 253
  analysing training, 259–261
  charting recruiting, 253–258

• I •

icons, 3
identifying
  measurement frequency, 267
  questions to answer, 265–266
  types of data, 76
  unanswered questions, 70–71
  what makes customers happy, 170
implementing key components of fact-based management, 30–36
Improve Six Sigma tool, 210
improvement and performance preview meetings, creating, 37–41
incentives
  hardwiring Key Performance Indicators (KPIs) to, 271
  initiating, 34–35
income statement, 140
increased market share, as benefit of brand equity, 195
indicator name
  about, 86–90
  in KPI design template, 83
information capital, as component of Learning and Growth perspective, 54

Information Technology (IT)
  about, 17
  importance of performance, 227–236
  measuring performance, 227–236
initiating rewards and incentives, 34–35
innovation, 222–225
Innovation Pipeline Strength (IPS), 222–224
insights
  about, 91
  analysing Key Performance Indicators (KPIs) to extract, 272
  analytics, 100–103
  business intelligence, 100–103
  extracting with Key Performance Indicators (KPIs), 272
  learning from business experiments, 96–97
  removing bias through experiments, 97–100
  testing cause and effect relationships, 92–96
intangible aspects, of Key Performance Indicators (KPIs), 23
intermediaries, data collection from, 186
internal efficiency
  calculating internal productivity, 213–222
  future planning, 222–225
  measuring, 207–225
internal process perspective, as perspective of Balanced Scorecard (BSC), 47, 51–53
internal productivity, calculating, 213–222
Internet, assessing impact of, 51
interval scale, 84
interviewing competitors, 185–186
inventory, 221–222
Inventory Shrinkage rate (ISR), 221–222
inventory waste, 208
investment activity, 137
IPS (Innovation Pipeline Strength), 222–224
isolating decisions, 71
ISR (Inventory Shrinkage rate), 221–222
IT (Information Technology) performance
  importance of, 227–236
  measuring, 227–236

IT Project Cost Variance (IT PCV), 233, 235–236

IT Project Earned Value (IT EV), 233, 236

IT Project Schedule Variance (IT PSV), 233, 234–235

• J •

James, Bill (baseball writer), 96

justifying cost and effort, 73, 267–268

• K •

Kaplan, Robert (author), 33, 46, 54, 55, 56

Key Performance Indicators (KPIs). *See also specific topics*

about, 7–8

Absenteeism Bradford Factor, 257

acting on, 273

analysing to extract insights, 272

Average Employee Tenure, 257–258

Capacity Utilisation Rate, 215

Cash Flow Solvency Ratio, 140

Cash Ratio, 142–143

challenging, 272

Cost Per Lead, 192–193

creating, 22–24

Current Ratio, 141–142

Customer Conversion Rate, 193

Customer Retention Rate (CRR), 174–175

Customer Turnover Rate (CTR), 175

Days of Working Capital, 143

deciding on, 70–75

developing, 65–90, 265–268

Earned Value (EV), 204–205

EBITDA, 128–129

Employee Churn Rate, 258

Employee Engagement Level, 243

Employee Satisfaction Index, 241–242

First Call Resolution (FCR), 232–233

Gross Profit Margin, 131–132

hardwiring to incentives, 271

Human Capital Value Added (HCVA), 251

Innovation Pipeline Strength (IPS), 223–224

IT Project Cost Variance, 235–236

IT Project Earned Value, 236

IT Project Schedule Variance, 234–235

linking strategies to, 270

linking to strategic objectives, 70

making them work in business, 11–14

measuring, 202–206

mistakes with, 26–28, 269–273

Net Profit, 128

Net Profit Margin, 131

number of, 23

Operating Profit Margin, 132

organising, 43–62

Process Level Waste, 215–216

Project Cost Variance, 204

Project Schedule Variance, 203

Quality Index, 212

Quick Ratio, 142

reasons for introducing, 32–33

Return on Innovation Investment (ROI²), 224–225

Revenue, 133

Revenue Growth Rate, 134

Revenue Per Employee (RPE), 251–252

Salary Competitiveness Ratio (SCR), 256

selecting, 271

Service Quality (SERVQUAL), 231–232

setting targets for, 24–26

Six Sigma Level, 211–212

strategic or operational nature of, 19–22

targets compared with, 25

Time to Hire, 255–256

top ten, 275–279

updating, 272

visualising with graphs and charts, 110–116

why companies need, 8–11

Working Capital Ratio, 139

Key Performance Questions (KPQs)

about, 31

assessing usefulness to answering, 72

developing, 66–69

examples of, 69

identifying unanswered, 70–71, 265–266

in KPI design template, 82

key skills/capabilitise, in 360-degree feedback, 248

Kirkpatrick, Donald (trainer), 259

KPI design template
applying, 81–90
sample, 88–90

KPIs (Key Performance Indicators). *See also specific topics*
about, 7–8
Absenteeism Bradford Factor, 257
acting on, 273
analysing to extract insights, 272
Average Employee Tenure, 257–258
Capacity Utilisation Rate, 215
Cash Conversion Cycle, 137–138
Cash Flow Solvency Ratio, 140
Cash Ratio, 142–143
challenging, 272
Cost Per Lead, 192–193
creating, 22–24
Current Ratio, 141–142
Customer Conversion Rate, 193
Customer Retention Rate (CRR), 174–175
Customer Turnover Rate (CTR), 175
Days of Working Capital, 143
deciding on, 70–75
developing, 65–90, 265–268
Earned Value (EV), 204–205
EBITDA, 128–129
Employee Churn Rate, 258
Employee Engagement Level, 243
Employee Satisfaction Index, 241–242
First Call Resolution (FCR), 232–233
Gross Profit Margin, 131–132
hardwiring to incentives, 271
Human Capital Value Added (HCVA), 251
Innovation Pipeline Strength (IPS), 223–224
IT Project Cost Variance, 235–236
IT Project Earned Value, 236
IT Project Schedule Variance, 234–235
linking strategies to, 270
linking to strategic objectives, 70
making them work in business, 11–14
measuring, 202–206
mistakes with, 26–28, 269–273

Net Profit, 128
Net Profit Margin, 131
number of, 23
Operating Profit Margin, 132
organising, 43–62
Process Level Waste, 215–216
Project Cost Variance, 204
Project Schedule Variance, 203
Quality Index, 212
Quick Ratio, 142
reasons for introducing, 32–33
Return on Innovation Investment (ROI^2), 224–225
Revenue, 133
Revenue Growth Rate, 134
Revenue Per Employee (RPE), 251–252
Salary Competitiveness Ratio (SCR), 256
selecting, 271
Service Quality (SERVQUAL), 231–232
setting targets for, 24–26
Six Sigma Level, 211–212
strategic or operational nature of, 19–22
targets compared with, 25
Time to Hire, 255–256
top ten, 275–279
updating, 272
visualising with graphs and charts, 110–116
why companies need, 8–11
Working Capital Ratio, 139

KPQs (Key Performance Questions)
about, 31
assessing usefulness to answering, 72
developing, 66–69
examples of, 69
identifying unanswered, 70–71, 265–266
in KPI design template, 82

laggers, 23–24
leaders, 23–24
lean, importance of being, 208–209
lean frameworks, 60–61
learning, from business experiments, 96–97

learning and growth perspective, as
  perspective of Balanced Scorecard
  (BSC), 47
life-time value, 277
Likert scale, 84
line graph, 112–113
linking
  Key Performance Indicators (KPIs) to
    strategic objectives, 70
  Key Performance Indicators (KPIs) to
    strategies, 270
liquidity
  about, 15
  measuring, 141–143
liquidity Key Performance Indicators
    (KPIs)
  about, 135, 140
  measuring liquidity, 141–143
  unseen risks, 141
long-term loyalty, as benefit of brand
    equity, 195
loss leader, 189
loyalty
  about, 16
  Net Promoter Score (NPS) and, 166–167

• M •

Machine Downtime Level, 214
macro ROI, 154
maintaining
  assumptions, 93
  rework levels, 216–217
  share price, 148–150
management dashboards, developing,
    116–119
managing
  assumptions, 93
  rework levels, 216–217
  share price, 148–150
mapping strategies, 55–60, 265
market
  about, 183
  charting brand power, 194–196
  customer acquisition Key Performance
    Indicators (KPIs), 190–194

market growth rate, 183–187
market share, 187–190
market growth rate
  about, 183–184
  market health, 184–185
  measuring, 185–186, 186–187
market health, 184–185
market share
  about, 16, 187
  importance of, 187
  measuring, 190
  problems with finding, 189
Measure Six Sigma tool, 210
measurement methodologies, 266–267
measuring
  about, 21–22
  brand equity, 195–196
  brand power, 194–196
  cash, 135–140
  cash conversion cycle (CCC), 137–138
  cash flow, 137–140
  churn, 174–175
  cost per lead, 192–194
  customer conversion, 191–192, 193–194
  customer engagement, 180–182
  customer Key Performance Indicators
    (KPIs), 16
  customers' lifetime value (CLV), 179–180
  delivery in full, on time rate (DIFOT),
    220–221
  Earned Value, 204–206
  eliminating fear of, 35–36
  employee Key Performance Indicators
    (KPIs), 18
  engagement of customers, 182
  engagement of employees, 241–243
  financial efficiency, 153–161
  financial Key Performance Indicators
    (KPIs), 14–15
  identifying frequency of, 267
  impact of Internet and social media, 51
  Innovation Pipeline Strength (IPS),
    222–224
  internal efficiency, 207–225
  internal productivity, 213–222
  Inventory Shrinkage rate (ISR), 222

IT performance, 227–236
IT project performance, 233–236
IT service delivery, 228–233
Key Performance Indicators (KPIs),
    202–206
liquidity, 141–143
market growth rate, 185–186, 186–187
market share, 190
mistakes with, 269–270
Net Promoter Score (NPS), 168–169
operational Key Performance Indicators
    (KPIs), 16–17
opportunity cost, 147–148
order fulfilment cycle time (OFCT), 219
people performance, 239–252
Price/Earnings (P/E) ratio, 149–150
profit margins, 129–132
profitability, 123–129, 176–178
Project Cost Variance, 204
Project Schedule Variance, 203
quality, 207–225, 210–211
recruiting, 253–258
recruitment effectiveness, 255–258
retention, 174–175
return on assets (ROA), 161
return on capital employed (ROCE),
    156–158
return on equity (ROE), 158–160
return on investment (ROI), 153–156,
    155–156
revenue growth, 132–134
rework levels, 216
Satisfaction Index, 171–172
satisfaction of employees, 241–243
service delivery, 229–230
Six Sigma Key Performance Indicators
    (KPIs), 211–212
staff advocacy, 245–246
360-degree feedback, 248–250
total shareholder return (TSR), 150–151
training, 259–261
trends, 244–245
usefulness to answering questions, 72
usefulness to decision-making, 72
waste, 213–215
whether projects are on budget, 201–202
whether projects are on time, 201

methods
    checking for existing data and, 71
    data collection, 75–81
micro ROI, 154
monitoring
    assumptions, 93
    rework levels, 216–217
    share price, 148–150
motion waste, 208
Motorola, 209
mystery shopping, 78

• *N* •

narrative, in reports, 109–110
NASA, 107
National Health Service
    (NHS), 271
The National Customer Satisfaction
    Index-UK (NCSI-UK), 172
net earnings. *See* net profit
net income. *See* net profit
net profit, 127, 128
net profit margin, 130–131
Net Profit Margin, as one of top ten Key
    Performance Indicators (KPIs),
    275–276
Net Promoter Score (NPS)
    about, 165–166
    formula, 167
    loyalty and, 166–167
    measuring, 168–169
    as one of top ten Key Performance
        Indicators (KPIs), 276–277
    profitability and, 166–167
NHS (National Health Service), 271
nominal scale, 84
Norton, David (management consultant),
    33, 46, 54, 55, 56
NPS (Net Promoter Score)
    about, 165–166
    formula, 167
    loyalty and, 166–167
    measuring, 168–169
    as one of top ten Key Performance
        Indicators (KPIs), 276–277
    profitability and, 166–167

• O •

observing situations, 79
OEE (Overall Equipment Effectiveness), 214
OFCT (order fulfilment cycle time), 218
Office of Strategic Management (OSM), 33
operating activity, 137
operating profit, 127
operating profit margin, 130, 132
operational Key Performance Indicators (KPIs), assessing, 16–17
operational nature, of Key Performance Indicators (KPIs), 19–22
operational performance improvement meetings, establishing, 39
opportunity cost
  about, 146–147
  measuring, 147–148
order fulfilment, 218–219
order fulfilment cycle time (OFCT), 218
ordinal scale, 84
organisation capital, as component of Learning and Growth perspective, 54
organising
  Key Performance Indicators (KPIs), 43–62
  reports, 110
OSM (Office of Strategic Management), 33
Overall Equipment Effectiveness (OEE), 214
over-processing waste, 208
over-production waste, 208
ownership, assigning, 267

• P •

passives
  about, 166
  employees as, 245
Pear Tree analogy, 20–21
peer-to-peer assessments, conducting, 78–79
people performance
  about, 239
  engagement, 240–243
  measuring, 239–252

recommendations from employees, 244–246
satisfaction, 240–243
360-degree feedback, 247–250
value generation by employees, 250–252
percentage target, 24
performance, human resource
  about, 253
  analysing training, 259–261
  charting recruiting, 253–258
performance, IT (Information Technology)
  importance of, 227–236
  measuring, 227–236
performance, people
  about, 239
  engagement, 240–243
  measuring, 239–252
  recommendations from employees, 244–246
  satisfaction, 240–243
  360-degree feedback, 247–250
  value generation by employees, 250–252
performance, poor, 36
performance, project
  about, 17, 199
  components of, 200–206
  importance of, 199–200
performance meetings, guidelines for productive, 40–41
performance thresholds, in KPI design template, 83
personal performance discussions, establishing, 39
Phillips ROI model, 260–261
photos, in reports, 109–110
pie chart, 113
present customer profitability, 177
present value, 277
price premium, as benefit of brand equity, 195
Price/Earnings (P/E) ratio
  about, 149
  measuring, 149–150
problem child products/services, 188
Process Downtime Level, 214
Process Level Waste, 215–216

processes, establishing, 33–36
product level, of measuring brand
        equity, 196
product mark up, compared with gross
        profit margin, 132
profit and profitability
    about, 14, 176
    advantages of, 125
    gauging, 123–129
    importance of, 127
    measuring, 128–129, 177–178
    measuring in practice, 128–129
    Net Promoter Score (NPS) and, 166–167
    perspectives on, 125–127
    sources of profit, 176
    top line compared with bottom line, 124
    tracking, 176–177
    types of, 126
profit margins, measuring, 129–132
Project Cost Variance
    about, 201–202
    measuring, 204
project management frameworks, 62
project performance
    about, 17, 199
    components of, 200–206
    importance of, 199–200
Project Schedule Variance
    about, 201
    measuring, 203
promoters, 166
proportional target, 24
Publishing analogy, 108–109
Purolator, 45

qualified lead, 191
qualitative data, weaknesses of, 79–80
qualitative methods, 77–80
qualitative surveys, conducting, 78
quality
    about, 17
    calculating internal productivity, 213–222
    future planning, 222–225

    importance of, 53
    measuring, 207–225
    tracking, 210–211
quality frameworks, 60–61
Quality Index, 212
quantitative data, weaknesses of, 77
quantitative methods, applying, 76–77
question number, in 360-degree
        feedback, 248
quick ratio, 142

rate of profit (ROP). *See* return on
        investment (ROI)
ratio scale, 84
Ratner, Gerald (CEO), 148
recommendations, from employees,
        244–246
recruitment
    charting, 253–258
    measuring effectiveness of, 255–258
Relative Market Share, as one of top ten
        Key Performance Indicators (KPIs), 278
relative to external benchmarks target, 24
relative to global best practice target, 24
relative to internal benchmarks target, 24
reliability, as dimension of SERVQUAL, 229
Remember icon, 3
removing bias through experiments, 97–100
Rent-A-Car, 180–181
reporting
    about, 105–106
    best practice performance in
        reports, 108
    decision makers, 106–110
    developing management dashboards,
        116–119
    graphs and charts, 110–116
responsiveness, as dimension of
        SERVQUAL, 229
retention
    about, 173
    importance of, 173
    measuring, 174–175

return on assets (ROA)
 about, 160
 importance of, 161
 measuring, 161
return on average capital employed
  (ROACE), 157
Return on Capital Employed (ROCE)
 about, 147
 measuring, 156–158
return on equity (ROE), measuring,
  158–160
Return on Innovation Investment (ROI^2),
  224–225
return on investment (ROI)
 assessing, 153–156
 measuring, 155–156
revenue
 about, 14
 defined, 125
revenue growth, measuring, 132–134
Revenue Growth Rate, as one of top ten
  Key Performance Indicators
  (KPIs), 275
Revenue per Employee (RPE), 251–252
revision date, in KPI design template, 86
rewards, initiating, 34–35
rework levels, monitoring, 216–217
risks, of business, 62
ROA (return on assets)
 about, 160
 importance of, 161
 measuring, 161
ROACE (return on average capital
  employed), 157
ROCE (Return on Capital Employed)
 about, 147
 measuring, 156–158
ROE (return on equity), measuring,
  158–160
ROI (return on investment)
 assessing, 153–156
 measuring, 155–156
ROI^2 (Return on Innovation Investment),
  224–225
ROP (rate of profit). *See* return on
  investment (ROI)

• S •

Salary Competitiveness Ratio (SCR), 256
sales profit. *See* gross profit
sales ready, 191
satisfaction, of employees
 about, 240
 importance of, 240–241
 measuring, 241–243
Satisfaction Index
 about, 169–170
 creating, 171
 identifying what makes customers
  happy, 170
 measuring, 171–172
scales
 in KPI design template, 84
 types of, 84
scatter chart, 113–114
schedule, as component of project
  performance, 200
Schneiderman, Art (management
  consultant), 46
SCR (Salary Competitiveness Ratio), 256
selecting
 frameworks, 44–45
 Key Performance Indicators (KPIs), 271
senior management buy-in, establishing,
  30–31
separating strategic Key Performance
  Indicators (KPIs), 270
service delivery, measuring, 229–230
Service Quality (SERVQUAL), 231–232
service recovery effect, 94
SERVQUAL, 229–230
setting targets for Key Performance
  Indicators (KPIs), 24–26
share price, monitoring, 148–150
shareholder Key Performance Indicators
  (KPIs)
 about, 145
 tracking total shareholder return (TSR),
  150–151
shareholder value
 about, 15
 defined, 24

shrinking inventory, 221–222
situations, observing, 79
Six Sigma, 13, 209–210
Six Sigma Key Performance Indicators (KPIs), measuring, 211–212
Six Sigma Level, 211–212
skill component/element, in 360-degree feedback, 248
social media, assessing impact of, 51
soft skills, 259
software tools, for management dashboards, 118–119
specific feedback questions, in 360-degree feedback, 248
speedometer dials/gauges, 115
Staff Advocacy Score
  about, 244
  measuring, 245–246
  as one of top ten Key Performance Indicators (KPIs), 278
star products/services, 188
statement of cash flows, 140
status day, 205
stock market, competition in, 150–151
strategic Key Performance Indicators (KPIs), separating, 270
strategic nature, of Key Performance Indicators (KPIs), 19–22
Strategic Objective
  in KPI design template, 82
  linking Key Performance Indicators (KPIs) to, 70
strategic performance preview meetings, 38
strategic profit model, 160
strategies
  linking Key Performance Indicators (KPIs) to, 270
  mapping, 265
Strategy Map
  about, 56–59
  customising, 59–60
strategy revision meetings, 37–38
supporting data, finding, 268
surveys
  creating, 76–77
  customers and end-users, 186

Sustainability Index, as one of top ten Key Performance Indicators (KPIs), 278–279

• T •

talent retention, 18
tangibles
  as dimension of SERVQUAL, 229
  of Key Performance Indicators (KPIs), 23
target audience, 107
targets
  absolute, 24
  compared with Key Performance Indicators (KPIs), 25
  examples of, 25
  in KPI design template, 83
  making realistic and achievable, 26
  setting for Key Performance Indicators (KPIs), 24–26
  specificity of, 25
Taylor, Bob (owner of Taylor Guitars), 52
Taylor Guitars, 52
template, 74–75
Tesco, 102
testing
  assumptions, 94–96
  business assumptions at Google, Inc., 95
  cause and effect relationships, 92–96
360-degree feedback
  about, 247
  importance of, 247–248
  measuring, 248–250
three-dimensional graphs, 116
tick-box, in 360-degree feedback, 248
Time to Hire, 255–256
Time to Market, 214
time-based activity-based profitability, 177
Tip icon, 3
top down NPS, 168
top line, 124, 132–134
Total Quality Management (TQM), 216
total shareholder return (TSR), tracking, 150–151
TQM (Total Quality Management), 216
training, 259–261

training ROI methodology, 259
transaction NPS, 168
transportation waste, 208
trends, measuring, 244–245
True Story icon, 3
TSR (total shareholder return), tracking, 150–151

• *U* •

unintended consequences, 87
United, 52
updating Key Performance Indicators (KPIs), 272

• *V* •

value
   generated by employees, 250–252
   shareholder, 15, 24
value-added Key Performance Indicators (KPIs)
   about, 145
   Economic Value Added (EVA), 145–148
   monitoring share price, 148–150
visualising Key Performance Indicators (KPIs) with graphs and charts, 110–116

• *W* •

waiting waste, 208
Wald, Abraham (statistician), 80–81
Warning! icon, 3
waste
   levels of, 213–216
   measuring, 213–215
Waste Recycling Rate, 214–215
Waste Reduction Rate, 214
websites
   Advanced Performance Institute, 4, 102
   Cheat Sheet, 3
working capital ratio, 139

• *X* •

Xerox, 180

• *Y* •

Yahoo!, 99

• *Z* •

Zappos, 169

About the Author

Bernard Marr is the founder and CEO of the Advanced Performance Institute, an organisation that specialises in KPIs, metrics and analytics as well as performance and strategy management.

Through his work at the Advanced Performance Institute, Bernard helps clients with their KPI, metrics and data needs. As a best-selling business author, keynote speaker, consultant and trainer, he is widely recognized as one of the world's leading experts on the topic.

Bernard is acknowledged by the CEO Journal as one of today's leading business brains and LinkedIn nominated him as one of the world's top 100 business influencers.

He has written a number of seminal books and over 300 high profile reports and articles. This includes the best-sellers '25 Need-to-Know Key Performance Indicators', 'The Intelligent Company', 'Doing More with Less – Measuring, Analyzing and Improving Performance in the Not-for-Profit and Government Sectors', 'Managing and Delivering Performance', and 'Strategic Performance Management'.

Bernard has worked with and advised many of the world's best-known organizations including Accenture, Astra Zeneca, Bank of England, Barclays, BP, DHL, Fujitsu, Gartner, HSBC, Mars, Ministry of Defence, Microsoft, Oracle, The Home Office, NHS, Orange, Tetley, T-Mobile, Toyota, Royal Air Force, SAP, Shell, the United Nations, among many others.

If you would like to talk to Bernard about any KPI project you require help with or if you are thinking about running a KPI event or training course in your organization, then contact him at www.ap-institute.com or via email at: bernard.marr@ap-institute.com

You can also follow @bernardmarr on Twitter, where he regularly shares his ideas or connect with him on LinkedIn, where he writes a regular blog.

Dedication

This book is dedicated to the people who give me meaning and pleasure beyond measure: My wife Claire and our three children Sophia, James and Oliver.

Author's Acknowledgments

I am so grateful to everyone who has helped me get to where I am today. All the great people in the companies I have worked with who put their trust in me to help them and in return give me so much new knowledge and experience. I must also thank everyone who has shared their thinking with me, either in person, in blog posts, books or any other formats. Thank you for generously sharing all the material I absorb every day! I am also lucky enough to personally know many of the key thinkers and thought leaders in the field and I hope you all know how much I value your inputs and exchanges. At this point I usually start a long list of key people but I always miss some off, so this time I want to resist that and hope your egos will forgive me. You are all amazing!

Finally, I want to thank the team at Wiley for all your support. Taking any book through production is always a challenging process and I really appreciate your input and help. A special thank you to Karen McCreadie for the amazing editorial support!

Publisher's Acknowledgments

Acquisitions Editor: Annie Knight/Claire Ruston

Project Editor: Simon Bell

Copy Editor: Kate O'Leary

Proofreader: Martin Key

Project Coordinator: Sheree Montgomery

Cover Image: ©iStock.com/Kalawin

Take Dummies with you everywhere you go!

Whether you're excited about e-books, want more from the web, must have your mobile apps, or swept up in social media, Dummies makes everything easier.

FOR DUMMIES®

A Wiley Brand

BUSINESS

978-1-118-73077-5

978-1-118-44349-1

978-1-119-97527-4

MUSIC

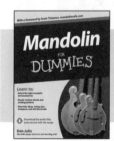
978-1-119-94276-4

978-0-470-97799-6

978-0-470-49644-2

DIGITAL PHOTOGRAPHY

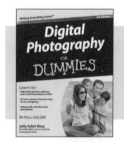
978-1-118-09203-3

978-0-470-76878-5

978-1-118-00472-2

Algebra I For Dummies
978-0-470-55964-2

Anatomy & Physiology For Dummies, 2nd Edition
978-0-470-92326-9

Asperger's Syndrome For Dummies
978-0-470-66087-4

Basic Maths For Dummies
978-1-119-97452-9

Body Language For Dummies, 2nd Edition
978-1-119-95351-7

Bookkeeping For Dummies, 3rd Edition
978-1-118-34689-1

British Sign Language For Dummies
978-0-470-69477-0

Cricket for Dummies, 2nd Edition
978-1-118-48032-8

Currency Trading For Dummies, 2nd Edition
978-1-118-01851-4

Cycling For Dummies
978-1-118-36435-2

Diabetes For Dummies, 3rd Edition
978-0-470-97711-8

eBay For Dummies, 3rd Edition
978-1-119-94122-4

Electronics For Dummies All-in-One For Dummies
978-1-118-58973-1

English Grammar For Dummies
978-0-470-05752-0

French For Dummies, 2nd Edition
978-1-118-00464-7

Guitar For Dummies, 3rd Edition
978-1-118-11554-1

IBS For Dummies
978-0-470-51737-6

Keeping Chickens For Dummies
978-1-119-99417-6

Knitting For Dummies, 3rd Edition
978-1-118-66151-2

FOR DUMMIES

A Wiley Brand

SELF-HELP

978-0-470-66541-1

978-1-119-99264-6

978-0-470-66086-7

LANGUAGES

978-0-470-68815-1

978-1-119-97959-3

978-0-470-69477-0

HISTORY

978-0-470-68792-5

978-0-470-74783-4

978-0-470-97819-1

Laptops For Dummies 5th Edition
978-1-118-11533-6

Management For Dummies, 2nd Edition
978-0-470-97769-9

Nutrition For Dummies, 2nd Edition
978-0-470-97276-2

Office 2013 For Dummies
978-1-118-49715-9

Organic Gardening For Dummies
978-1-119-97706-3

Origami Kit For Dummies
978-0-470-75857-1

Overcoming Depression For Dummies
978-0-470-69430-5

Physics I For Dummies
978-0-470-90324-7

Project Management For Dummies
978-0-470-71119-4

Psychology Statistics For Dummies
978-1-119-95287-9

Renting Out Your Property For Dummies, 3rd Edition
978-1-119-97640-0

Rugby Union For Dummies, 3rd Edition
978-1-119-99092-5

Stargazing For Dummies
978-1-118-41156-8

Teaching English as a Foreign Language For Dummies
978-0-470-74576-2

Time Management For Dummies
978-0-470-77765-7

Training Your Brain For Dummies
978-0-470-97449-0

Voice and Speaking Skills For Dummies
978-1-119-94512-3

Wedding Planning For Dummies
978-1-118-69951-5

WordPress For Dummies, 5th Edition
978-1-118-38318-6

Think you can't learn it in a day? Think again!

The *In a Day* e-book series from *For Dummies* gives you quick and easy access to learn a new skill, brush up on a hobby, or enhance your personal or professional life — all in a day. Easy!